MW01679123

HAROLD MORTIMER-LAMB

# the art lover

ROBERT AMOS

TouchWood Editions

Copyright © 2013 Robert Amos

All rights reserved. No part of this publication may be reproduced, stored in a retrieval system, or transmitted in any form or by any means—electronic, mechanical, recording, or otherwise—without the prior written consent of the publisher or a licence from The Canadian Copyright Licensing Agency (ACCESS Copyright). For a copyright licence, visit accesscopyright.ca.

TouchWood Editions
touchwoodeditions.com

This book was produced in partnership with the Art Gallery of Greater Victoria (aggv.ca) and accompanied an exhibition presented there from November 15, 2013, to February 23, 2014.

LIBRARY AND ARCHIVES CANADA CATALOGUING IN PUBLICATION
Amos, Robert, 1950–
Harold Mortimer Lamb : the art lover / Robert Amos.

Issued also in electronic formats.
ISBN 978-1-77151-018-9

1. Mortimer-Lamb, Harold, 1872–1970. 2. Mortimer-Lamb, Harold, 1872–1970—Friends and associates. 3. Painters—British Columbia—Biography. 4. Journalists—British Columbia—Biography. 5. Photographers—British Columbia—Biography. 6. Art, Canadian—History. I. Title. II. Title: Art lover.

ND249.M67A46 2013 759.11 C2013-902126-4

Editor: Marlyn Horsdal
Proofreader: Vivian Sinclair
Design: Pete Kohut
Front cover images:
John Vanderpant, *Harold Mortimer-Lamb*, 1926, photograph, 38.0 x 25.4 cm (support) (AGGV 1981.095.002) (detail)
Harold Mortimer-Lamb, *Vera with a glass globe*, n.d., photograph (Royal BC Museum, BC Archives I-66773) (detail)
Back cover images:
F.H. Varley, *Vera*, 1930, oil on canvas, 61.0 x 50.6 cm (National Gallery of Canada, Ottawa, Vincent Massey Bequest, 1968, no. 15559, © Varley Art Gallery, City of Markham, Photo © NGC)
Unnamed street photographer, *Harold Mortimer-Lamb and Vera in Vancouver*, April 1954 (Molly Lamb Bobak collection)
Interior images: see List of Illustrations, pp. 174–178
The artwork from the Art Gallery of Greater Victoria was photographed by Stephen Topfer.

Canadian Heritage Patrimoine canadien Canada Council for the Arts Conseil des Arts du Canada British Columbia Arts Council CRD Making a difference...together

TouchWood Editions gratefully acknowledges the financial support for our publishing activities from the Government of Canada through the Canada Book Fund, Canada Council for the Arts, and the province of British Columbia through the British Columbia Arts Council and the Book Publishing Tax Credit. The Art Gallery of Greater Victoria acknowledges the support of the Canada Council, the CRD Arts Development Service, the British Columbia Arts Council, and the Associates of the Art Gallery of Greater Victoria.

MIX
Paper from responsible sources
FSC® C016973

This book was produced using FSC®-certified, acid-free paper, processed chlorine free and printed with soya-based inks.

1 2 3 4 5 17 16 15 14 13

PRINTED IN CHINA

To Sarah, as ever.

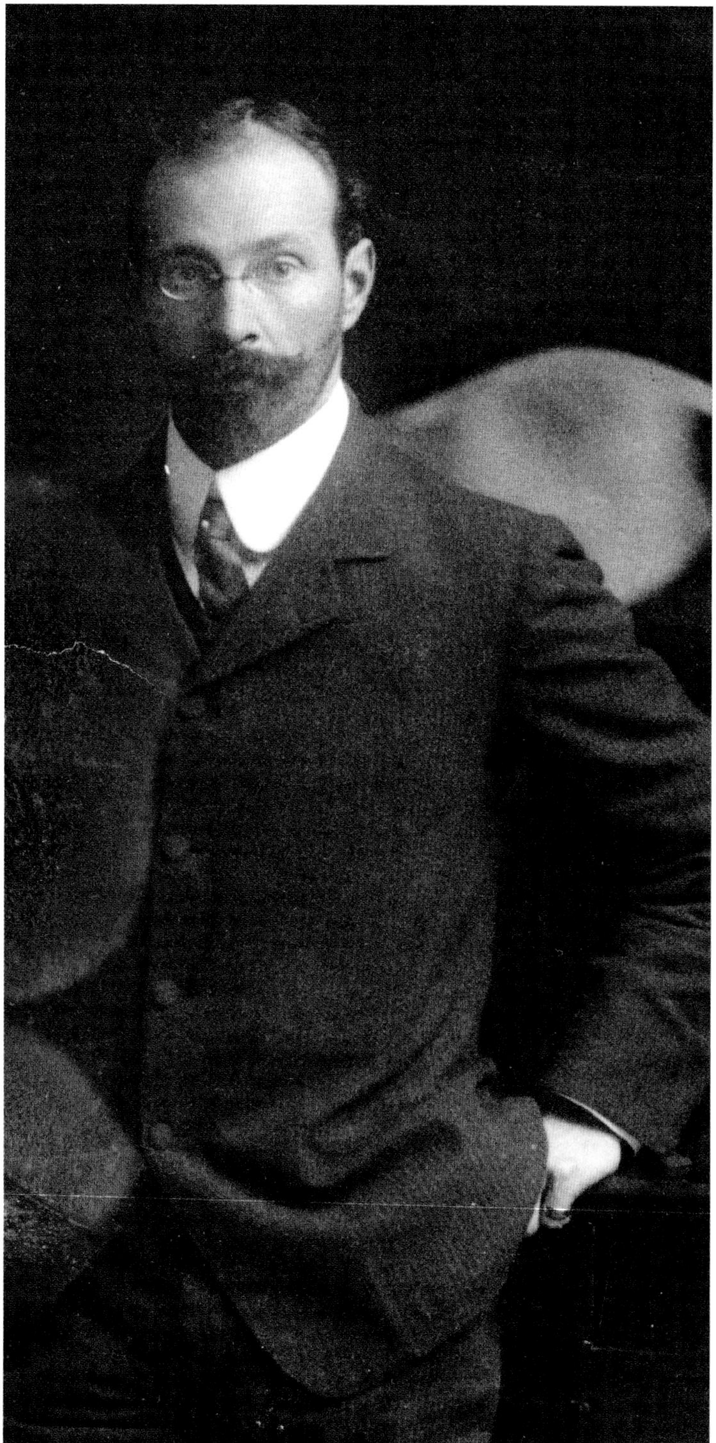

Mortimer-Lamb, *self portrait*.

# CONTENTS

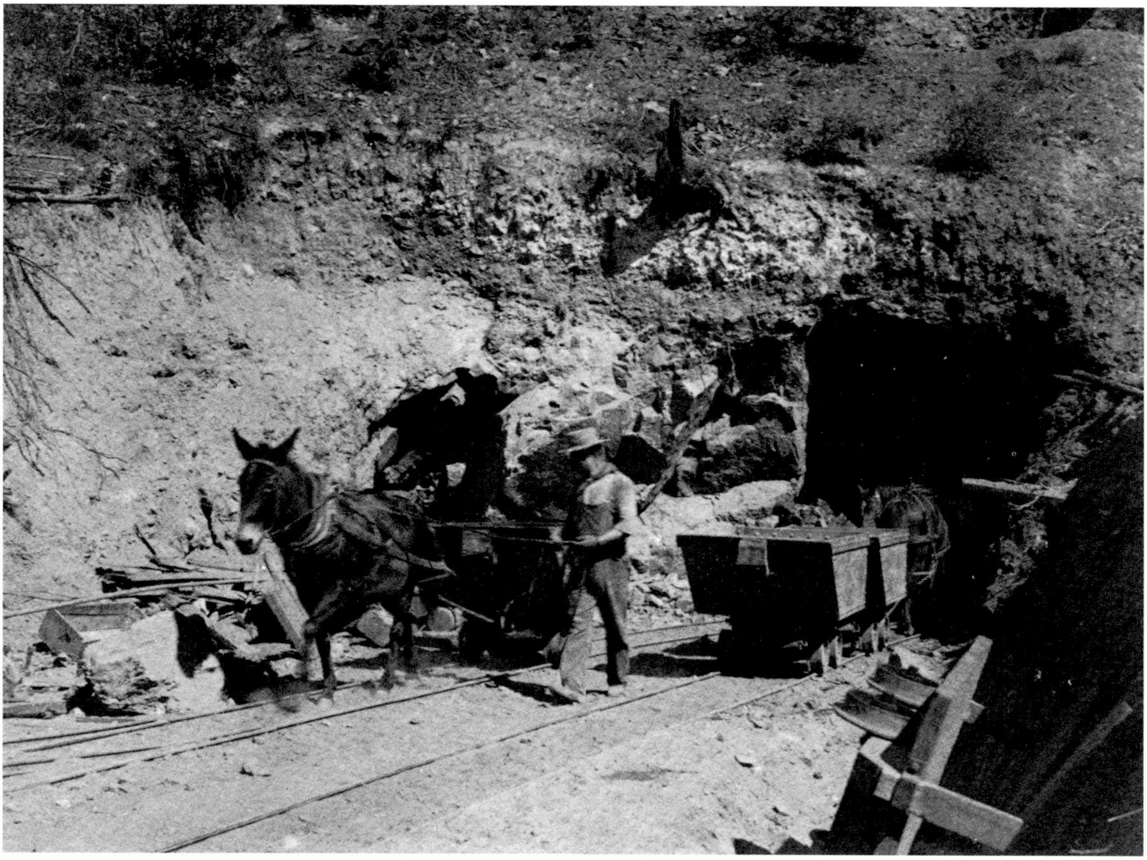

1 Mortimer-Lamb, *a mine in British Columbia.*

# Introduction

One day in 1978 Colin Graham, director emeritus of the Art Gallery of Greater Victoria, drove up to the gallery with a small moving van and proceeded to unload the estate of Harold and Vera Mortimer-Lamb. Scores of artworks were unpacked in the basement storage area; papers and photographs were carried to the library; household items were set aside for the volunteer committee's Classy Cast-Off sale. A considerable amount of money was deposited in the bank for the purchase of Canadian art. I took a well-used Windsor chair from the van to my office upstairs and sat down to write about the donation for the gallery's *Arts Victoria* magazine. That was my introduction to a fascinating story of love and Canadian art.

In stature Mortimer-Lamb was small, with spectacles and a little goatee. With his first wife, Kate, he fathered six children, and at the time of her death they had been married for forty-five years. During that time he also fathered a child by his housekeeper, Mary Williams, who lived with the family for the next twenty-three years. Their daughter is the artist Molly Lamb Bobak. Then, a widower at the age of seventy, Mortimer-Lamb married the legendary beauty Vera Weatherbie, who was just thirty, and they shared twenty-eight years of happily married life, until his death at the age of ninety-nine.

Mortimer-Lamb loved art: the artworks, the people who made them, and those who inspired them. He was a photographer, a painter, a patron, and a promoter of art. He is mentioned in the index of many books about Canadian art history but—until now—has remained a figure in the background.

It was Mortimer-Lamb who first championed A.Y. Jackson, writing about him as early as 1911. It was Mortimer-Lamb who, in 1921, first brought Emily Carr to the attention of the National Gallery of Canada, and he was instrumental in bringing Frederick Varley to Vancouver in 1926, where he became his patron and supporter. Mortimer-Lamb was constantly in the company of the best artists—he befriended Sophie Pemberton in Victoria in 1904 and Laura Muntz in Montreal in 1907; he kept in touch with Arthur Lismer and the Group of Seven from the 1920s on and was at home to Jack Shadbolt in Vancouver from 1939. He was a neighbour of Lawren and Bess Harris. There are portraits of him by William Notman, John Vanderpant, Frederick Varley, E.J. Hughes, B.C. Binning, Fred Amess, Vera Weatherbie, Jack Shadbolt, Harry Upperton Knight, Joe Plaskett, Bruno Bobak, and others. His photographs are in the collections of the Royal Photographic Society in London, the National Gallery of Canada, the Vancouver Art Gallery, and the University of British Columbia. In the end, he and Vera left a collection of art numbering 192 pieces in every curatorial department in the Art Gallery of

Greater Victoria. The British Columbia Archives holds more than 260 of his photographs.

Mortimer-Lamb was an exponent of what was called Pictorial photography, a soft-focus aesthetic tinged with soulful symbolism. In the 1920s Pictorialism was superseded by the hard edge of Modernism, at which time Mortimer-Lamb's considerable achievements were deemed passé. Yet in the first years of the twentieth century, he was the leading artistic photographer in Canada. His work was regularly exhibited and published in London and New York, and he was the Canadian correspondent for the leading art and photography journals.

Why is he not better known?

Mortimer-Lamb was not a tortured romantic soul. During his entire working life, he was fully and usefully employed by various divisions of the Canadian Mining Institute, and so was able to support and encourage the arts with his own resources. Thus he has been seen as a dilettante. As this story shows, he was not a trifler, but a man with a lifelong and profound commitment to art.

For fifty years Mortimer-Lamb was involved with Vancouver's galleries and museums, as founder, board member, donor, and champion. In the end, he felt that his contributions would be more effective in Victoria, where the Art Gallery of Greater Victoria showed a serious interest in his vision. Building on the basis of his donations, that gallery's collections of Asian art, decorative art, and Canadian painting have given it unique strength. Thus he is better known in Victoria than Vancouver.

I took up the story of Mortimer-Lamb because I wanted to learn about his life. Why was Kate sequestered in the back room? What went on between Mortimer-Lamb and Mary Williams? Was Vera really Varley's lover? How did the old codger catch the almond-eyed beauty? In the end, Mortimer-Lamb took up painting dreamlike songs of joy and lived to be ninety-nine years old. It was a wonderful life. How did he do it?

The simple answer seems to be—he was an art lover.

## MORTIMER-LAMB OR MORTIMER LAMB?

How shall we name the central figure of this study? On his birth certificate, he was Harold, son of Captain Henry Lamb and his wife, Emily, née Mortimer. His marriage certificate from 1896 spelled his name with a hyphen (Harold Mortimer-Lamb), yet the records from the British Columbia Provincial Archives now name him Harold Mortimer Lamb, without the hyphen. His contributions to the Royal Photographic Society's annual shows and publications began, in 1904, as by Mortimer Lamb, changed to Mortimer-Lamb in 1905, and switched back and forth many times in subsequent years. On the letterhead of the Canadian Mining Institute, he was always Mortimer-Lamb. Colin Graham, who knew him well, accepted the first donation to the Art Gallery of Victoria in 1957 as from Mortimer Lamb, yet published a posthumous catalogue there in 1978 titled *Paintings of H. Mortimer-Lamb*. For many years, the gallery, known today as the Art Gallery of Greater Victoria, catalogued his donations as "gift of Harold Mortimer-Lamb" but now refers to him as Mortimer Lamb. The National Gallery of Canada files his work under Mortimer-Lamb, while the Vancouver Art

Gallery knows him as Mortimer Lamb. Jack Shadbolt's obituary in the Vancouver *Sun* in 1971 used Mortimer Lamb in the title and Mortimer-Lamb in the body of the story.

Mortimer-Lamb or Mortimer Lamb? It is an open question. While legally he was Lamb, his signature reads Mortimer-Lamb. His most important writings, his exhibited photographs, the publicity for his art gallery, and the letterhead of his professional occupation all name him as Mortimer-Lamb. So we shall too.

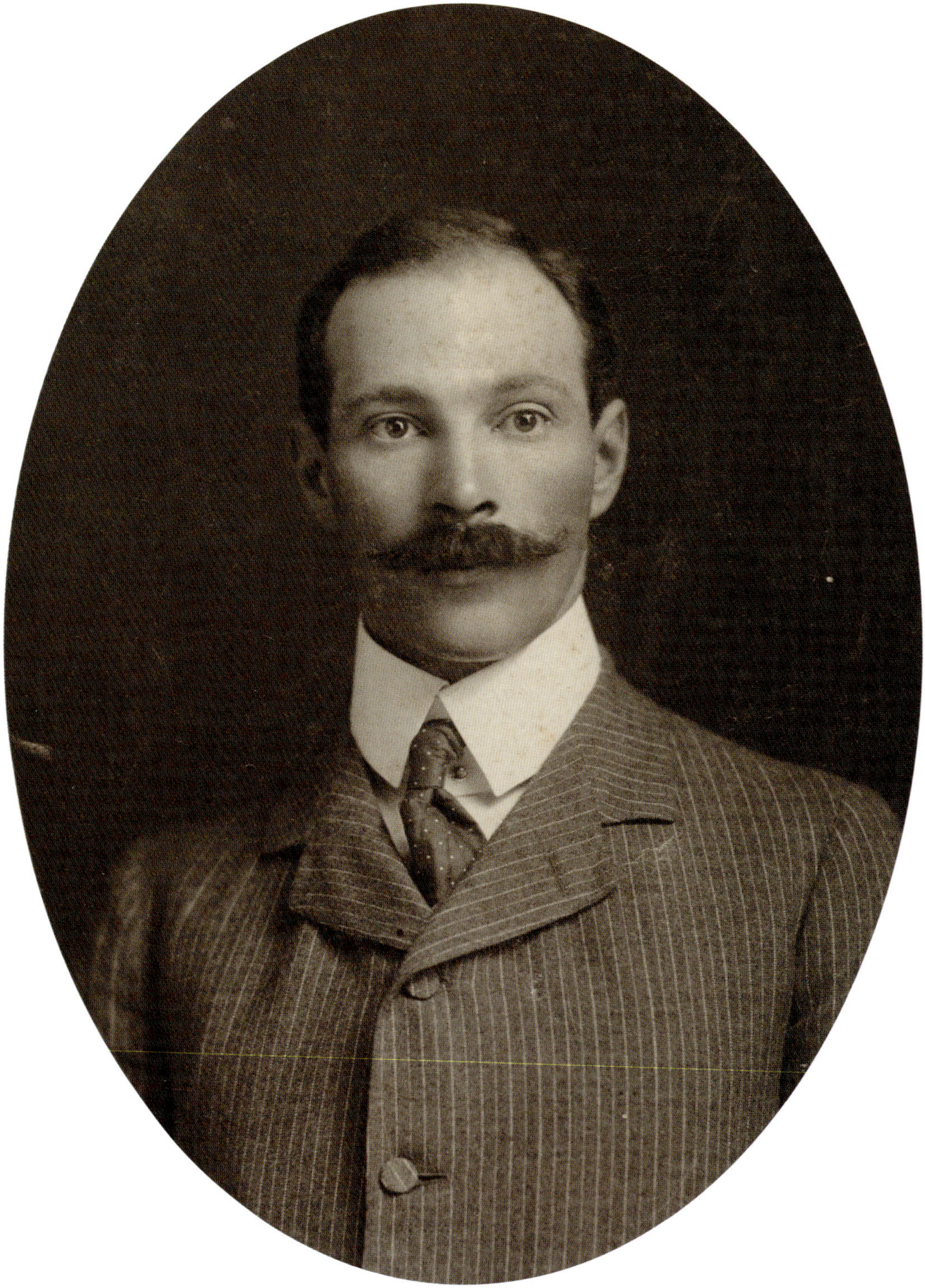

2 J. Savannah, *portrait of Harold Mortimer-Lamb.*

CHAPTER ONE

# The Early Years in British Columbia

Harold Mortimer-Lamb was born May 21, 1872, in Leatherhead, Surrey, England. The family home was just west of London, south of the current Heathrow Airport. Mortimer-Lamb's father, Captain Henry L. Lamb, served as a lieutenant in the Indian navy and rose to become naval director of India House in London. He shared his home there with his wife, Emily (née Mortimer), and named it Coonoor after a hill station in southwest India. There they raised their sons, Harold, Malcolm, and Stanley. In his extensive papers, Harold Mortimer-Lamb made almost no mention of his family or his upbringing.

Young Harold was educated at Hurstpierpoint, a village in mid-Sussex, and later at Grosvenor School in Twickenham. Subsequently he studied in Bruges in Belgium, where, according to his daughter, Molly, he almost died of scarlet fever. "His only memory of it," she said, "was a huge black cloak which opened up and enwrapped him—it was his father, come to take him away in a coach, to the boat and back to England."[1]

With a solid education behind him, at the age of seventeen Mortimer-Lamb was sent to British Columbia, ostensibly to learn farming. It was 1889 and he made his way over the continent by travelling across Lake Superior on a packet boat and then continuing west on the recently completed Canadian Pacific Railway. Its west-coast terminus, the new city of Vancouver, was not much more than a clearing on the shores of Burrard Inlet.

Mortimer-Lamb had come to Canada to learn farming from Captain L.N. Agassiz, an Englishman who had sold his commission in the Royal Welsh Fusiliers to join the gold rush on the Fraser River in 1858. By 1866 Agassiz had built his home, Ferny Coombe, on the fertile lands of the Fraser Valley. The town of Agassiz is named after him, and his original home is still standing, the oldest building in the Abbotsford area. In fact, Captain Agassiz did not teach Mortimer-Lamb much about farming. The young Englishman was put to work with the lowest of the farmhands and lived in a shack with the Chinese labourers. He enjoyed their company, but this education was not what he had in mind. "Dadda had to work so hard," Molly explained, "that he always said it stunted his growth."[2] As soon as possible, he freed himself from the clutches of Agassiz and, three months after arriving, left to make his own way.

In the rough-and-tumble world of the new province he worked as a labourer and a cook and found intellectual stimulus in the company of Reverend H.G. Fiennes-Clinton, rector of the St. James Anglican Church in Vancouver. There he became a lay reader, a post in which he served for three years, until his widening knowledge of the world undermined his Christian faith. About this time he tried his hand at journalism, taking the opportunity to visit on horseback the burgeoning mining communities along the Canada–United States border.

Mortimer-Lamb enjoyed his new-found freedom and, as a freelance reporter, discovered a natural gift for writing prose of style and clarity. In addition to his fluency with the written word, he was ambitious and showed an entrepreneurial spirit. At the age of nineteen, in 1891, he reinvented himself as the founding editor of the Chilliwack *Progress*. Moving farther into the mountains to the east, he initiated the Midway *Advance* and, in 1894, moved to the community of Greenwood, where he started the *Boundary Creek Times*.

Greenwood is a little town near the American border, between Osoyoos and Grand Forks. At the time Mortimer-Lamb arrived, mining fever was raging along those borderlands, and Greenwood was at the centre of the mining district. As an educated young Englishman and the editor of the local newspaper, he was an eligible bachelor and was soon courting Kate Lindsay, daughter of a military officer newly arrived from Winnipeg. She was a very pretty country girl from the Kettle Valley. Kate and Harold were married on June 24, 1896, at a ceremony in Vancouver, and they remained married until her death in 1939. Kate bore six children—two girls and four boys.

Because Mortimer-Lamb was on the scene in the mining country, he soon became correspondent on mining matters for *The Province*, a leading newspaper published in Victoria. This brought him to the attention of mining promoters in the provincial capital. Mining was a powerful force, at the very heart of growth and settlement in the province. In 1895 the first provincial mineralogist was appointed, and in 1897 private enterprise responded by creating the Mining Association of British Columbia; Mortimer-Lamb was invited to come to Victoria to become the association's first director and secretary. At the same time he became

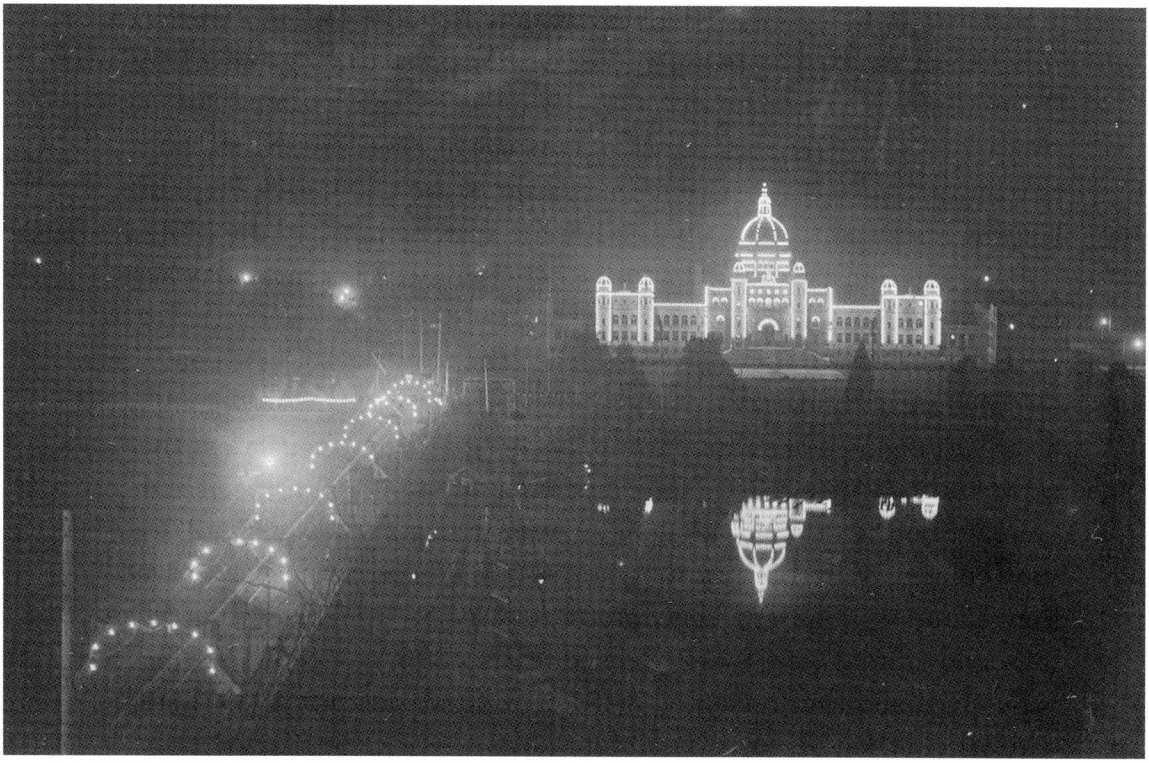

3 Mortimer-Lamb, *Parliament and Causeway illuminated,* Victoria.

the founding editor of the *British Columbia Mining Record*, an industry newspaper published at the offices of *The Province* on Broughton Street.

In addition to the responsibilities of his new work, Mortimer-Lamb became a family man. The first child of his union with Kate was a girl named Molly, who died in infancy. In 1898 Kate gave birth to Dorothy, always known as Dolly. Dolly's arrival coincided with Mortimer-Lamb's discovery of photography, and as a model she was one of his favourites. With the following years came the four boys: John Haliburton, known as Hal, was born in 1899, followed by Oliver, Lawrence, and, in 1908, Willoughby, known as Abby.

Though Vancouver eventually eclipsed Victoria in size and prestige, in 1897 Victoria celebrated the Queen's Jubilee year by opening the splendid new Parliament Buildings. Still indisputably the hub of the province, Victoria was also the jumping-off point and supply depot for the Klondike gold rush of 1897. City merchants were enriching themselves by outfitting the intrepid explorers who were setting off in search of mineral wealth. Information about mining was in demand, and at the turn of the century the *British Columbia Mining Record* was a journal of considerable significance to many in the community. Mortimer-Lamb, as its editor, was well positioned to mix with influential people. Not long after he arrived in Victoria in 1897, he bought his first home, on the south side of Oak Bay Avenue near Newport.

Across the road from Mortimer-Lamb's house was the sixteen-acre estate of a fellow countryman, Clive Phillipps-Wolley. There the owner lived like a country gentleman in a fine brick-and-half-timbered home overlooking the waters of Oak Bay. A keen big-game hunter, Phillipps-Wolley had left England and travelled across the continent, eventually settling in the Kootenays, where he published a newspaper, *The Nelson Miner*. From this base on the Canada–US border he had been a prolific contributor to the London *Mining News* before moving to Victoria.

Considering their shared interests, it was inevitable that Mortimer-Lamb would meet up with his neighbour. Among the first photographs of his distinguished career as an artistic photographer was a series of surprisingly sophisticated portraits of the Phillipps-Wolley family: bewhiskered father; mother and child; solemn infant. Phillipps-Wolley provided a splendid example for the young Mortimer-Lamb. Here was an Englishman who had turned his literary bent to advantage as a journalist, focusing his attention on mining. Moving into Phillipps-Wolley's orbit was a stroke of luck for Mortimer-Lamb.

Among the people he met in the vigorous young town of Victoria were others with artistic leanings, and in 1895 they founded the Victoria Art Society, a rather loose grouping of artists that was the first art club in the province. Variously known as the Art Union and the Victoria Brush and Camera Club, it eventually matured in 1909 to become the long-lived Island Arts and Crafts Society.

In his "Reminiscences," an autobiography Mortimer-Lamb wrote when he was over ninety years of age, he looked back fondly to the time he had spent with art-club members. There was Sam Maclure, "who painted watercolours getting a pleasant diffuse effect by applying the colour on damp paper."[3] Maclure was the leading residential architect in the city, and an unsigned watercolour by him was found tucked into an early Mortimer-Lamb photo album. Another member of the club, James Bloomfield, painted murals for Government House and had completed designs for the stained-glass windows in the new

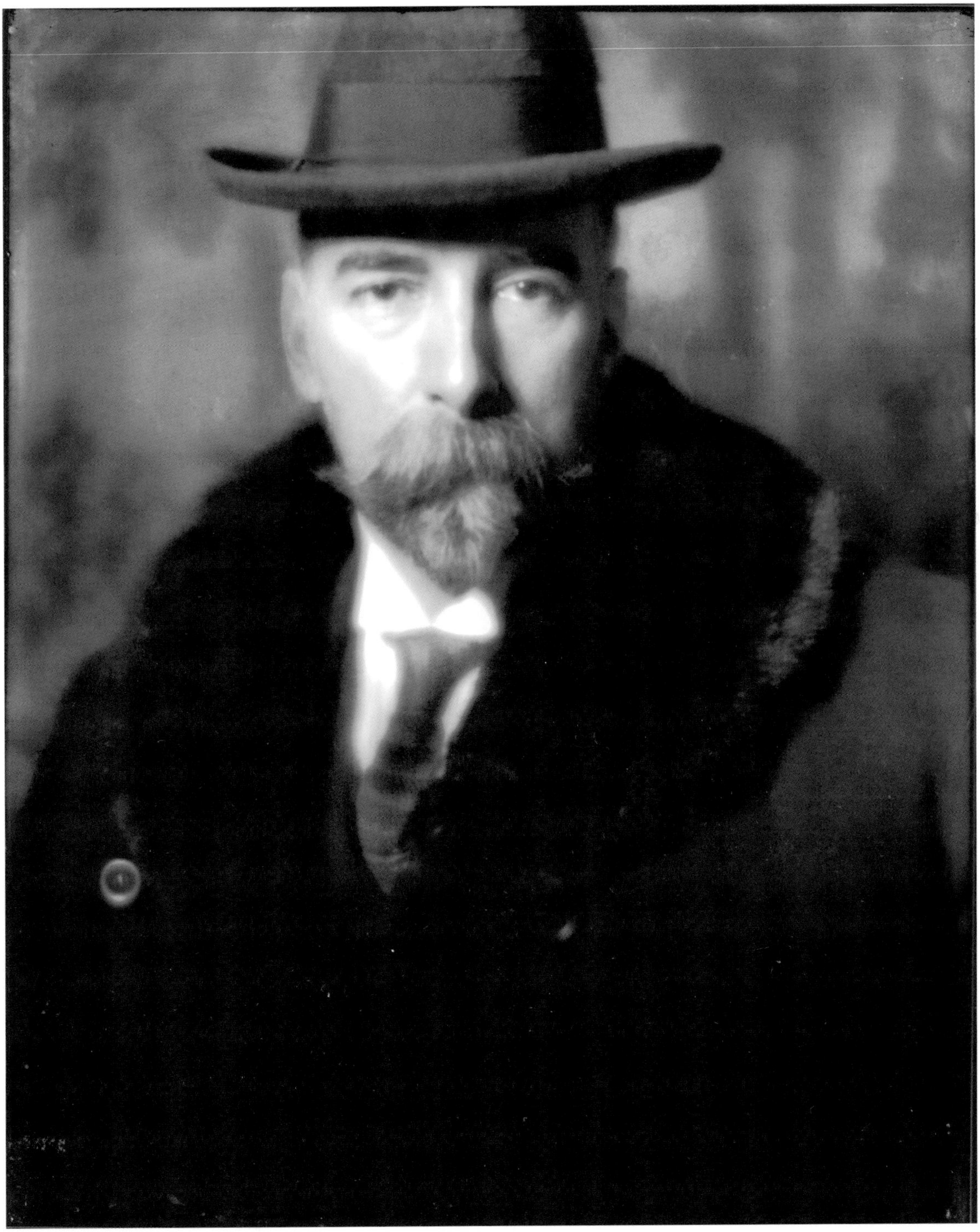

4 Mortimer-Lamb, *Clive Phillipps-Wolley*.

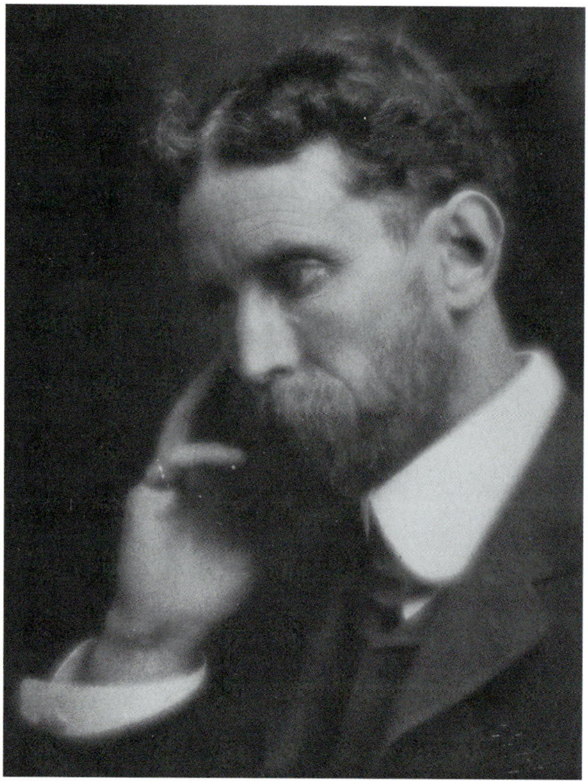

5 Mortimer-Lamb, *Samuel Maclure*.

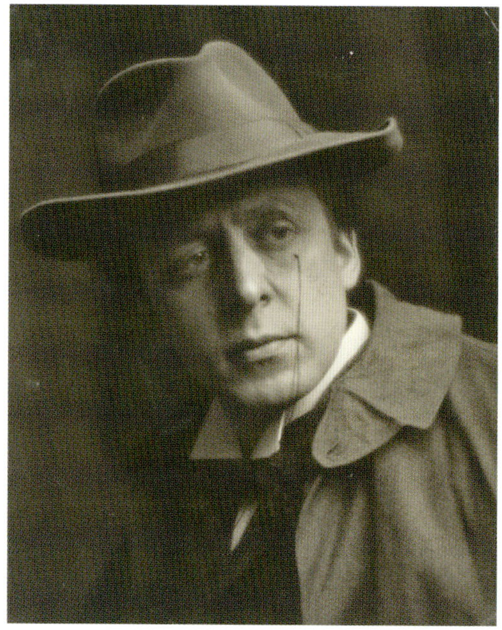

6 Mortimer-Lamb, *James Bloomfield*.

Parliament Buildings. The glass itself was executed in his family's studio and workshop in Vancouver. Bloomfield had recently returned from a two-year tour sponsored by Canada's Governor General, Lord Aberdeen, in the course of which he had studied in New York, Chicago, New Orleans, London, and Manchester. There was probably much eager sharing of information among members of the art club upon his reappearance. Certainly Mortimer-Lamb was open to the information his companions could offer.

In addition to editing regular issues of the *British Columbia Mining Record*, Mortimer-Lamb took evident delight in creating an annual Christmas supplement of the *Record*, which was noted in the best circles. The supplement for 1899—"a literary miscellany of a local and locally historic character"—presented, among much else, his first published photograph, a study of his beloved daughter, Dolly. Also included were ethnology by Charles Hill-Tout, poetry by Phillipps-Wolley, and a short story by Mortimer-Lamb himself. In a more sober vein, the supplement for the following year offered a thirty-three-page essay by Mortimer-Lamb on "The History and Progress of Mining in British Columbia," notable because it was illustrated with twenty-eight of his photographs.

Looking back on those carefree times was always a pleasure for Mortimer-Lamb. He enjoyed cycling around town on smooth roads not yet cluttered with automobiles and recalled stopping at The Little Brown Jug tavern, where for the price of a drink patrons were free to enjoy the complimentary roast beef buffet. At a memorable New Year's Eve party at the Victoria Badminton Club, things got out of control. He recalled "a duel with cues on top of the billiard table. Finally, I was carried up to bed. So sound was the liquor I consumed that next morning I awoke as fresh as a daisy."[4]

Of a different temper was his friendship with Sophie Pemberton, which was one of the highlights of the time Mortimer-Lamb spent in Victoria. Pemberton has been described as British Columbia's first professionally trained artist, and she opened Mortimer-Lamb's eyes to the look of large, academically accomplished oil paintings. Born in 1869, Sophia Theresa Pemberton was the daughter of the surveyor-general of British Columbia, Joseph Pemberton. Unlike the parents of Emily Carr, who was her near contemporary, Sophie's allowed her to study in London, where she exhibited at the Royal Academy's annual exhibitions. She moved on to Paris, attending Académie Julian, where she won the Prix Julian for best picture submitted. Further prestigious showings included the glamorous St. Louis Exhibition of 1904, immediately preceding her glorious return to Victoria.

In the meantime, Mortimer-Lamb had moved in from Oak Bay to be closer to town and was now living in Rockland, Victoria's toniest neighbourhood. In fact, he was living on Pemberton Road, named for Sophie's family, who lived in a mansion nearby. Sophie kept a studio in the turret, which looked across to the Olympic Mountains. In the fall of 1904, about forty of Pemberton's paintings, including some of the large oils she had exhibited in London and Paris, were featured at the Annual Provincial Agricultural Exhibition held at the Willows Fairgrounds. "They were a revelation to me," Mortimer-Lamb exclaimed, "as I had never seen competent examples [of oil painting] of any kind, modern or otherwise."[5]

He was inspired to commission a portrait of Dolly by this talented artist, and Sophie painted the eight-year-old in a lovely white dress and

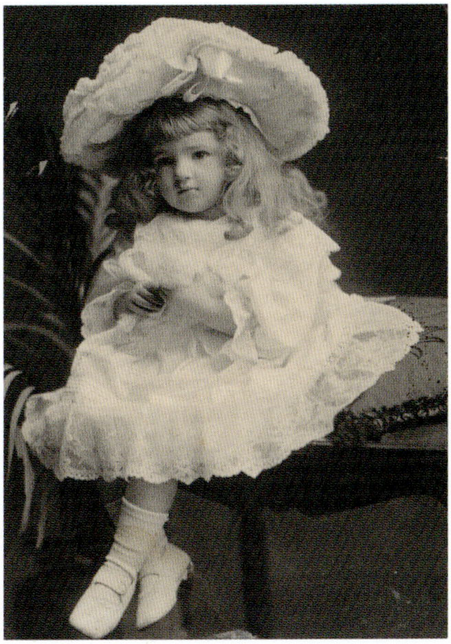

7 Mortimer-Lamb, *Dolly with a wide hat*.

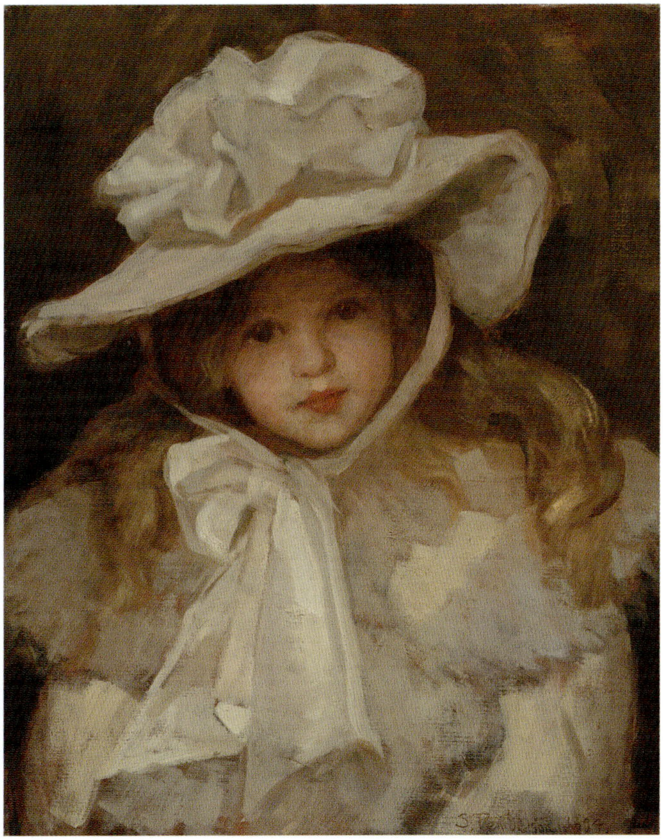

8 Sophie Pemberton, *Portrait of a Child*.

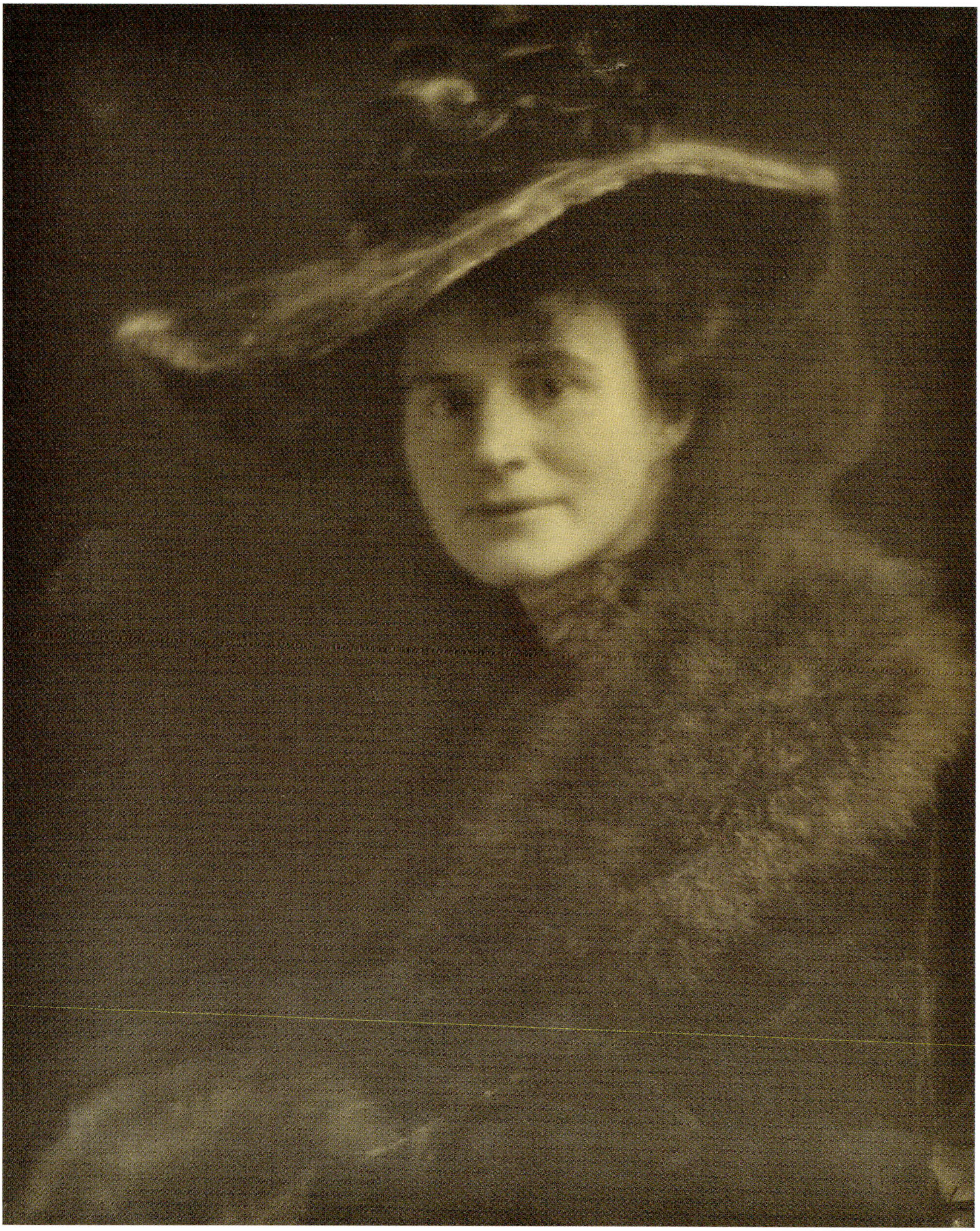

9 Mortimer-Lamb, *Untitled (Portrait of Sophie Deane-Drummond).*

broad-brimmed hat. The oil is an endearing portrait of a pretty girl, her face framed in a cascade of dark golden hair. Mortimer-Lamb presented it to the Vancouver Art Gallery in 1946. For his part, at the time of the painting, Mortimer-Lamb made a haunting portrait photograph of Pemberton, also wearing a broad-brimmed hat.

His friendship with Sophie Pemberton was the first of a series of relationships that enormously enriched Mortimer-Lamb's life. Their close connection was lifelong, as attested to by the correspondence they maintained over more than fifty years. After Sophie married, she and her husband, Canon Arthur Beanlands, moved to England. During the First World War she wrote to Mortimer-Lamb from her estate at Sevenoaks, Kent, with intriguing tales of Christmas in a country house during wartime. Her final note, written after her return to Victoria and dated 1954, is illustrated with a watercolour of a dry and curling red maple leaf above the message "wishing that you were at Pemberton Road instead of so far off!"[6]

Given the evidence of his first photograph albums, Mortimer-Lamb was not, in the beginning, a Pictorialist photographer. There are two little books full of sharp and arresting images: farmhouses amid Garry oaks, a ship aground off Trial Island, the Parliament Buildings with ceremonial arches illuminated for the visit of the Duke of Connaught in 1901. In this he was like almost any other shutterbug. But soon Mortimer-Lamb became involved with a different, consciously artistic sort of picture-making. He built a darkroom and studio in the Pemberton Road house and there photographed Lieutenant-Governor Henri-Gustave Joly de Lotbinière looking dour. In his insightful picture of Sir Richard McBride, the premier of the province appears to be somewhat more cheerful.

These portraits of important Victorians were exhibited in the first show of photography as art in the new city of Vancouver. It took place in the studio of his friend, James Bloomfield, in the Fairfield Building during February 1905. In an admiring column, the Vancouver *News-Advertiser* named the subjects of the pictures, including Reverend Baugh-Allen and Reverend Fiennes-Clinton of St. James Anglican Church in Vancouver and, from Victoria, Clive Phillipps-Wolley, Samuel Maclure, and Mrs. Lindsay, Mortimer-Lamb's mother-in-law. Regarding the images of Dolly, the journalist effused: "In his little daughter the artist is happy in possessing a most graceful model, fitted to his purpose from all points of view, and the most delicate bits of his collection are studies of the pretty child."[7] Also included in the show were landscapes and nudes.

From the start, Mortimer-Lamb took his photography very seriously. As early as 1903 he submitted images to the Royal Photographic Society's annual London Salon, and a picture of his daughter holding an apple, titled *Little Eve*, was accepted. Two years later he placed seventh in a field of twenty thousand during the annual photo contest in London. Beginning in 1904, Mortimer-Lamb contributed reports on the state of the art in Canada, which were published in *Photograms of the Year*, an annual published by the society. Through these efforts he took his place in the worldwide movement of artistic photography.

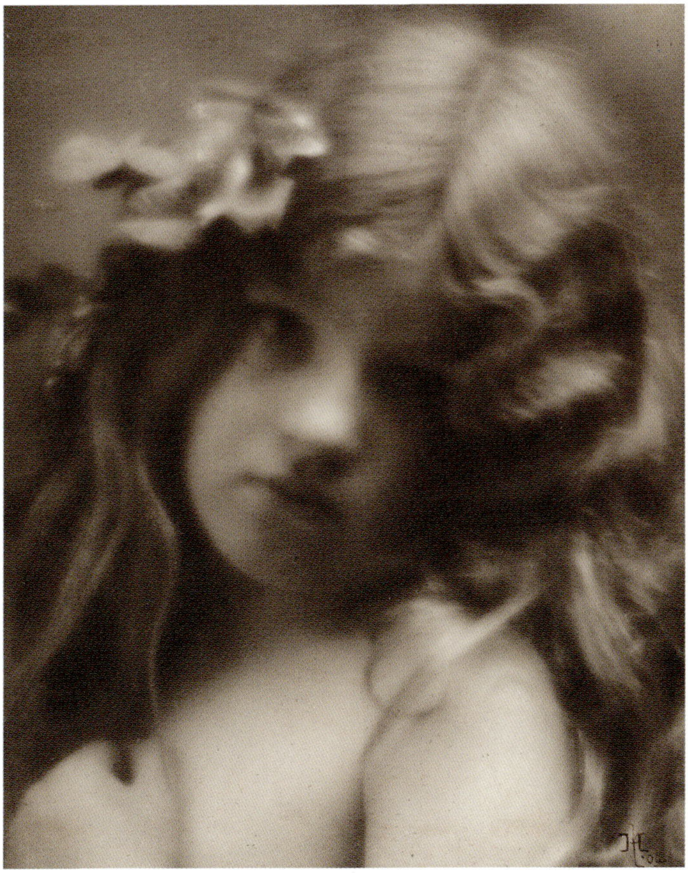

10 Mortimer-Lamb, *Dolly*.

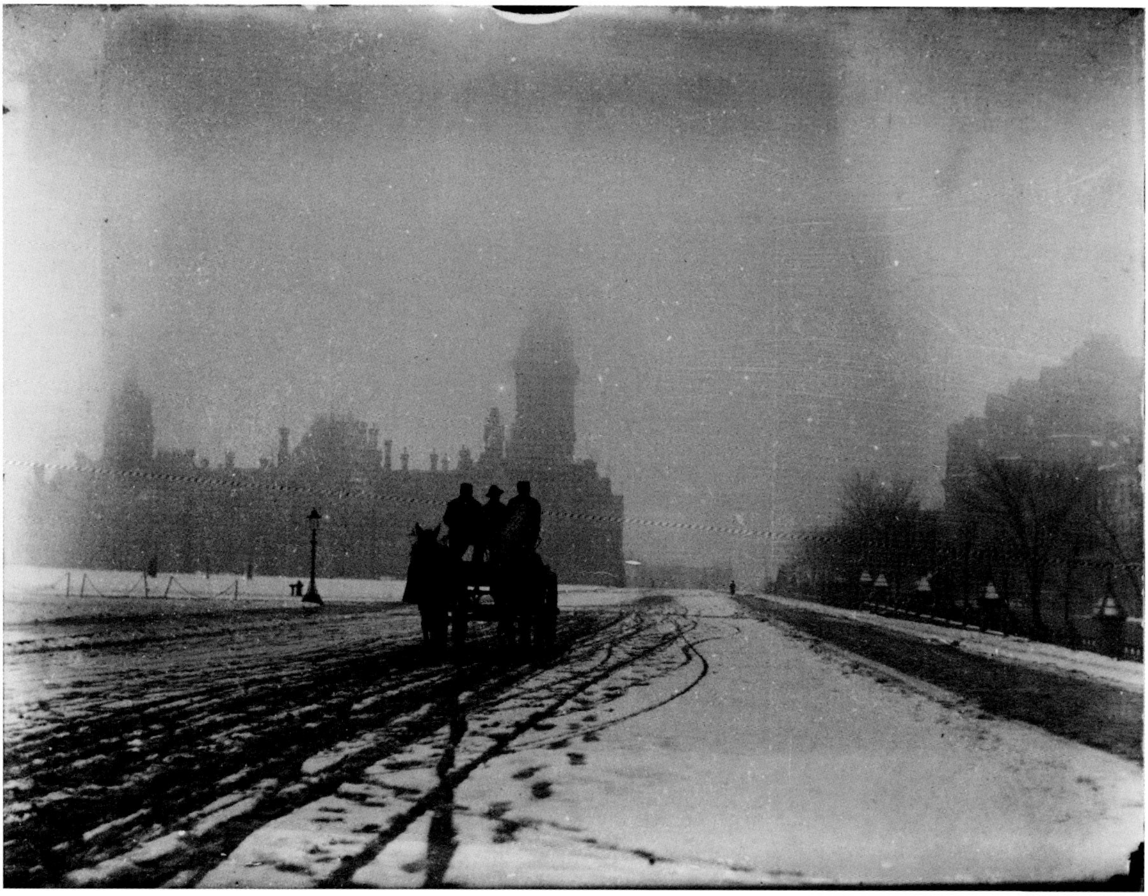

11 Mortimer-Lamb, *Parliament Hill, Ottawa in snow.*

CHAPTER TWO

# Montreal

In his professional life, Mortimer-Lamb also took a place in the wider world. Recognized for his facility as a writer and for his managerial skills, in 1903 he was named secretary of the Canadian Mining Institute's national body. This entailed, in 1905, a move to Montreal, the business capital of Canada, where he took over the institute's head office. Just ten years after he had left Greenwood in the Kettle Valley, Mortimer-Lamb established his family in a substantial home at 310 Grosvenor Avenue in Westmount, the anglophone stronghold of Montreal. The four-bedroom home, named White Birches, had lots of space for his growing family and soon boasted a well-equipped darkroom.

Most days, Mortimer-Lamb went to work at the institute, which was at first located in the Ritz-Carlton Hotel and eventually expanded to a suite of offices in the Drummond Building. He had a staff, and seemed a little surprised by the power he was given in his role as secretary and later secretary-treasurer. "When I first went to Montreal," he reminisced, "the secretary of the Institute was an initiator, and almost a dictator.

For example, for the first few years of my residence there, during January every year, I would prepare a list of those I thought would constitute a desirable Council or directorate, including a president, then take a sleigh and go round to invite Montreal members to endorse my list with their signatures. This would be issued as the recommendations of a nominating committee and would be invariably approved."[1] In this way Mortimer-Lamb became familiar with the most important mining men in Canada, who were also the nation's wealthiest men, and he learned a great deal from these experiences.

Mortimer-Lamb kept the membership informed with regular bulletins and became editor of the *Canadian Mining Review*. Volume XIV was dedicated to a long technical article titled "Photography for Mining Engineers and Geologists," written and illustrated by the editor. He represented the institute at international congresses and, in 1908, arranged and supervised a five-week tour across Canada for thirty-five industrialists and investors from Britain, Belgium, France, and Germany. They travelled on their own train and visited a series of mining sites and cities from Cape Breton to British Columbia. The tour was commemorated in a special issue of the institute's journal that contained more than three hundred pages and was profusely illustrated with photographs and tales of their spirited adventures.

The Germans reciprocated by inviting Mortimer-Lamb to a week-long conference in Dusseldorf in 1909. At the conclusion of that trip he was one of five men honoured at a testimonial banquet, given by a sister institution in London, at the Savoy Hotel. There he was also presented with a silver tea service. In a biographical sketch written after Mortimer-Lamb's death, Colin Graham, director emeritus of the Art Gallery of

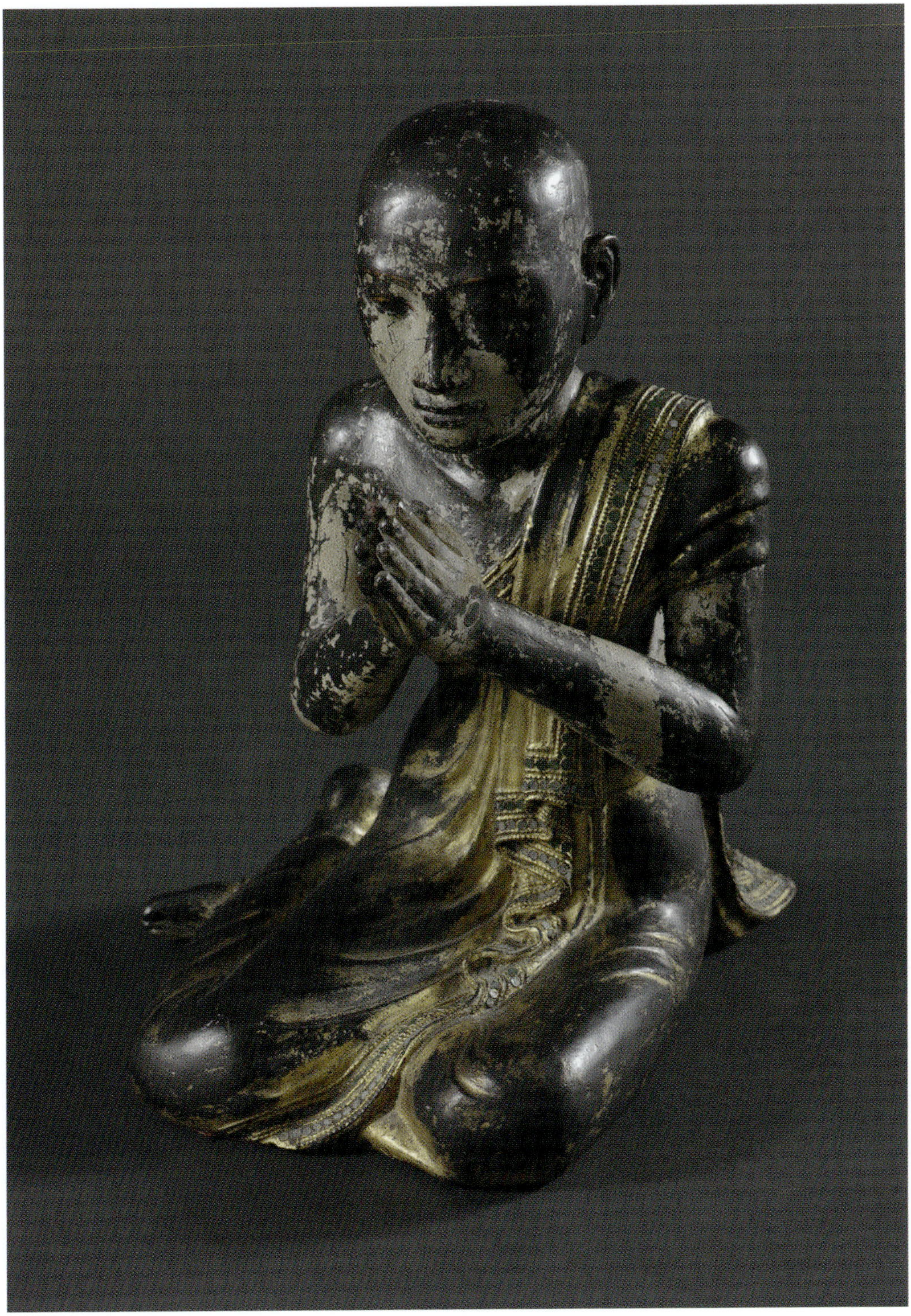

12 *Praying Monk*, Burma, early nineteenth century.

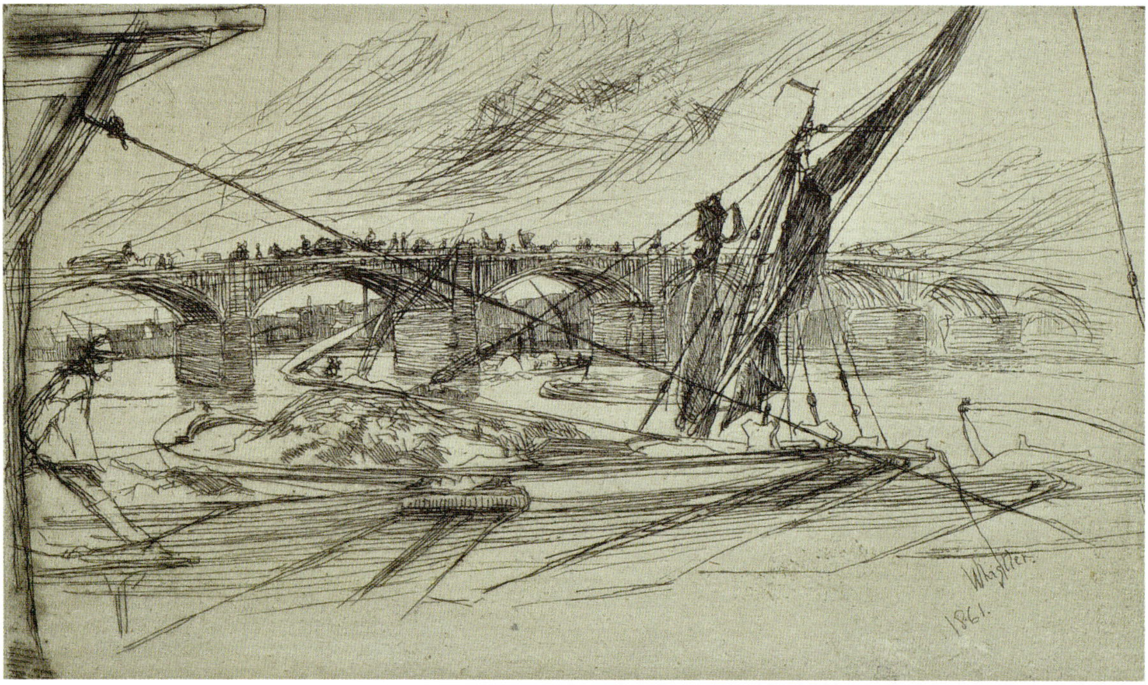


13 J.A.M. Whistler, *Vauxhall Bridge*.

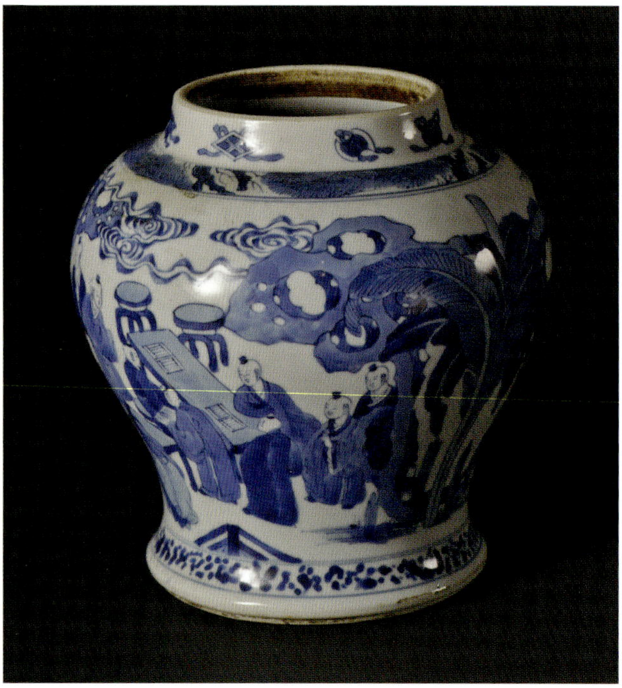

14 *Enjoying the Polite Arts*, China, eighteenth century.

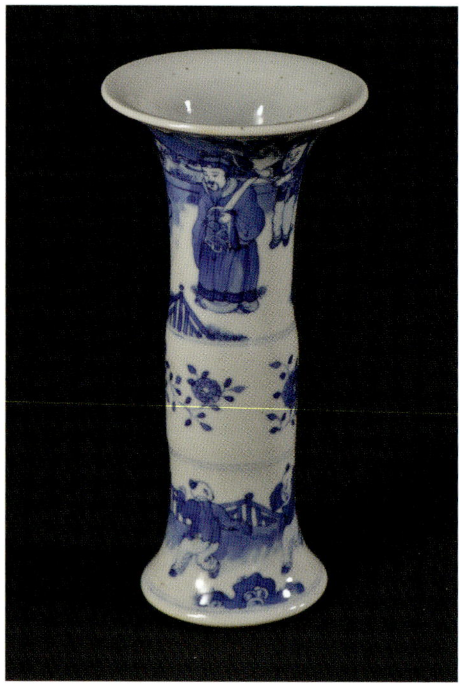

15 Blue and white vase with figure design, China, nineteenth century.

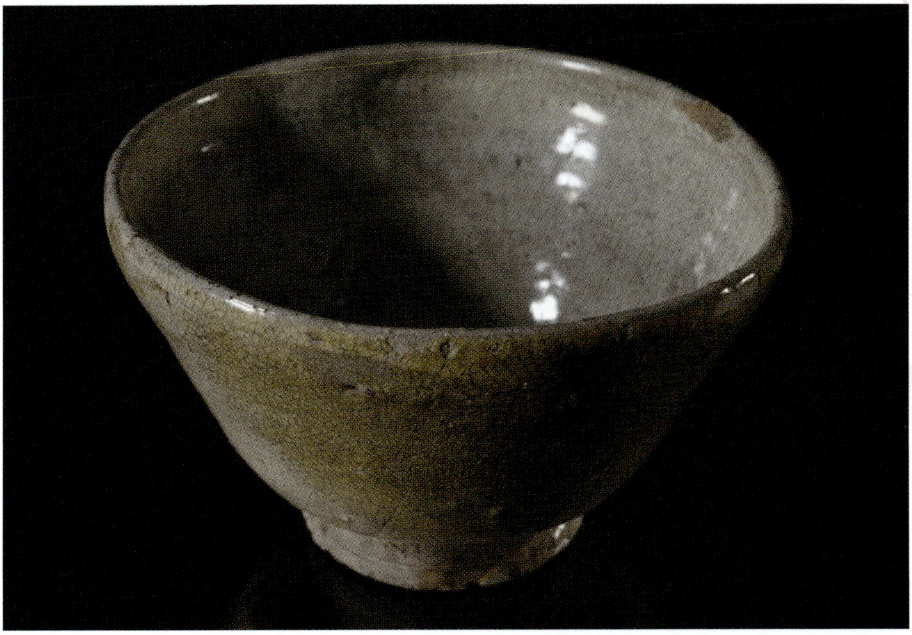

16 Tea bowl, Hagi ware, Japan, late seventeenth-early eighteenth century.

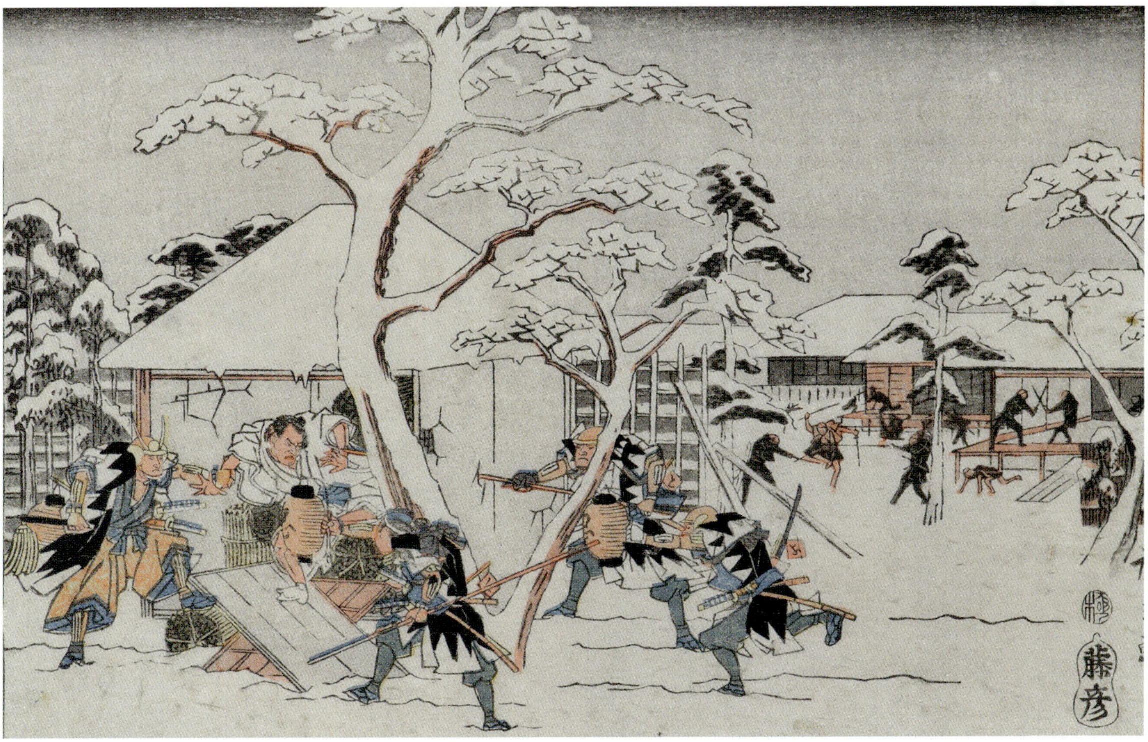


17 Ando Hiroshige, *Tale of the Forty-Seven Ronin: Act XI, Sixth Episode* (Fuji-Hiko series), nineteenth century.

Greater Victoria, offered a rounded view of his character, which few in the art world saw: "He was blessed with abundant energy and a rugged constitution, not to mention high spirits. He possessed the rare ability to live comfortably in two totally disparate worlds, that of the esthete and that of the rough-and-tumble mining world."[2]

The trip to Europe and Britain may have inspired Mortimer-Lamb to pursue his interest in art, for that is when his art collection really got under way. As he moved about foggy London, immersed in a dream of the Aesthetic Movement, he may have picked up souvenirs such as his little etching by J.A.M. Whistler of Vauxhall Bridge, which showed a young man lounging under the bridge on the tidal flats of the Thames. He also found a published edition of Whistler's *Ten O'Clock Lecture* in which the artist defended himself against the charge of having thrown a pot of paint in the public's face. His collection was further expanded by his acquisition of a number of pieces of Chinese porcelain decorated with under-glaze blue, some subtle Japanese tea wares, and a group of colour woodcut prints by the nineteenth-century master of the form, Ando Hiroshige. Combined with a diverse gathering of small Buddhist statuary, these treasures set the mood in Mortimer-Lamb's home for years to come.

In Montreal, the captains of industry with whom Mortimer-Lamb associated were also the most prominent art collectors in the country. Sir William Van Horne, the financier behind the Canadian Pacific Railway, was chief among them. Mortimer-Lamb photographed him in a memorable portrait (now in Canada's National Gallery) and even offered to write his biography. George Drummond, the key figure in the Cape Breton iron and steel industry, was also a leading collector of European

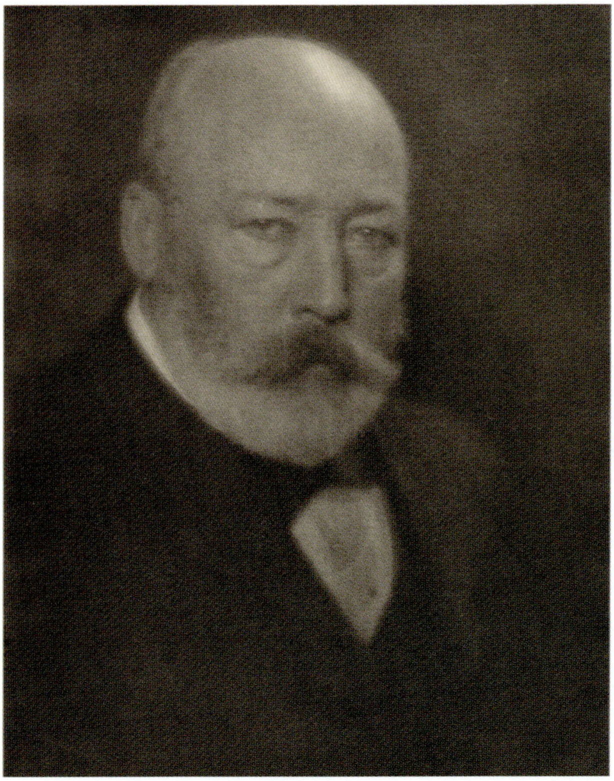

18 Mortimer-Lamb, *Sir William Van Horne.*

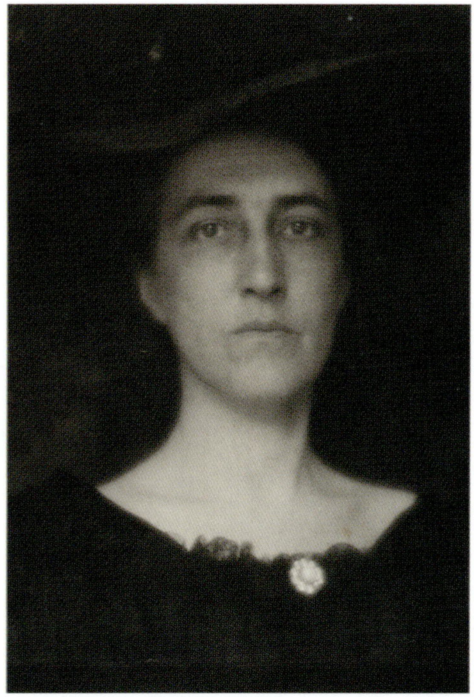

19 Mortimer-Lamb, *Lady Drummond.*

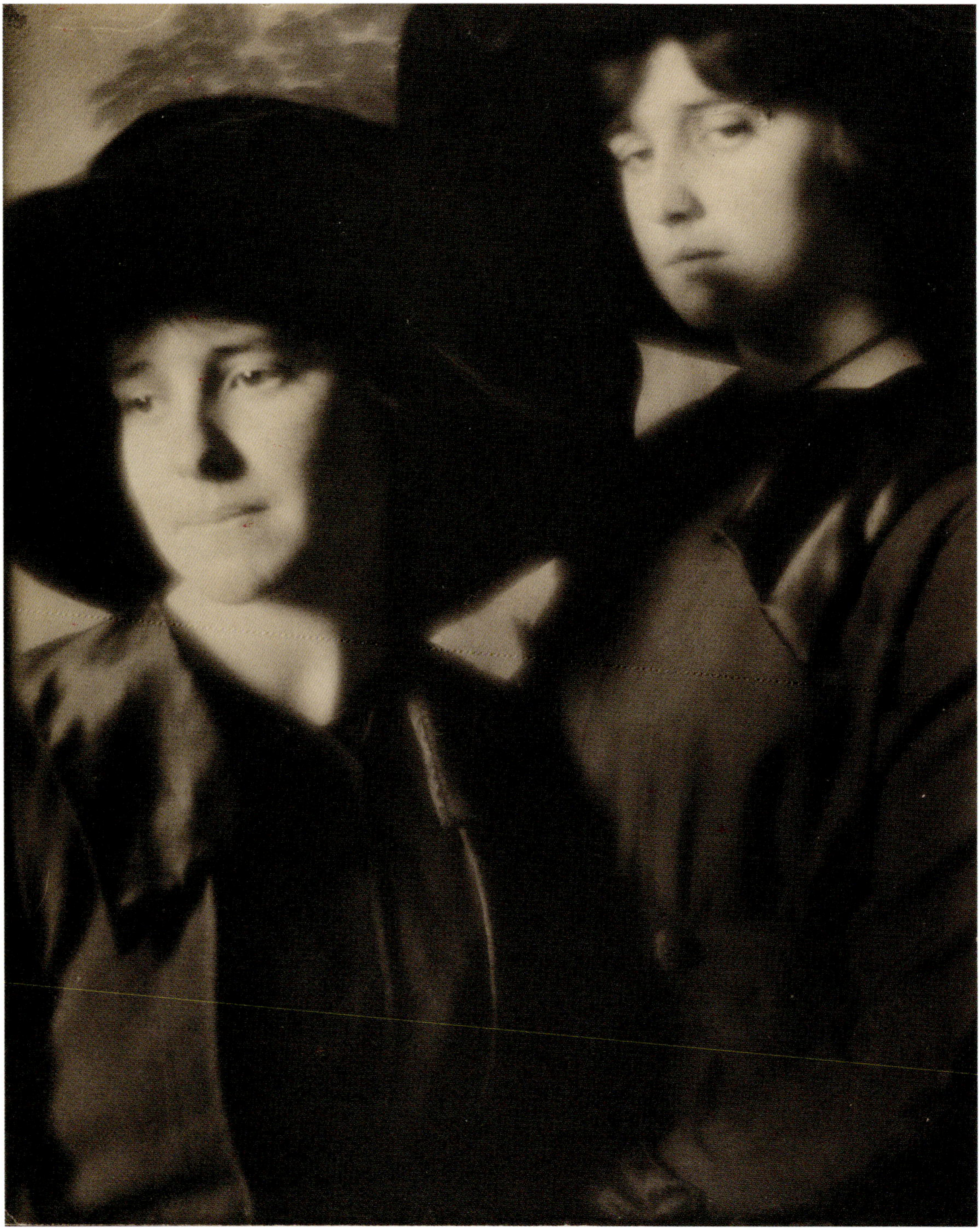

20 Mortimer-Lamb, *Two Sisters (daughters of Mr. and Mrs. George Drummond)*.

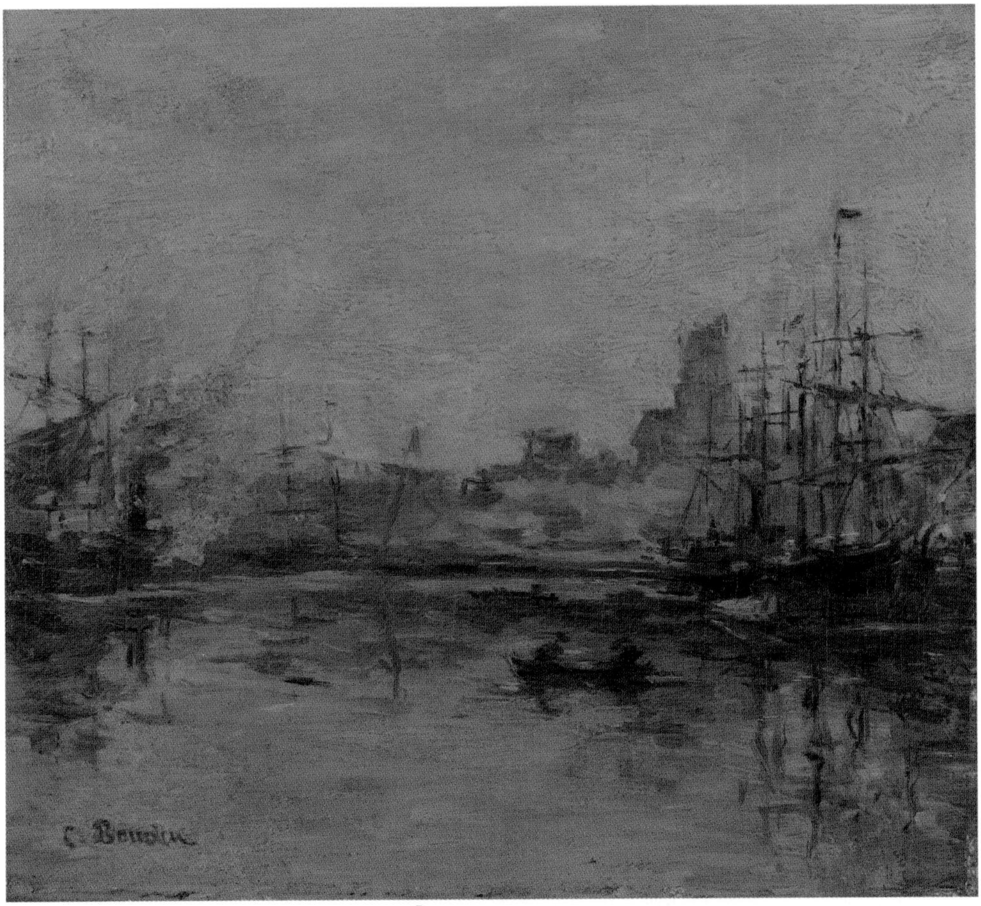

21 Eugène Boudin, *The Harbour of Fécamp*.

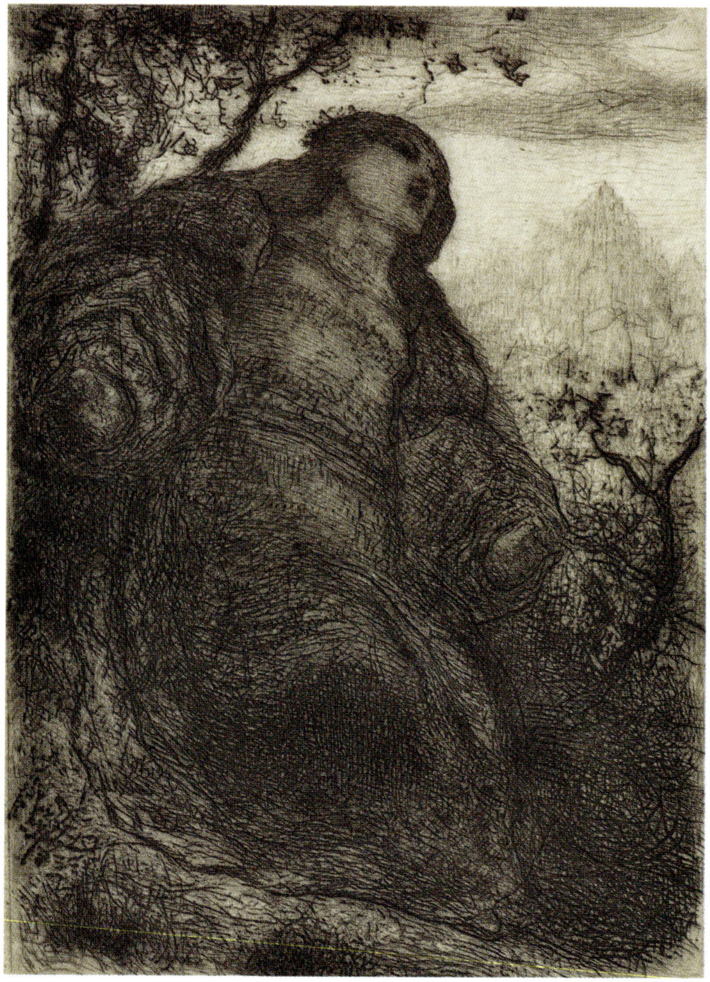

22 Matthijs Maris, *Under the Tree*.

masterworks. Mortimer-Lamb's fine photograph, which captures the tempered gaze of Lady Drummond, is also part of Canada's national collection, and the family appreciated his picture of the Drummond daughters. Drummond's preference for the paintings of the French Impressionist Eugène Boudin, of which he owned four, is reflected in Mortimer-Lamb's astute purchase at that time of a small Boudin panel, *The Harbour of Fécamp*. E.B. Greenshields, president of Amalgamated Asbestos, had perhaps the strongest influence. Greenshields's taste for late nineteenth-century Hague School paintings is echoed with smaller examples in Mortimer-Lamb's collection—for example, a watercolour by Jan Weissenbruch and an etching by Matthew Maris. Greenshields too was the subject of a Mortimer-Lamb photographic portrait.

According to Mortimer-Lamb, the high point of his varied artistic career was his election to The Brotherhood of the Linked Ring, a mystical-sounding subgroup of the Royal Photographic Society with whom he exhibited in the London Salon. The society, established in 1853, was essentially a democratic and educational organization dedicated to the furtherance of the art and science of photography in all forms, most notably as a rather practical "handmaiden of the arts." The Linked Ring took exception to this and believed photography was, first and foremost, a means of artistic expression. They aligned themselves with the Photo-Secession group headed by Alfred Stieglitz in New York and called their style of image-making Pictorialism.

Avoiding anything topical, political, or controversial, the Pictorialists concentrated on portraiture and figure studies, landscapes, and genre scenes. The principal subject of the picture was seen with relative clarity while everything else was subdued and hazy. Taking inspiration from the

23 Mortimer-Lamb, *Dolly in white.*

realm of painting, such as the portraits of Rembrandt, the Pictorialists included simple symbolic elements in their compositions—the globe, the veil, the mirror. The soft context that enwraps the central image seems to owe something to an Impressionism in which atmosphere is more important than form. Mortimer-Lamb made every effort to render the essence of his subjects, going beyond simple portraiture to create figurative mood pieces to which he gave titles like *Beata*, *Meditation*, and *Reflection*.[3]

Mortimer-Lamb first wrote on the state of Pictorial photography in Canada for the Royal Photographic Society's annual, *Photograms of the Year*, in 1904. The magazine also featured a charming photo of his daughter Dolly, altogether creating an auspicious entry for him into the international world of artistic photography. The next year, he had moved to Montreal, and his report on the Canadian scene for *Photograms* of 1905 had a more national scope. But to Mortimer-Lamb, the prospect was bleak. "I have been strongly tempted," he wrote, "to abandon the task as one utterly without hope or profit. In a word, Pictorial Photography in Canada is so poorly represented that it is hardly worth talking about it at all."[4] That said, he continued and things in Canada improved.

The members of the Royal Photographic Society came to a division in about 1908. It was during that year that The Linked Ring faction curated the annual exhibition for the society and showed photographs by only eight entrants. They took the high road, favouring the most advanced trends in photographic art. Those who supported a more broadly populist approach to photography regained control of the salon's exhibition the following year and named themselves The London Salon Club. Though he continued to exhibit in the annual salon, Mortimer-Lamb's sympathies were with the artistic principles of The Linked Ring, and in this, he

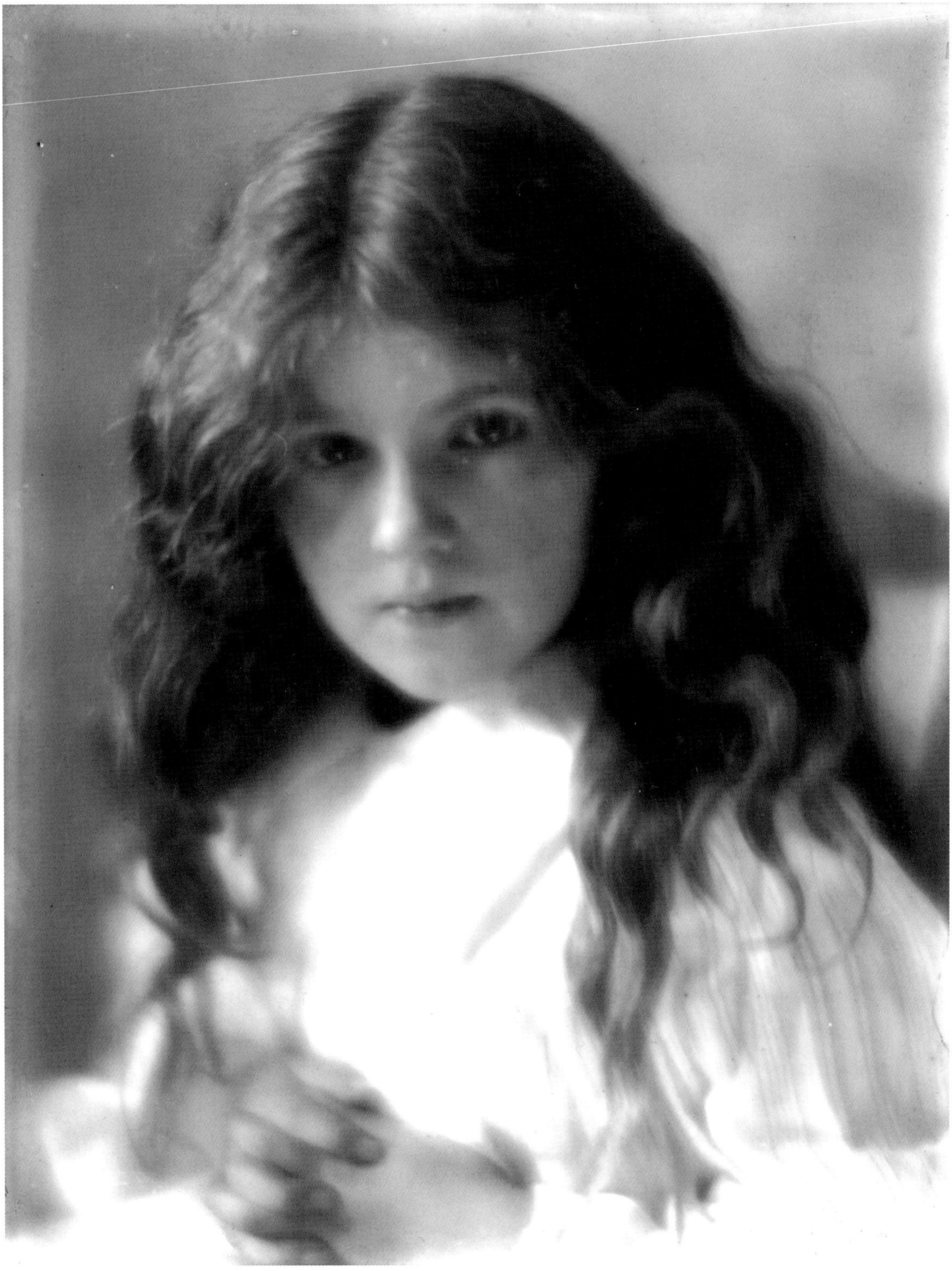

allied himself with the renowned masters of Pictorial photography from Germany, Britain, and, in particular, the United States. Mortimer-Lamb's work was described at the time as being "of the American school. It is characterized by freshness of outlook and breadth of treatment that stamps it with a quality that compels attention."[5]

Mortimer-Lamb continued to provide a voice for Canadian photography in *Photograms of the Year* until 1919. His comments in the 1913 issue described Canada as "grim and majestic, forbidding and beautiful, but never insignificant. To the photographer the problem is exceptionally difficult. To photograph the big things in Nature so that the suggestion of their bigness is not lost demands more than mere skill. It has yet to be done successfully in this country."[6] The grandeur of Canada: that was the challenge the future Group of Seven painters were to face. Mortimer-Lamb's insight into a truly Canadian art was acutely visual, for, as the editor in the same issue noted, Mortimer-Lamb himself was "an artist to the fingertips." His photographs were "always characterized by painter-like qualities."

As a writer, his contributions appeared most frequently in *The Amateur Photographer and Photographic News*, a weekly founded in London, England, in 1884. The *News* was a chatty and enthusiastic little newspaper in which he made his debut on August 11, 1904, with a story titled "Control—For the Beginner." "Now, let it be clearly understood at the outset that I do not set myself up as an authority on matters photographic," he humbly began, and then went on to describe his efforts with the gum-bichromate, carbon, and ozotype processes for making photographic prints.[7] Mortimer-Lamb's ability to present technical matters in a clear and accessible manner was perfect for the publication.

Most notable among his contributions was Mortimer-Lamb's description of his technique for night photography. At the time he wrote about it, taking a picture after sunset was a challenging problem. Setting up his cumbersome tripod and heavy view camera outdoors in the dark, he focused "by lighting a candle which was placed on a convenient root [of a tree] at what I judge to be about the right distance under the circumstances. Then, leaving the lens open at full aperture, I exposed my plate by blowing magnesium powder through an alcohol lamp, and moving from place to place outside, of course, the area embraced by the lens."[8] The glass plate was exposed by the flare of ignited magnesium powder, repeated at different locations. His pioneering efforts in this field were later the subject of an article by Ariane Isler-de Jongh in the journal *The History of Photography* in 1996.[9]

*The Amateur Photographer and Photographic News* frequently included Mortimer-Lamb's photographs. The July 6, 1909, issue carried a full-page reproduction of his portrait of Laura Muntz, a celebrated Canadian painter, as shown in its first *Exhibition of Colonial Photography*, and he won a medal in the second annual exhibition. "Of the pictures from Canada," the *News* reported, "indisputably the premier position is held by H. Mortimer-Lamb. In fact, in one or two of his pictures . . . we have the finest productions in the exhibition."[10] Referring to his *Mother and Child*, Anthony Guest noted that "its sympathetic rendering of a Pre-Raphaelite theme in modern language gives it its distinction."[11] Among the thousands of entries to this international show, Mortimer-Lamb's photographs were always given thoughtful consideration. Writing in the *News* about the colonial exhibition in 1911, Guest asked, "Who can say what is in the mind of the young woman depicted in 'Portrait'?

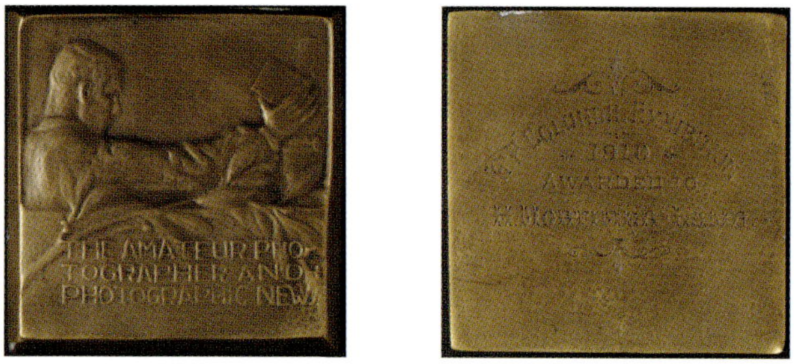


24 Medal presented to Mortimer-Lamb by *The Amateur Photographer and Photographic News, Exhibition of Colonial Photography*.

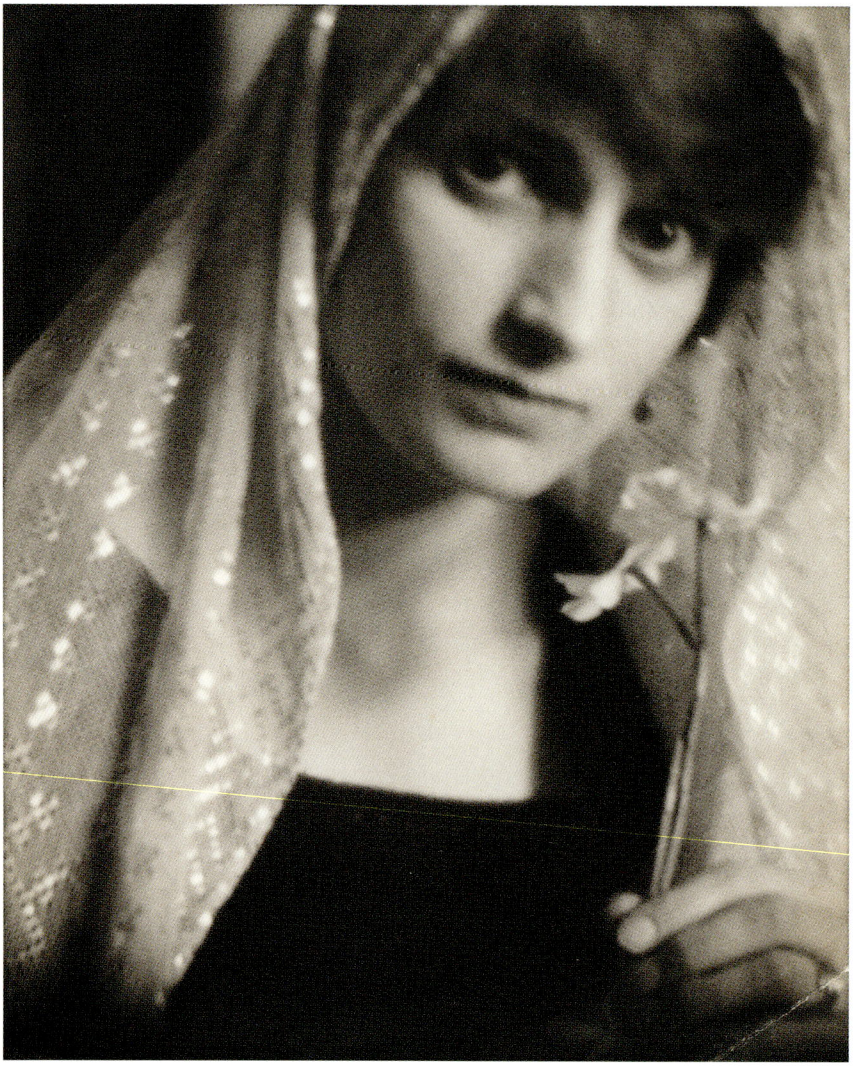

25 Mortimer-Lamb, *The Silver Veil*.

It is the picture of an expression, nothing more; the reflection of a mysteriously beautiful thought tinged by sadness. How does it happen that Mr. Mortimer-Lamb's sitters have these strange emotions? Or can it be that he is merely expressing his own sense of something beyond the veil?"[12] The taste of the times is evident in these references to "the Pre-Raphaelite theme" and "something beyond the veil."

His work got the attention not only of other amateur photographers but the wider public as well. *The Tiger and The Boy*, his entry to the 1910 London Salon of Photography, was reproduced in *The Sketch*, a popular British weekly. The caption succinctly expressed Mortimer-Lamb's intentions: "The photographer, who may fairly claim the title of 'photographic artist', is striving to create something of far more interest than the stiff, old-fashioned commonplace print of other days . . . He makes it his business not only to release the shutter of his camera, but to have so arranged the pose of the sitter, the accessories and the lighting that he produces a picture worthy of the name."[13] Mortimer-Lamb was truly a Pictorialist photographer.

There were not many other Pictorialist photographers in Canada, though Sidney Carter of Toronto had already been attracting attention. Carter's work was seen in *Photograms of the Year* in 1901, and in 1903 he was elected to Alfred Stieglitz's Photo-Secession group based in New York. Carter at that time worked at a bank in Toronto, and in 1907, after the bank failed, he moved to Montreal at the invitation of Mortimer-Lamb. The two formed a partnership, hoping to find an audience and a market for their Pictorial portraiture. For a promising first subject, they arranged a sitting with Rudyard Kipling, who was then on a tour across Canada. Other subjects from Mortimer-Lamb's circle of acquaintances

26 Mortimer-Lamb, *Sidney Carter.*

followed. And, ever eager to promote international photography and their own associated interests, Carter and Mortimer-Lamb began preparations for a remarkable exhibition of prints by the world's leading photographers.

To lend credibility to their enterprise, they grandly named it *An Exhibition of Pictorial Photography Arranged by the Photo-Club of Canada*, though in truth no such club existed. They arranged for a show from November 23 to December 7, 1907, in the galleries of the Art Association of Montreal (an organization later known as the Montreal Museum of Fine Arts). Mortimer-Lamb and Carter called on their associates far and near to loan prints and marshalled an extraordinary 279 exhibits by fifty-six photographers, including the biggest names from Vienna, Paris, London, and New York. Those among them who are still famous a century later include Alvin Lang Coburn, E.S. Curtis, Robert Demachy, F.H. Evans, David O. Hill, A.H. Horsley, Gertrude Kasebier, Edward Steichen, Alfred Stieglitz, and Clarence H. White. The organizers themselves were prominently featured, Carter showing thirty photographs and Mortimer-Lamb thirty-two. The public apparently enjoyed the event, but it was not repeated.

Mortimer-Lamb's work with the Canadian Mining Institute allowed him to pursue his photography without the need to make it pay. Unfortunately, Carter did not succeed as a professional portrait photographer. His partnership with Mortimer-Lamb broke up within the year and he took work as a salesman at Montreal's prestigious commercial art gallery W. Scott & Sons. This gallery was the source of a number of elements in the art collection that Mortimer-Lamb was building at the time.

In addition to a certain fame in the photography world, Mortimer-Lamb was constantly involved with painters and painting. He mentioned

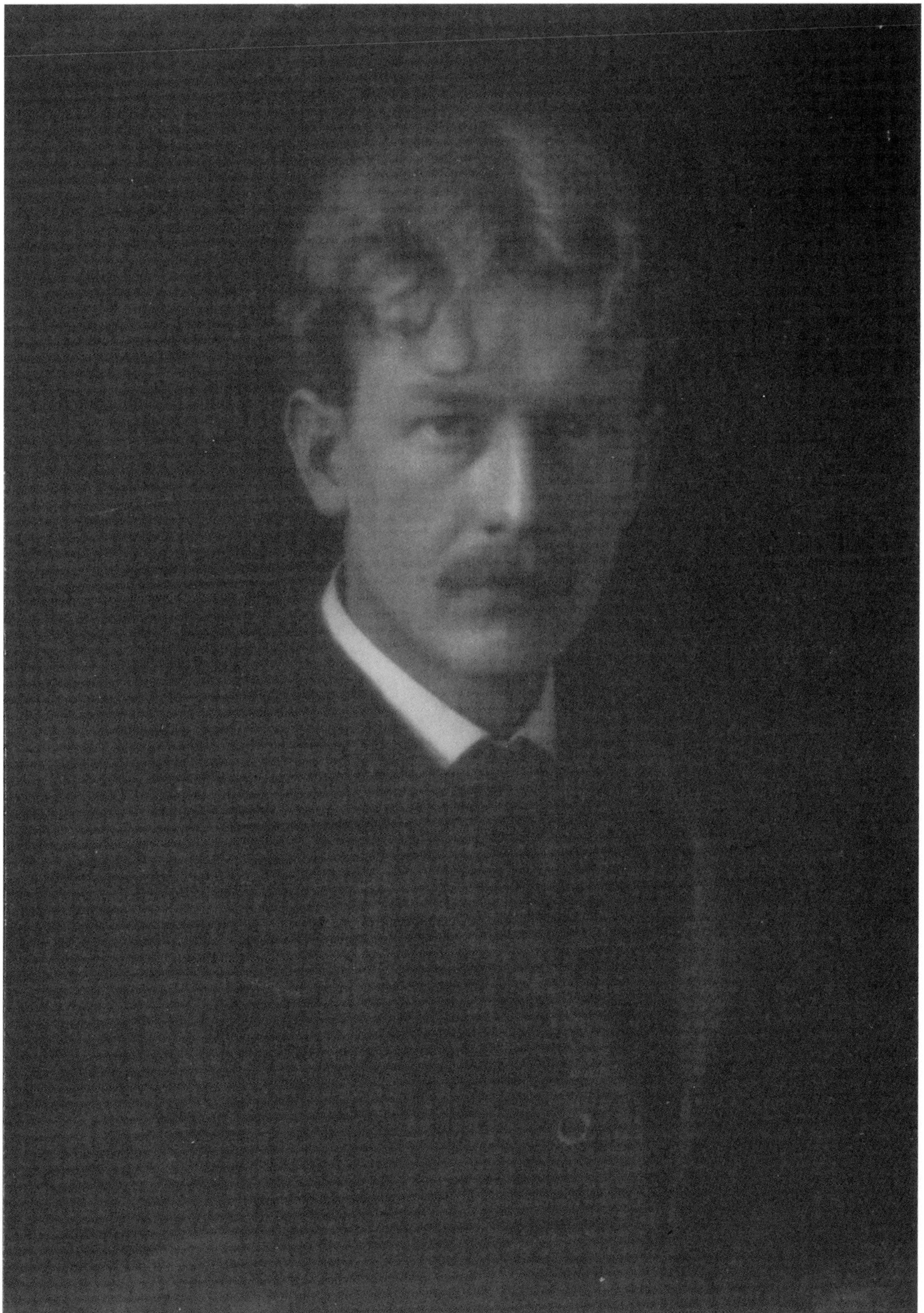

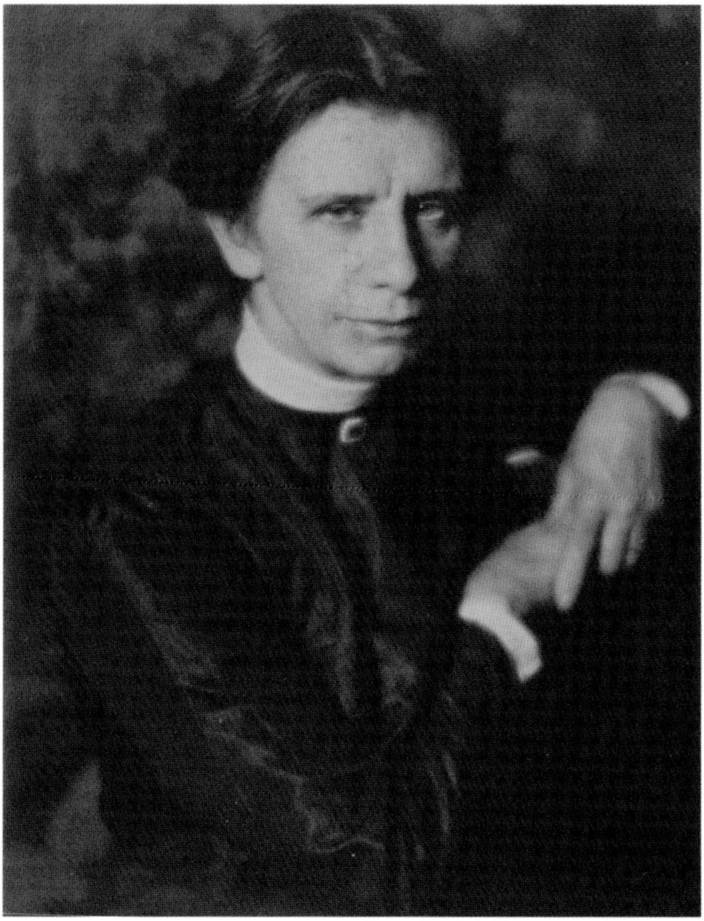

27 Mortimer-Lamb, *Laura Muntz*.

in his memoir that he studied with Maurice Cullen and formed connections with William Brymner and H. Mabel May, the foremost artists in Montreal at that period. His most important relationship was with Laura Muntz, a painter very sympathetic to Pictorialism. Born in Warwickshire, England, in 1860, Muntz came to Canada as a child and had her early training in Hamilton, Ontario. Moving to Paris, in 1891 she studied with the best teachers available, developing what was described as a fluid Impressionist style. Indicative of the high respect in which she was held at home, in 1895 she became one of the first women elected to membership in the Royal Canadian Academy of Arts. When she later returned to live in Canada, she settled in Montreal, the indisputable centre of the arts in the country, and immediately became a member of the recently formed Canadian Art Club.

Her career in Canada was based on her paintings in a Pictorialist mode rather than the more open and airy Impressionism, and Muntz and Mortimer-Lamb developed a bond of affection. He began by studying painting with her and included a reproduction of her work in an article he contributed, in March 1908, to *The Studio*, a London-based periodical founded in 1894 and the foremost art magazine in the world. He also made a profoundly evocative photograph of her, which was seen in the Royal Photographic Society's annual salon and published in *Photograms of the Year* in 1909. At this time he commissioned her to paint his young son Lawrence, the first of many artworks he acquired from her studio. *Portrait of a Girl* (which he donated to the Vancouver Art Gallery in 1946) is the most fully realized among them, while a tender and personal tone is conveyed in *Mother and Child*, now part of the collection of the Art Gallery of Greater Victoria. Among Mortimer-Lamb's prized possessions throughout his life was a Greek icon with the subject of the Virgin and Child. Both the icon and the Muntz painting share many qualities beyond the title—an emotive power, a rich gold ground, and an elaborate, gilded frame. Much about the interrelated imagery within the Pictorialist tradition can be discovered by a comparison of her painting, his photograph, and that icon.

Additionally, Mortimer-Lamb's collection included a number of gifts from Muntz's studio, items of little commercial value but cherished for the artistic insight they provide. There is a beautiful fragment torn from a much larger canvas showing a mother and child in the Impressionist mode; a tiny oil painting of a sultry woman, held safe in a miniature wooden frame; and a sketch on paper of a little girl, nude, touching her toe in a pool of water. Muntz later acknowledged a photo by Mortimer-Lamb of his little daughter, nude, lost in thought by the water's edge. "Thanks so much for the lovely photo you sent me," she wrote. "Molly Joan is the sweetest thing. She looks something like Peter Pan must have looked amongst the flowers—with her clever whimsical little face. I love the little nude studies in the wood."[14] Mortimer-Lamb's daughter Molly (the Molly Joan who was photographed by the pool) later said that her father "had a good eye for women, and paintings" and that Muntz may have been "the love of his life."[15]

As it happened, his friendship with Muntz was growing deeper while his personal life was under duress. Sidney Carter, in a letter to Alfred Stieglitz dated February 6, 1907, reported that Mortimer-Lamb "had just gone to England a nervous wreck just out of hospital and was further distracted by the death of his daughter."[16] Dolly died of measles when she was just ten years old. Almost from birth she had been Mortimer-Lamb's

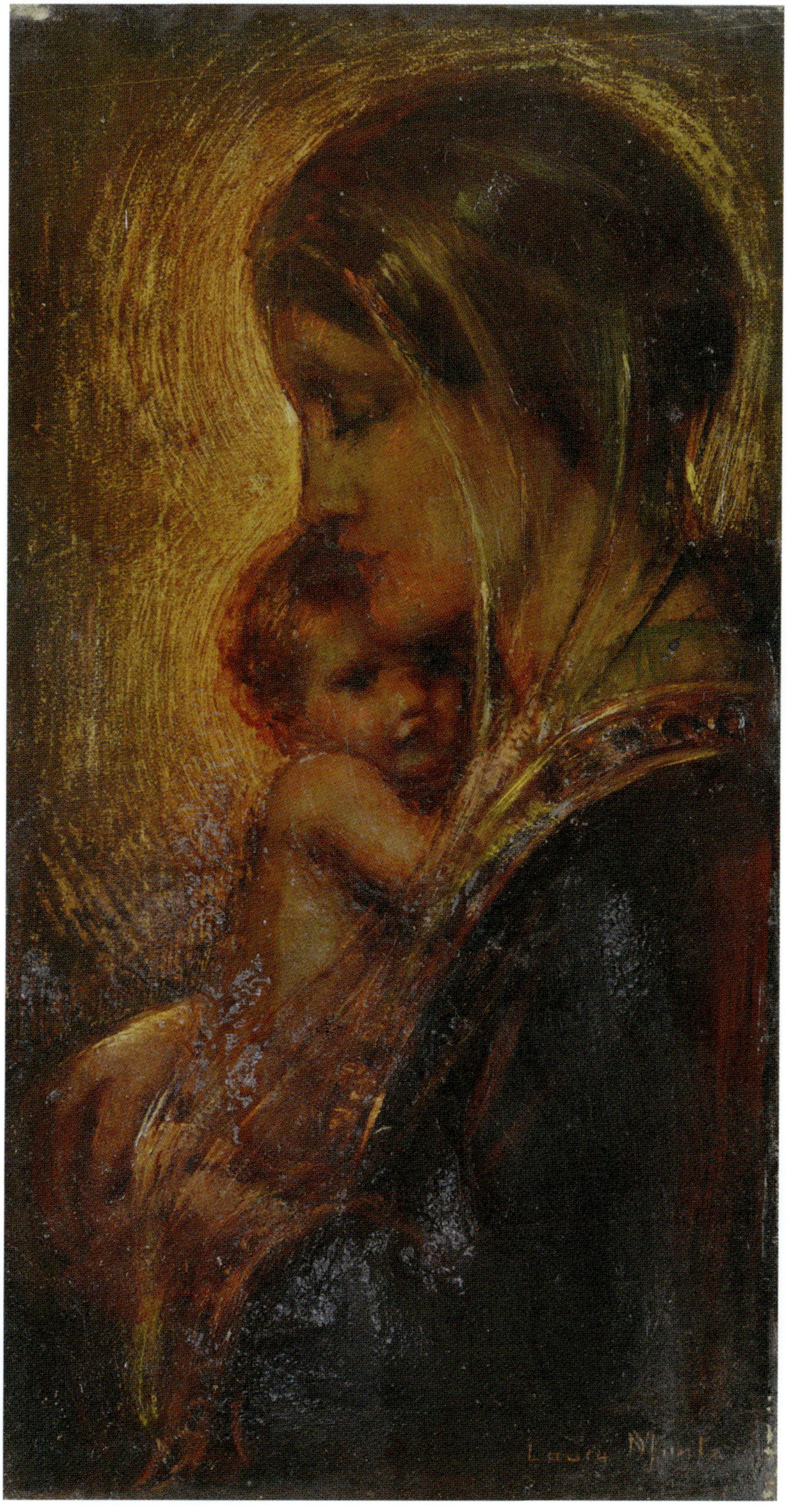

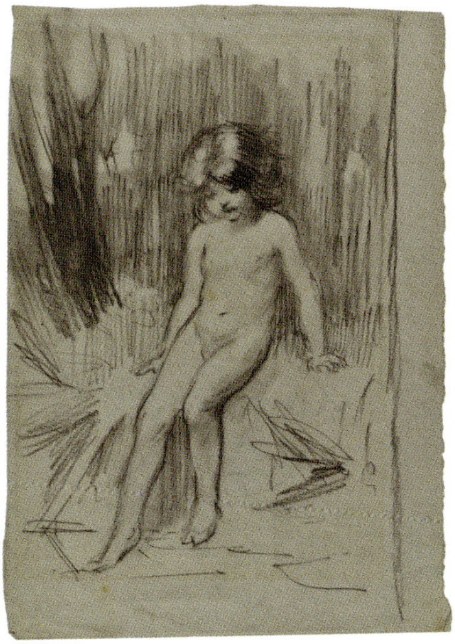

29 Laura Muntz, *Wader*.

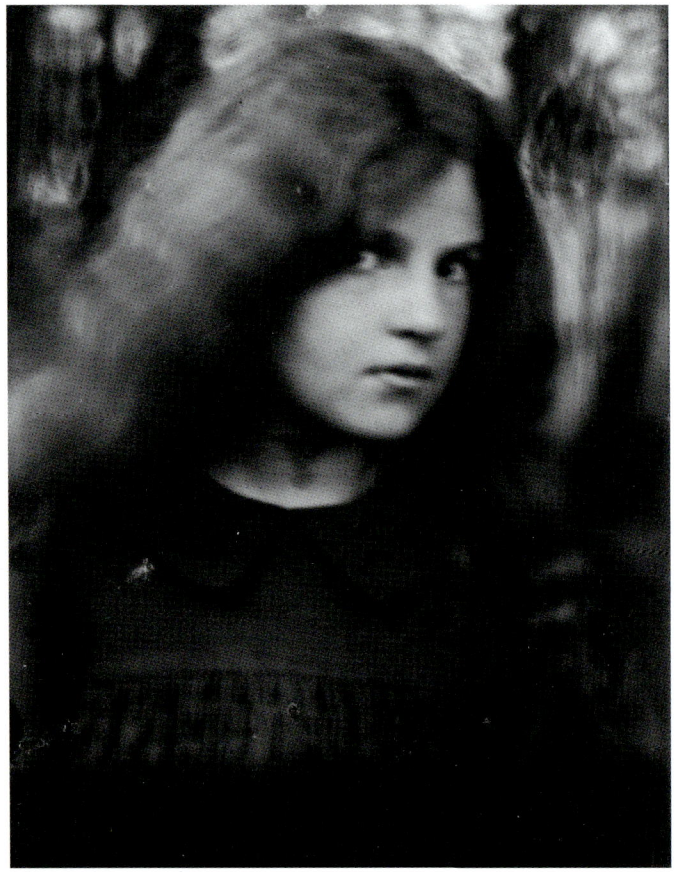

30 Mortimer-Lamb, *Dolly in a dark smock*.

most valued model and his dearest companion, and her death was the saddest event of his life. This tragedy shook him just as his professional responsibilities were at a peak and things were unusually stressful at home. Kate Lamb, his "country girl" from the British Columbia interior, was out of her depth among the sophisticates of Westmount. She was also going through her sixth pregnancy when her husband was away a great deal for his work, this being the year that he led the contingent of industrialists on a tour by train across Canada. Managing the household was increasingly beyond her.

Whatever the situation at home, Mortimer-Lamb's association with Muntz continued. She was the subject of an illustrated article he wrote for the popular *Canadian Magazine* in May 1912. Their times together came to an abrupt end when, at the age of fifty-five, Muntz married her widowed brother-in-law and moved to Toronto, there to become stepmother to his eleven children. Clearly unhappy with her new lot in life, in 1926 she wrote to Mortimer-Lamb: "Oh dear. I wished you lived near and could come in to see me now and again." She described her husband as "a nice mild chap . . . but how can you talk of pictures and art to someone it bores stiff?"[17] Mortimer-Lamb tried to keep her spirits up by sending her books by their favourite authors—Pushkin, Gorky, and Flaubert.

In the midst of his busy life, Mortimer-Lamb found time to do a little painting and showed two works in the annual exhibition of the Art Association of Montreal in both 1912 and 1913. A reviewer in the Montreal *Star* took note of his "two small but finished canvases full of feeling," though none of his early paintings have survived.[18] His position in the art world at the time is more accurately reflected by his membership in the Canadian Art Club, created in 1907 by a group of artists who had studied in Europe. They were disappointed by the tired, old-fashioned look of the art that prevailed in Canadian exhibitions, in particular those of the Royal Canadian Academy of Arts. The Canadian Art Club was a private exhibiting society whose invited professional members were dedicated to modern "subjective" work of the highest calibre. Members included J.W. Morrice and Horatio Walker. The founder of the club, Edmund Morris, wrote to Mortimer-Lamb on May 8, 1911, confirming his membership as a supporting lay member.

Homer Watson, once described by Oscar Wilde as "the Canadian Constable," was perhaps the most prominent Canadian artist of his day and was the obvious choice as president of the club. Mortimer-Lamb purchased a fine little oil by him, *The Ploughman*, and wrote to ask about his artistic philosophy. He received a lengthy letter in reply, in splendid handwriting, from the man some people called The Sage of Doon. Among Watson's considered comments was this: "It is in the nature of things to be true to influences and if we are to have art in Canada peculiar to us it may not have the refinement of European art, but certainly it should not lack virility." Looking ahead to the plein air painting which came to define the Canadian landscape, he was of the opinion that "no large picture of a transitory mood of nature can be seriously painted outside. Nature never poses. It is a joy to work and live over again some emotion felt in nature's presence."[19] These words were to influence Mortimer-Lamb's opinions regarding an indigenous Canadian art.

As part of his professional life at the mining institute, Mortimer-Lamb found occasion to visit New York City. Through his own exhibiting career and perhaps with Sidney Carter's introduction, he met and collected the

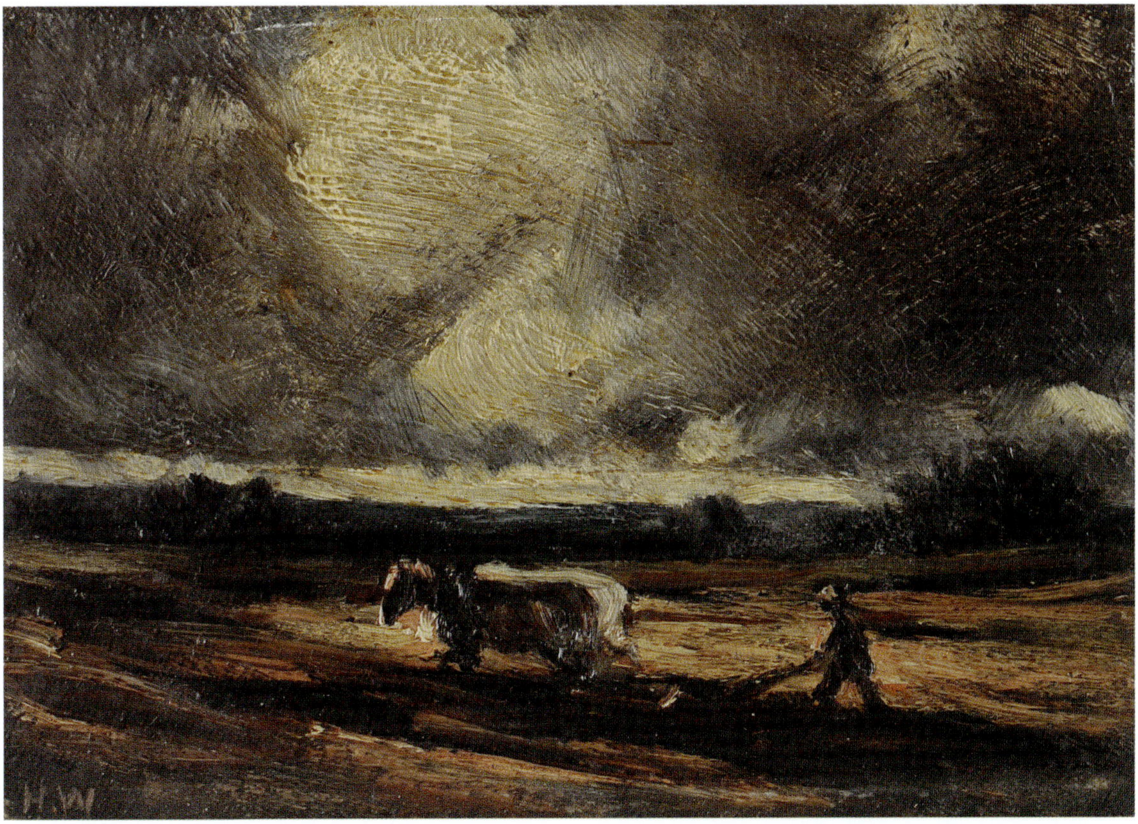

31 Homer Watson, *The Ploughman*.

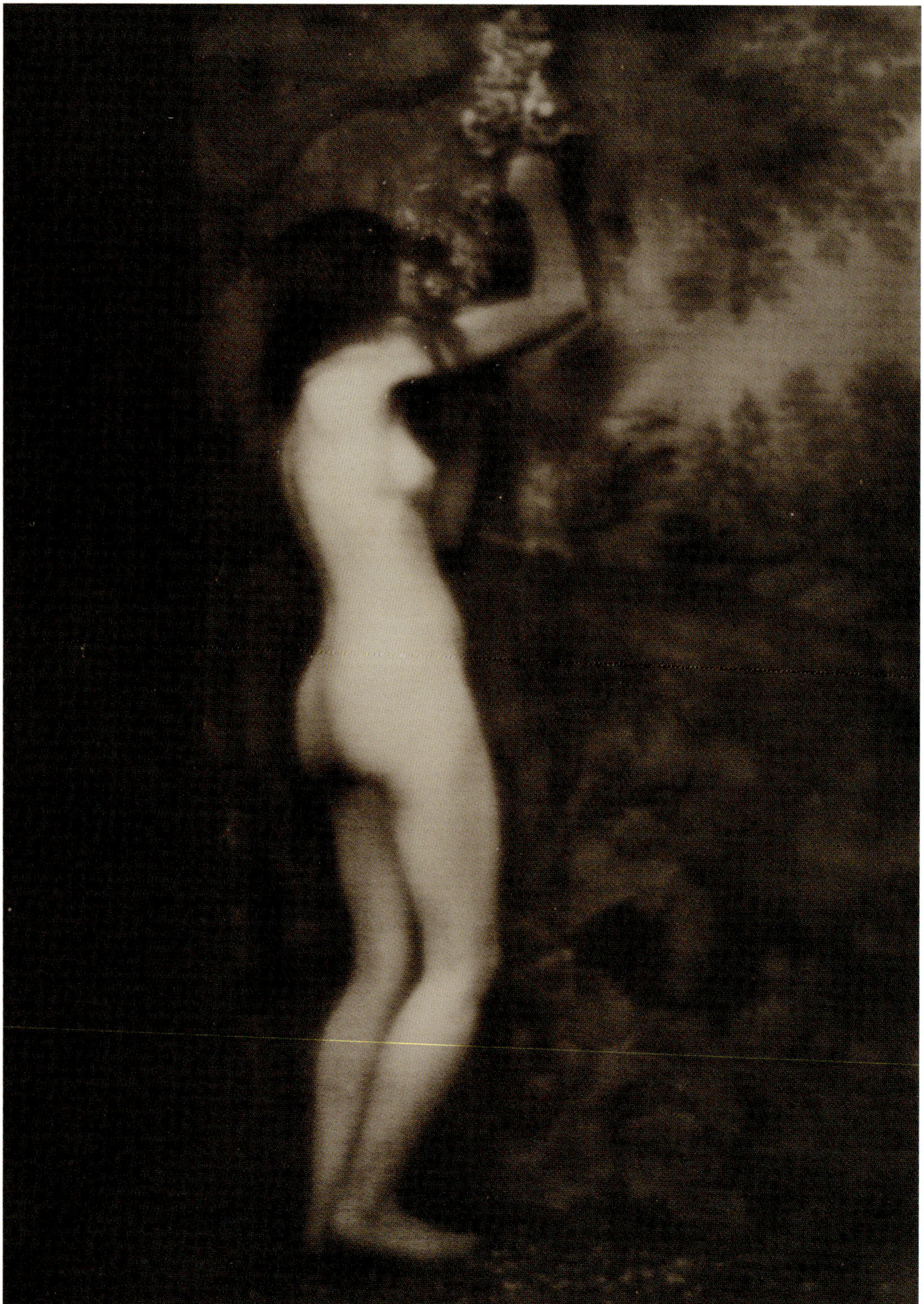

32 Mortimer-Lamb, *nude in the studio.*

work of the leading photographers at work in the city—Edward Curtis, Edward Steichen, and Alfred Stieglitz. Looking back, Mortimer-Lamb recalled that "whenever I went to New York I invariably went to a small upstairs gallery called I think 291 on Fifth Avenue established by Alfred Stieglitz . . . Stieglitz was most hospitable and always invited me to lunch with him when I called. As a rule he would have one or another guest and in this way I met Steichen, who brought photography to a high state of artistry."[20] It is certainly a mark of Mortimer-Lamb's renown in photographic circles that Stieglitz published one of his photographs in the legendary quarterly magazine *Camera Work*. It was included in Number 34–35 of the quarterly, published in 1911, which also presented new drawings by Matisse and photos of sculpture by Rodin. Later, Stieglitz wrote a note to Mortimer-Lamb, on December 11, 1913, saying: "[T]hat thing of yours in *Photograms of the Year* is very good. It was one of the best things in the book. It is what it professes to be and is well done." Closing on a familiar note, Stieglitz signed off with "it was fine to have you with us these few days."[21]

*Camera Work* was coming to the end of an illustrious run, and Stieglitz canvassed his contributors for their comments on his tiny perfect gallery: what did 291 mean to them? He published the replies in the final issue, Number 47 of July 1914. Thirty-five people replied, including Djuna Barnes, Marsden Hartley, and Mabel Dodge. "It means to me a personality," Mortimer-Lamb wrote. "I go not to see the latest extravagance in pictorial expression, but to hear, be inspired by a Man."[22] The man was Stieglitz, of course. When, twelve years later, it came time for him to open his own small upstairs gallery, Mortimer-Lamb kept Stieglitz's 291 in mind.

Upon its demise, *Camera Work* was followed by a series of eight broadsheet issues of Stieglitz's radical and avant-garde publication titled *291*. This was a brilliant and erratic sequence of printed art that appeared between April 1915 and January 1916, and with it, Stieglitz created a platform for contemporary work by Pablo Picasso and Georges Braque, Francis Picabia, and John Marin, among others. It was far ahead of its time, and most of the print run of eleven hundred copies was eventually pulped. A complete set of this rare creation, held in a red cardboard portfolio, was presented to Mortimer-Lamb by Stieglitz and is now in the collection of the Art Gallery of Greater Victoria.

In Montreal, Mortimer-Lamb played an active role in the art life of the city. He lectured on art to students at McGill University and various social organizations and was a charter member of the Arts Club of Montreal, which he joined in 1912. His active engagement with modern art and his skill as a writer allowed his voice to be heard in the journals of the day. Mortimer-Lamb had begun in 1908 to write from a Canadian perspective for *The Studio*, and the issue for March 1911 included his survey of Montreal artists. He mentioned A.Y. Jackson's painting *Edge of the Maple Wood*, the first notice of that young painter. Among the many accomplishments of Mortimer-Lamb's long life, it is this act for which he is most often remembered—he was the first writer to champion the work of the "modern" school of Canadian painters.

*The Studio* was up to date, but back in Montreal, the public was not prepared for the latest trends. The regular critic for the Montreal *Star*, S. Morgan-Powell, wrote a column on March 29, 1913, that began "Post-impressionism is a fad—an inartistic fetish for the amusement of bad draughtsmen, incompetent colourists, and others who find themselves

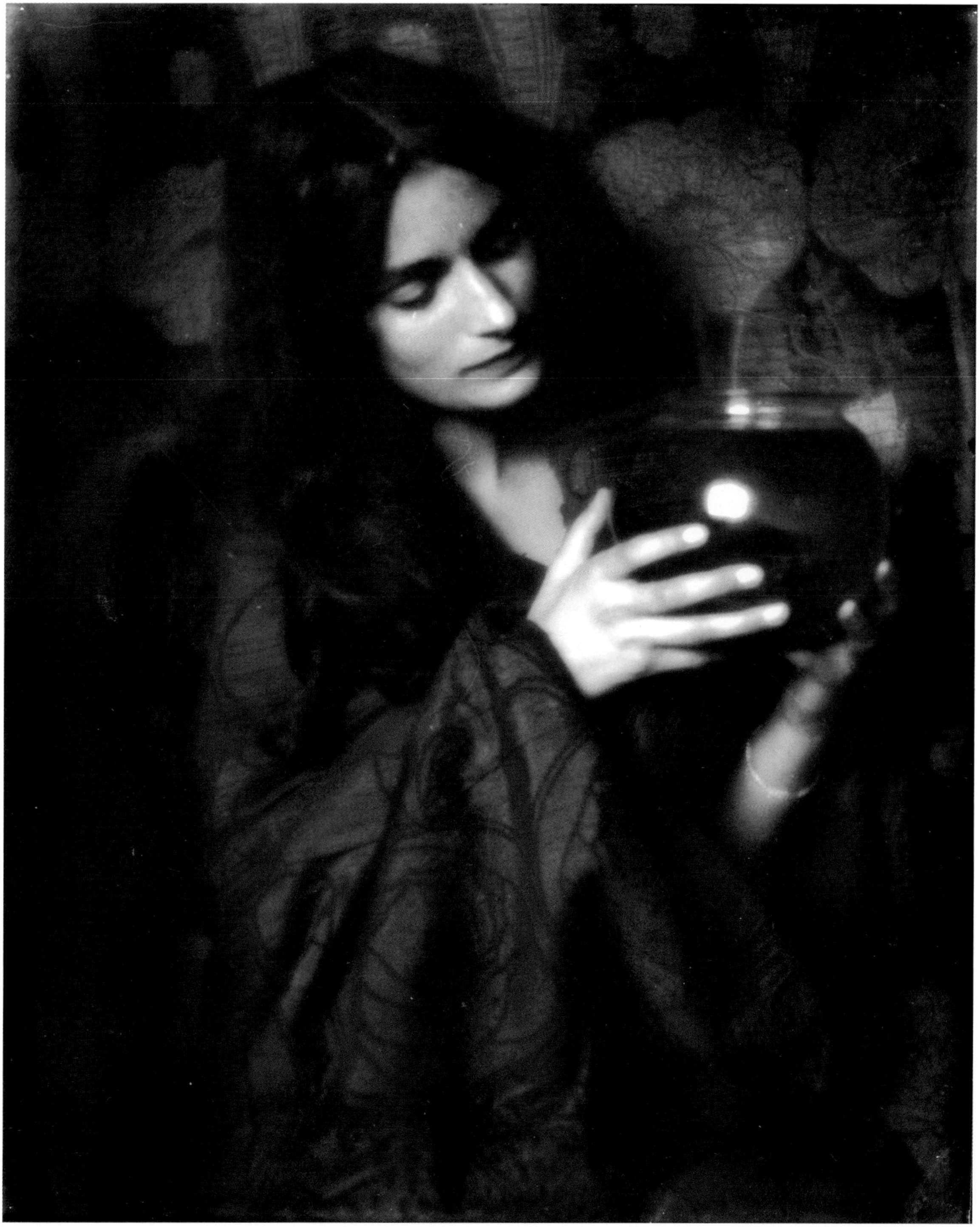

33 Mortimer-Lamb, *The Vase*.

unqualified to paint pictures."[23] Responding to this in a letter to the editor on April 7, 1913, Mortimer-Lamb requested that the newspaper refrain from "publishing the futile dogmatisms of self-opinionated and generally incompetent scribblers."[24] His spirited defence brought him a letter of thanks on April 15, 1913, from Jackson, who expressed his "sincerest appreciation for the part taken by you in defending the younger artists against the would-be critic. It is regrettable that it should have been necessary and fortunate that one there was who could do it so thoroughly."[25] Their correspondence would endure throughout their long lives.

Later, in the Montreal *Star* of April 24, 1913, Mortimer-Lamb offered a more considered rebuttal to Morgan-Powell: "The work of two young artists, that of Messrs. [Randolph] Hewton and [A.Y.] Jackson, was made the subject of special attack, on the score, presumably, of its extreme modernity. The work in each case evidences sincerity of purpose, and is distinguished by qualities that any student of art should be able to recognize. The influence of Manet is very manifest in Mr. Jackson's essays; and by no stretch of fancy can these efforts be classified as 'post-impressionistic.'" Mortimer-Lamb concluded that "if we must have art criticism, let us be sure that it is competent."[26] The antipathy that had grown between himself and Powell was never resolved.

In *The Studio* of September 1914, Mortimer-Lamb wrote at greater length about the talented young Canadian painter: "For the past year Mr. Jackson has sought and found inspiration in the lonely places of Northern Ontario. His sketches and pictures suggest poetically, yet strongly and truthfully, the grim silent beauty and bigness of this wilderness."[27] He again mentioned Jackson, and also Laura Muntz, in *The Studio* of February 1914, naming, for the first time, Lawren Harris.

Then, in one of his ever-more-detailed reports on Canadian art, in *The Studio* of August 1915 he included reproductions of paintings by Harris and Jackson, who, he wrote, "may properly be called the leaders of the Canadian school."[28] In February 1917, *The Studio* devoted ten full pages to his observations regarding the *Thirty-eighth Annual Exhibition of the Royal Canadian Academy of Arts*. Thus, a worldwide audience was informed about what was happening in the Dominion of Canada.

Closer to home, Mortimer-Lamb made it his personal mission to see that the holdings of the National Gallery were shared equitably among Canadian citizens. The first salvo of his long-running campaign was a letter he wrote on December 9, 1913, concerning the promotion of art in "the minor centres of the country." His letter was addressed to Eric Brown, then director of the National Gallery, proposing "a series of exhibitions periodically, at every town or village throughout the country" to display a collection that the federal government would acquire, including "representative examples of the major schools of artists." Mortimer-Lamb went on to say that he had spoken of this to Sir Edmund Walker, a powerful trustee of the (later-named) Art Gallery of Toronto, but nothing came of his proposal.[29]

At about this time he gave the first indication that he was longing to put Montreal behind him and return to the fresh fields of British Columbia. On September 30, 1913, he sent a letter "in confidentiality" to H.E. Young, BC's provincial secretary and minister of education, suggesting that a provincial art gallery be established there, and that he would be the person who could put it all together. He asked that Young appoint him to inaugurate it; he would then be in charge of the work under Young's direction. "I am now receiving a salary of $3200.00 per annum," he revealed, "and my post is one of independence and responsibility. I am, however, most anxious to return to BC, which I regard as my home." He went on to explain that he was "well-known to all the more important Canadian and to some British artists," a boast that few others could make. Further, he informed Young of a "small but select collection of pictures and oriental pottery of my own, to the value of some thousands of dollars. This collection I should be glad to loan to a British Columbia collection if formed."[30]

Young replied that, regarding the establishment of a provincial art gallery, the time was not opportune, though he hoped to build a new museum on one of the floors in the east wing of the Parliament Buildings. The plans had already been drawn up and provided for an art gallery in one of the rooms.[31] Though this gallery was never established, Mortimer-Lamb did not let go of his dream. Through his advocacy with the BC Art League, he came to play a role in the founding of the Vancouver Art Gallery in 1931. And, beginning in 1954, his efforts toward building the Art Gallery of Greater Victoria in the provincial capital were substantial.

The promise Mortimer-Lamb saw ahead for a truly Canadian art culture was dampened by dark clouds of conflict. When war was declared in 1914, the forty-four-year-old Mortimer-Lamb was too old to be considered for active service, but his inborn Britishness would not let him stand idle. On February 25, 1915, he wrote to the chief clerk of the Army Service Corps at Whitehall in London to offer his services. Nothing came of this, but on the home front, he was able to put his abilities to use. During the war he worked with five departments of the Canadian government regarding special services, including approving candidates for commissions in tunnelling companies. He was also named chairman of the Central

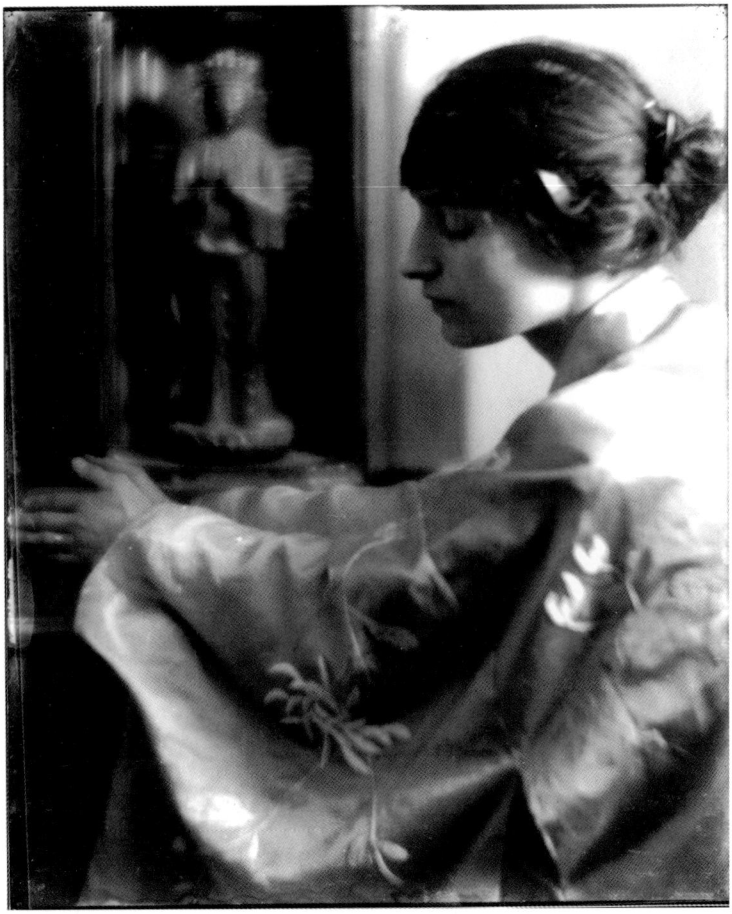

34 Mortimer-Lamb, *Meditation*.

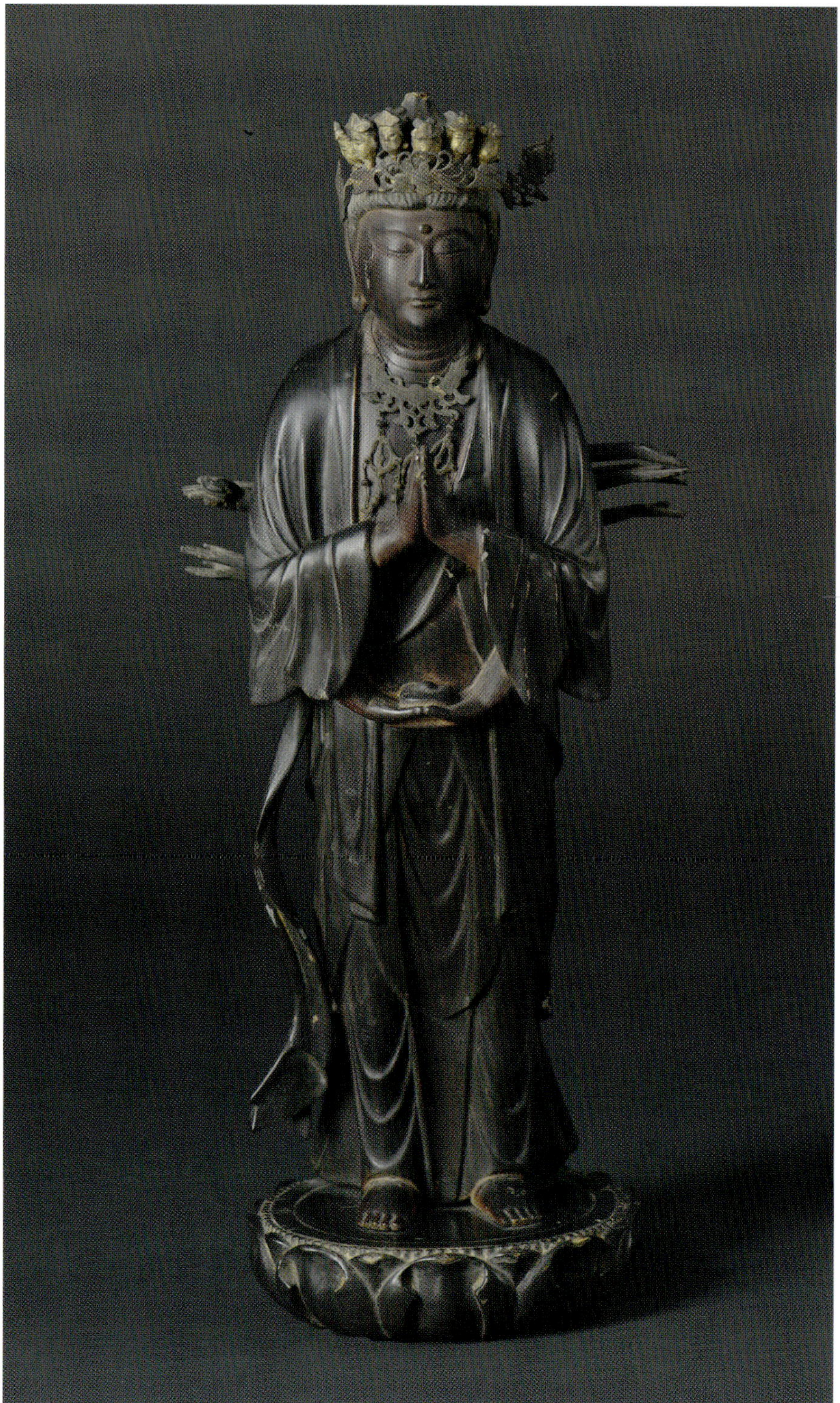

35 *Senju Kwannon Bosatsu*, Japan, eighteenth century.

Directing Committee of Technical Organizations, co-operating with the Advisory Council for Scientific and Industrial Research.

During this time he continued his photographic work, making studio images of his sons and hired models, sometimes using artifacts from his art collection as props. Many of these images were accepted for the annual salon in London and were published in *Photograms of the Year*. Perhaps Mortimer-Lamb's most significant contribution as a writer appeared in *The Studio* in August 1919, in which he presented a seven-page story on Tom Thomson. The story was accompanied by five large reproductions of the painter's work, some in colour. A Canadian artist who mysteriously drowned in Canoe Lake, Thomson produced hundreds of sketches and many finished pictures of extraordinary individual charm and power. Thomson's paintings were "remarkable chiefly in that they express a typically Canadian spirit, in a degree never before so concentrated and consistently maintained."[32] Though now generally accepted, in 1919 this was a view ahead of its time, and it spoke of a theme close to Mortimer-Lamb's heart. It was remarkable to find an international publication paying its full attention to a young Canadian.

Mortimer-Lamb kept busy during the war years with his mining-institute work, his writing, and his photography, but it seems he was letting things slide with his family. In particular, his wife, Kate, was not prospering. Her first baby had died in 1895, and her second child, the adored Dorothy, in 1908. Of the four sons who succeeded Dolly, all were alive and three were at home. The eldest, Hal, had been working on a cattle ranch outside Kamloops when, at the age of sixteen, he enlisted in the machine-gun sector of a western battalion. Then, in a Montreal newspaper, a small notice on November 30, 1916, reported that Private J. Haliburton Mortimer-Lamb had been wounded at the front by gunshot in the right arm, shoulder, and hip. Uncertainty about his wounds and his whereabouts brought a pall of gloom to the family. For some years, Kate had not been able to cope with life in Montreal, and a variety of housekeepers had taken on the task of keeping the boys in line. In her later days Kate was referred to as Gombo, a childish mispronunciation of "godmother," and following what was called "a paralytic seizure," she retired to a shadowy existence in the back rooms of the family home.

As the war dragged on, Mortimer-Lamb allowed himself to become totally absorbed by his many activities, and the running of the household was left to a housekeeper named Ruth. According to Molly Lamb Bobak, Ruth "took his money and neglected the boys."[33] It was at this time, in late 1918, that a new figure entered the scene.

She had been born Alice Salter Price in Kent, England, in 1886, but during her first years in Canada changed her name to Mary Williams. Williams grew up in Canterbury, where she was educated at King's College. At the onset of the war years, she answered an advertisement in an English newspaper for a mother's helper in Canada and went to St. Andrews, New Brunswick, a summer place frequented by the wealthy of Montreal. There she worked for an architect and his family and was invited to return to Montreal with them at the end of the summer. She rented a room for herself and, to make ends meet, took in hand laundry—washing the dainty garments of rich women. Through her connection with the architect, she met Mortimer-Lamb at a party and learned that he needed a housekeeper.

Molly said that when Mary Williams arrived at the Mortimer-Lamb residence to offer her services, she found that Ruth, the housekeeper, had locked the children outside in the below-zero weather of wintry Montreal. Williams was outraged and kicked Ruth out. From then on she looked after the boys.[34] Family legend adds that at this time Mortimer-Lamb suffered "a terrible nervous breakdown" and was no longer part of family life. Kate, in her seclusion, needed peace and quiet, despite the three young boys still living at home. Later, Mary Williams caught influenza, an alarmingly deadly disease at that time. And another factor must have contributed strongly to everyone's anxiety: Mary was pregnant with Mortimer-Lamb's child. As he later reported, he was advised to go out west.

He was ready to go—driven out of Montreal by personal issues, including his impending fatherhood, and drawn back to BC by the siren song of the Pacific coast. His public departure took place on a positive note. The Canadian Mining Institute's report for the year 1920 put it this way: "Owing to continued ill health, Mr. Harold Mortimer-Lamb, who had been granted six months' sick leave from the end of November 1919, was forced to forward his resignation to council early in the year . . . It was with feelings of regret and with full appreciation for Mr. Mortimer-Lamb's 15 years' devoted service to the Institute that council accepted his resignation on the expiry of his leave of absence on May 31, 1920. In recognition of his valuable services to the Institute and to the mining industry during his term of office, the Council had much pleasure in appointing Mr. Mortimer-Lamb Secretary Emeritus of the Institute."[35]

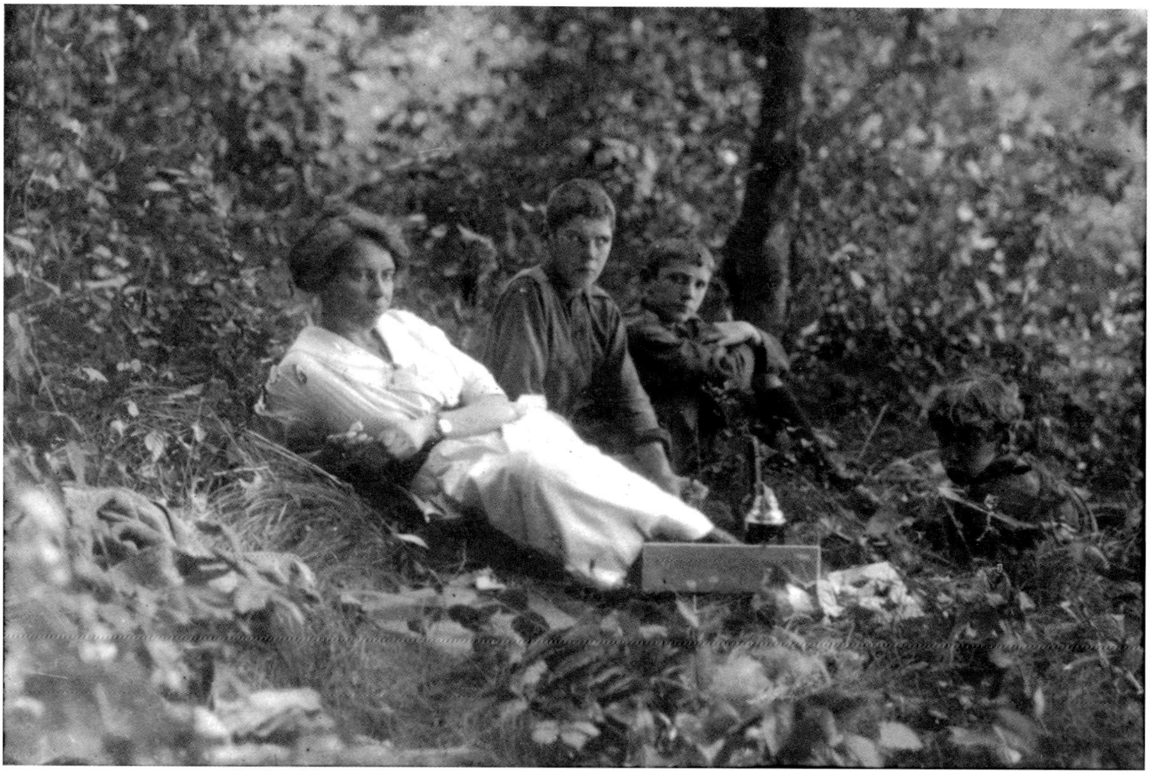

36 Mortimer-Lamb, *Mary Williams, Hal, Lawrence and Willoughby Lamb.*

CHAPTER THREE

# Vancouver

Mortimer-Lamb moved the family to British Columbia early in 1920, and after he arrived showed no further signs of a nervous breakdown or ill health. He brought with him his invalid wife Kate, sons Oliver, Lawrence, and Willoughby, and his housekeeper Mary Williams, who, on February 25, 1920, gave birth to their daughter, Molly. A new chapter in everyone's life was about to begin.

Mortimer-Lamb first purchased a small four-bedroom house down among the cottages on Lulu Island, on the delta of the Fraser River. Finding it unsuitable, he sold it the following spring and purchased Hill Cottage, a farm of eight acres on Rayside Avenue on the south shore of Burnaby Lake. This attractive property had good roads, city water, electric light, and telephone service. Hill Cottage proved to be another in the succession of astute real-estate investments Mortimer-Lamb made throughout his life. Positioned on a gentle slope running down toward the lake, it was the subject of a glowing article in *Farm and Home* magazine in 1925.

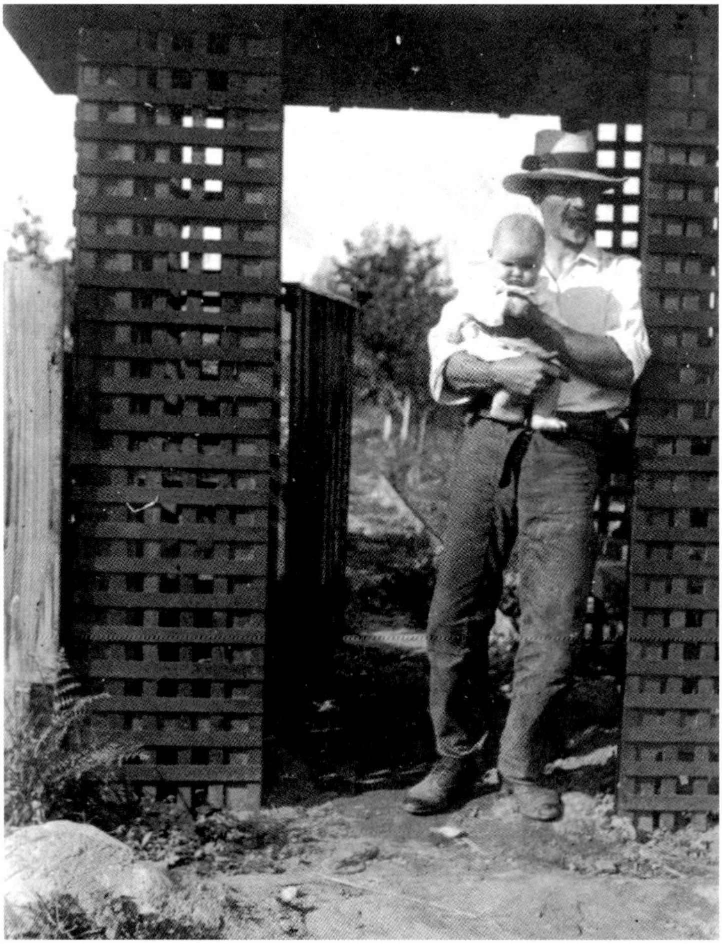

37 Unknown photographer, *Mortimer-Lamb and baby Molly at Rayside*.

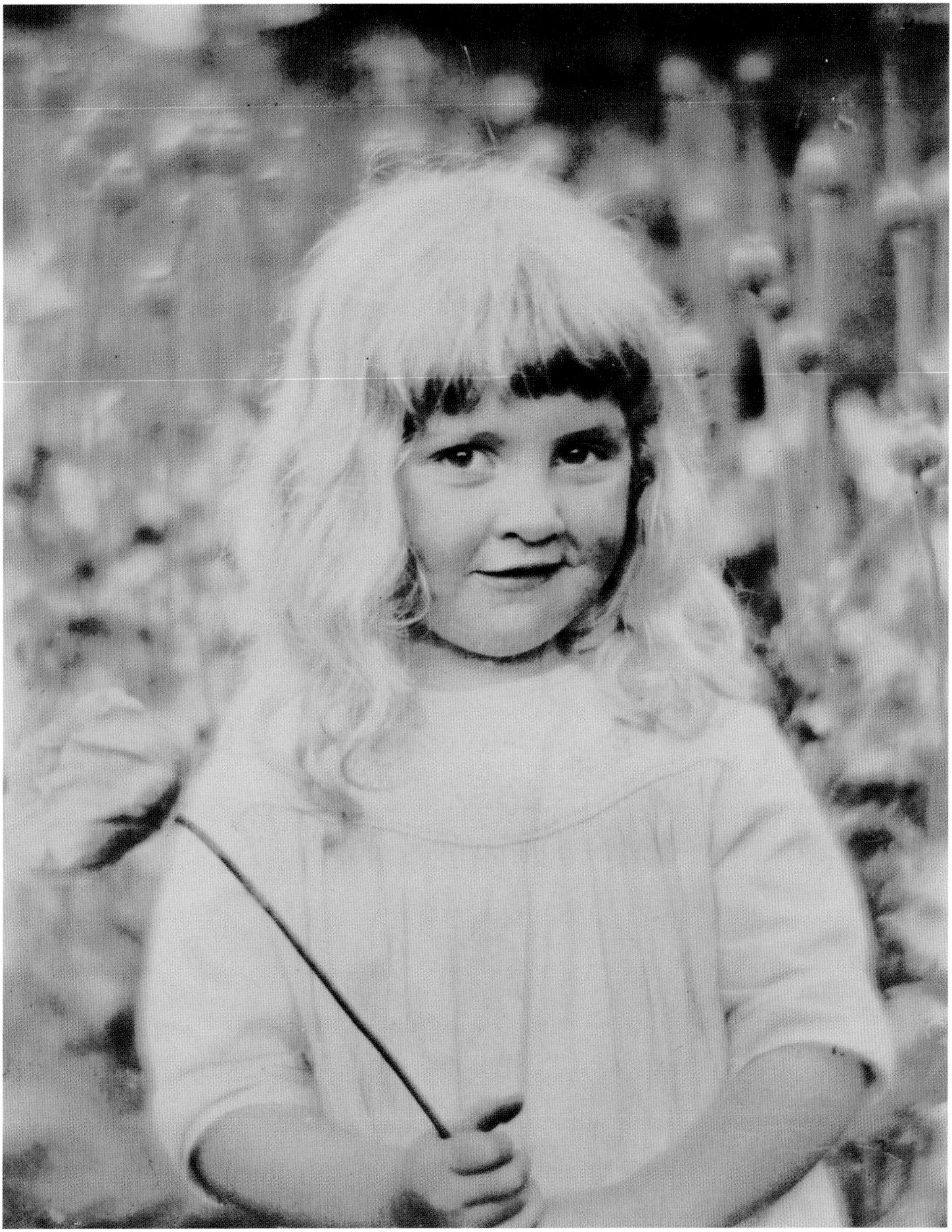

38 Mortimer-Lamb, *Molly among poppies*.

"A striking demonstration of what land in that vicinity will do," the writer gushed. "An absolute revelation of unexcelled fertility and growth . . . The location of a new residence which [Mortimer-Lamb] is erecting on the former country club land on the lakeside was chosen both with artistic as well as utilitarian ideas. The result is a happy combination such as no beauty spot in BC can excel and few equal."[1] Four acres were sold off to allow the family to better manage the intensive agriculture that Mortimer-Lamb proposed.

Mortimer-Lamb had already demonstrated a formidable range of talents; now he seriously applied himself to animal husbandry and agriculture. In his "Reminiscences" he listed among his responsibilities the following: "three Jersey cattle; ten goats, pure bred Toggenburg; and rabbits, sixty in all, pure silver grey ones; and two hundred pullets. Unfortunately, all the chickens and rabbits were killed by the hired man's setter dog. Under cultivation were raspberries, strawberries (half an acre) and Bartlett pears . . ."[2]

Molly Lamb Bobak, in her own reminiscences, had a different impression of Hill Cottage. "The house was an ugly-looking brute of a thing, with a tamarack tree in front. My mother [Mary Williams] used to garden—you can see it all in Dadda's pictures. The living room had a raised piece, a sort of stage, at one end. Father bought a horse called Peter and he ploughed the field. That was Father's therapy—he ploughed. And it worked. He got over his breakdown." Molly admitted that she had really very little to do with her father, who had a nervous disposition and "smoked like a chimney . . . and he took funny-looking medicine from a lot of different bottles."[3]

In a short time it became clear that Mortimer-Lamb was too ambitious for a rural retirement. Leaving his family almost entirely in the care

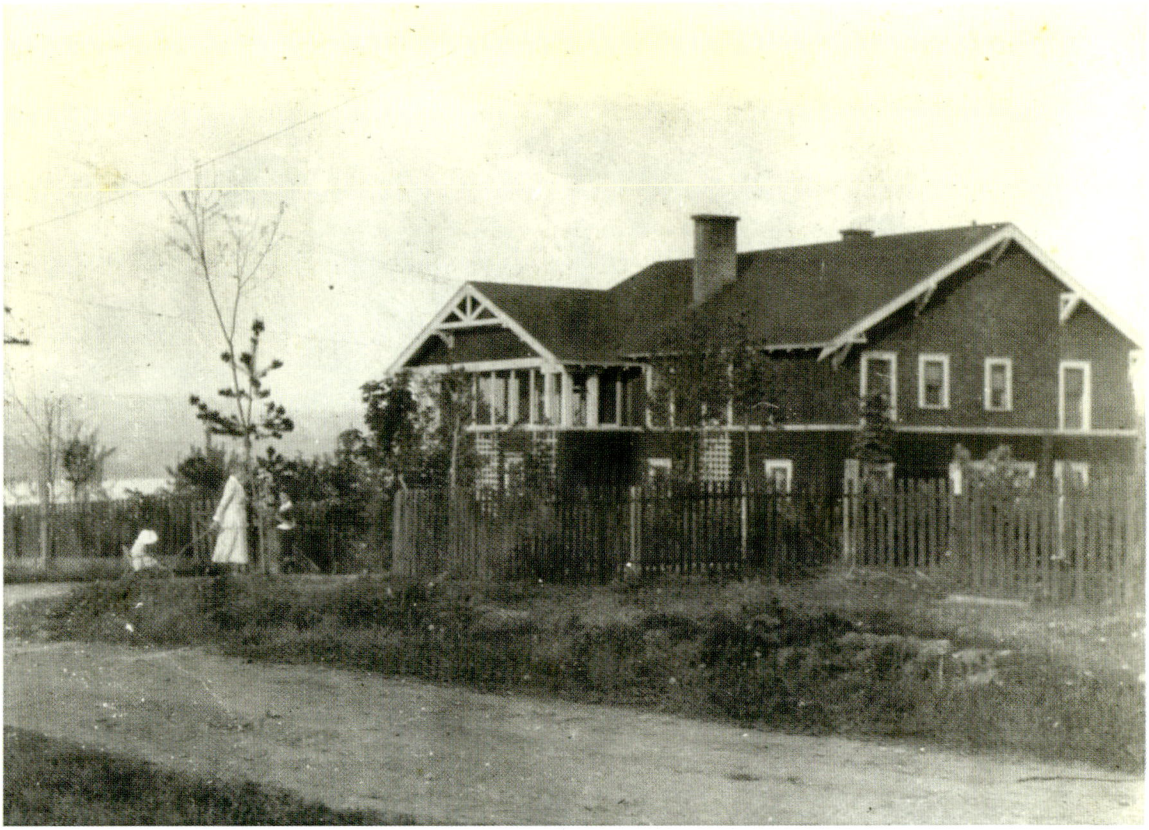

39 Mortimer-Lamb, *Hill Cottage, Rayside, Burnaby.*

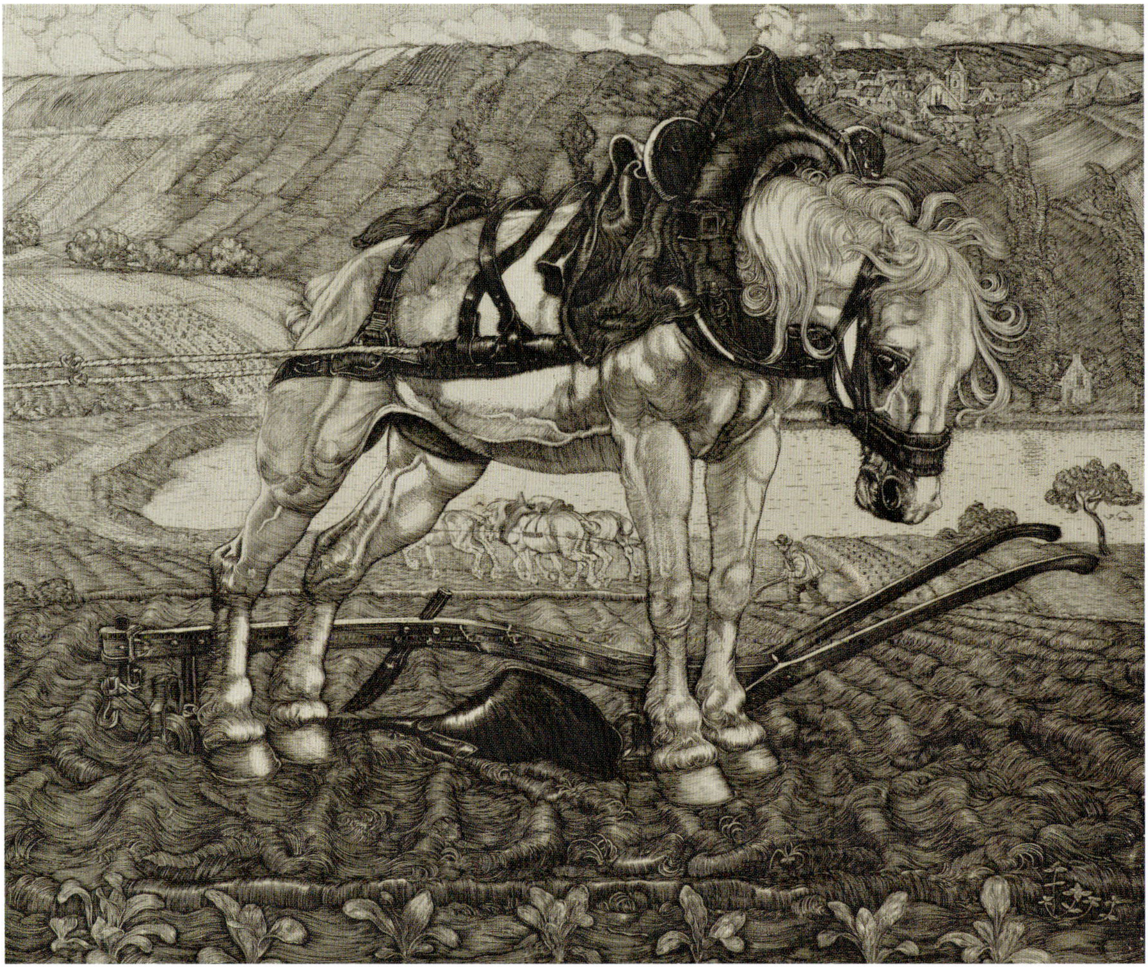

40 P. Dupont, *L'outillage*.

of Mary, he once again pursued his activities with the mining industry. He soon became secretary-treasurer of the Canadian Mining Institute's British Columbia division, and, acting in that position, he invited the Canadian Society of Civil Engineers and the mining, forestry, and agricultural departments of the University of British Columbia to co-operate in a special report for the provincial government. Soon afterward he was hired by the Geological Survey of Canada, but, when that work was delayed by political realities in Ottawa, in 1922 he became the executive secretary of the Mining Association of British Columbia. In addition, a few years later he became the founding editor of its journal, *The British Columbia Miner* (later *Western Miner*), and served as local correspondent for technical journals in eastern Canada, the United States, and Great Britain.

Mortimer-Lamb's home in Burnaby was near the new interurban railway, which he used to commute to his office; the mining association's headquarters were in suite 507 of the Pacific Building in downtown Vancouver. In February every year, he took up comfortable lodgings in Victoria's Union Club during the sitting of the provincial legislature.

Life at Hill Cottage was a wonderful change for the family after Montreal. Molly grew up to be very much her mother's child, and the first ten years of her life were idyllically happy. Her parents were never very close and mostly went their own separate ways. "Mum had a habit of sneaking into his bedroom and going through his trouser pockets looking for change, which was a game they played. But they weren't very fond of each other. She served him his meals and looked after the house and eight acres. Not being married to Mortimer-Lamb certainly must have made things more difficult for her, but I didn't know anything about it at the time." They were together twenty-two years. Throughout, Molly said that her stepmother, Kate, "was not capable of doing much, but some Sundays she went to St. James Anglican Church in Vancouver and sometimes to Chinatown."[4] The reference to Chinatown is telling, for Molly explained that Kate would on occasion snitch some of the family silverware and, with her little stepdaughter in tow, take the interurban train to Chinatown, where she could trade it for opium.

"I think [Kate] resented my mother, although she needed her," Molly wrote. "She always pretended Mother was a servant."[5] As time went on, Kate retired further into her little room, with a reproduction of Leonardo's Christ on the wall above her bed, and sang hymns to herself. Her youngest son, Willoughby, was dutiful to his mother and took good care of her right to the end.

Outside on the family farm, Mary was "just the merriest woman you ever met in your life," according to Jack Shadbolt.[6] She made butter from the milk their Jersey cows gave and preserves from the berries they grew. And when Mortimer-Lamb was away at "the sessions" in Victoria she would invite her women friends from Vancouver, who would come out with their men and share some of Mary's homemade beer. "I remember," Molly wrote, "Uncle Bill went outside to the rabbit hutch and brought in a couple of rabbits and did magic tricks with the washing machine."[7] They were marvellous parties, with the young people gathering around the piano and phonograph to sing and dance.

Mortimer-Lamb had his friends, too. A.Y. Jackson came to see him whenever he was in western Canada, bringing tales of the northern wilderness where he went to paint in the company of geologists. His dirty boots made an unfortunate impression on Mary's clean kitchen floor. In this

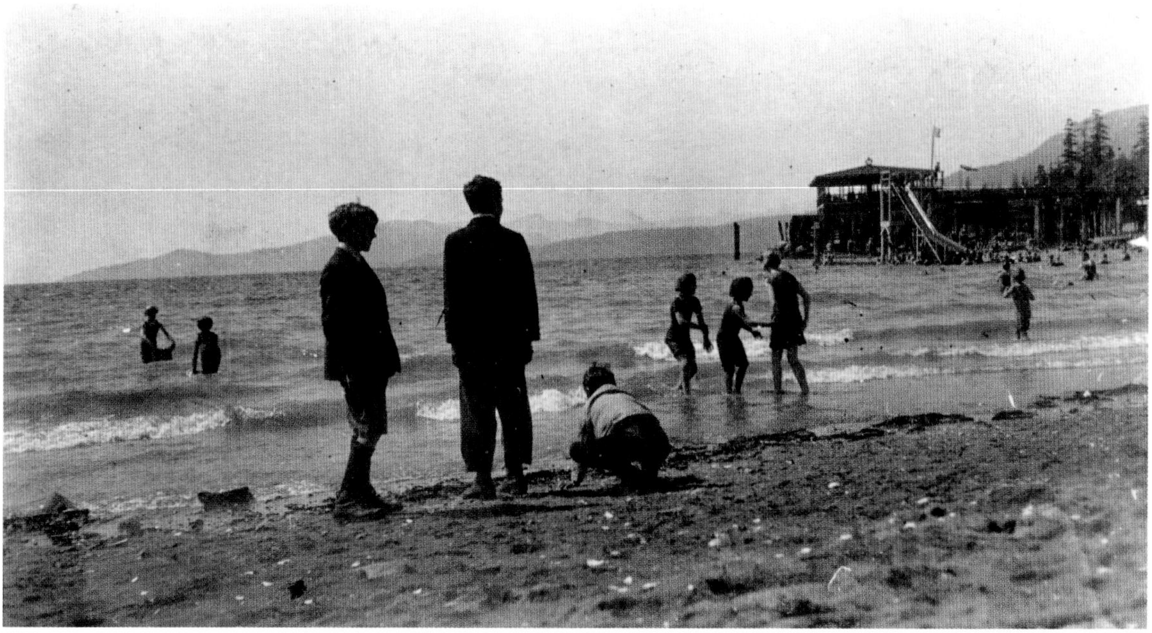

41 Mortimer-Lamb, *at English Bay, Vancouver.*

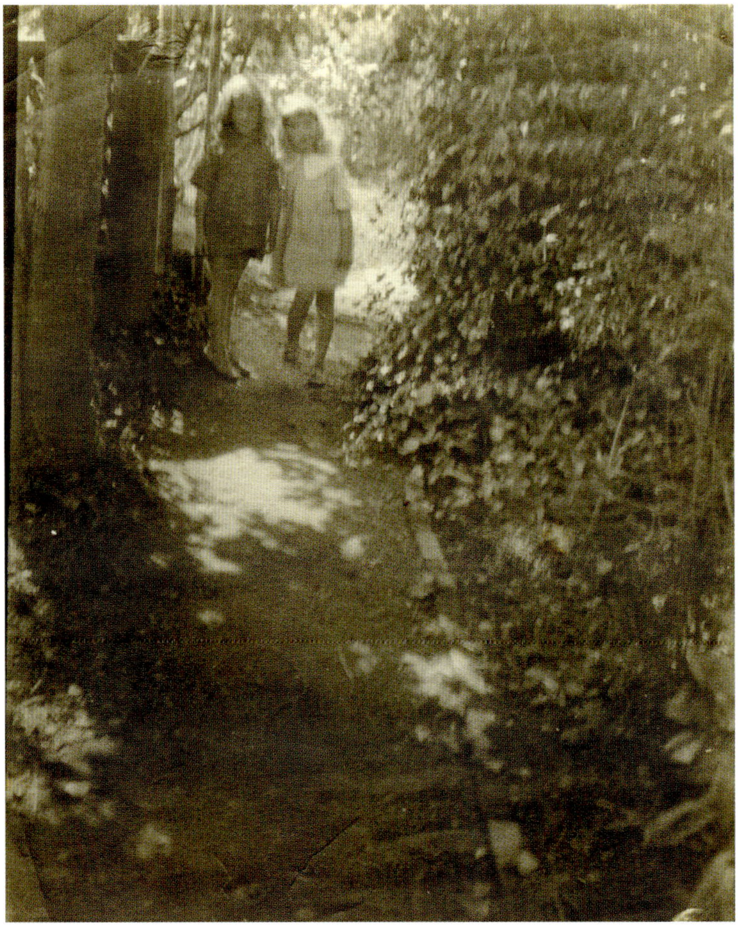

42 Mortimer-Lamb, *Molly and Betty Biart on the path.*

new milieu on the coast, Mortimer-Lamb broadened his involvement with the world of art. Having recently been in the thick of it in Montreal, he was soon lecturing on contemporary Canadian art. "When I came to Vancouver," he wrote, looking back, "the Group's work was anathema and I did my best to change this by articles and an address or two at the University [of British Columbia]."[8] These addresses were illustrated with photographic transparencies that he borrowed from the National Gallery in Ottawa.

He was also instrumental in arranging a show of recent Canadian art from the National Gallery, which toured many western cities. In 1922, the gallery loaned sixteen paintings by the Group of Seven to supplement its other loans to agricultural exhibitions in what they called "the western fair circuit." The works were shown in the Fine Arts Building at the New Westminster Provincial Exhibition, at East Hastings Park exhibition grounds in Vancouver, and at the Willows Fairgrounds in Victoria. Finally, they were seen at the gallery recently established by the British Columbia Art League at 309 East Cordova Street in Vancouver. Mortimer-Lamb had been one of the founders of the league, which was incorporated in 1920. Similar touring shows reached the coast in 1923 and again in 1925.

When the show from the National Gallery arrived on the coast in 1922, Harry McCurry, secretary of the gallery, accompanied it; he reported on the great interest expressed by artists, and the nascent plans to set up new municipal galleries. He particularly mentioned the support given by Mortimer-Lamb and John Vanderpant, a photographer on the art committee in New Westminster. Mortimer-Lamb, in the Vancouver *Province* of September 15, 1922, wrote a long article titled "The Modern Art

Movement in Canada," in which he outlined the history of the Group of Seven and offered his readers a useful approach to understanding their ideas.

Inevitably, during the early years of his return to the west, Mortimer-Lamb was encouraged to seek out Emily Carr and her art by his friend Sophie Pemberton. It seems he did so on one of his trips to Victoria. Carr's home and studio were just four blocks south of the Union Club, his home base when he was in town. Exactly who was the first to champion the work of Carr on the national level is an issue that has been subjected to considerable scrutiny. A.Y. Jackson, in his book *A Painter's Country*, says "the first person to realize the potentiality of Emily Carr's work was Mortimer-Lamb."[9] Maria Tippett, in an article titled "Who 'Discovered' Emily Carr?" in the *Journal of Canadian Art History*, states unequivocally that "Harold Mortimer-Lamb must be given credit for first raising her name in the East."[10] More evidence is revealed in a letter dated October 24, 1921, which Mortimer-Lamb wrote to Eric Brown, then director of the National Gallery in Ottawa. He recommended that Carr's collection of paintings from her trips to the Skeena River and the Queen Charlotte Islands be purchased by the Dominion or Provincial Government.[11] While this purchase did not take place, his advocacy did have some influence when, in 1926, Marius Barbeau again brought Carr to the attention of Eric Brown and the National Gallery. Subsequently, forty-four of Carr's artworks were included in a show at the gallery in Ottawa and the Art Gallery of Toronto in 1927, and this encouraged her to return to painting.

Meanwhile, Mortimer-Lamb continued his efforts to spread the influence of the National Gallery in Ottawa throughout the west; his ideas are shown in a series of articles in Canadian newspapers. Writing in the Vancouver *Province* on February 8, 1925, he made his case under the heading "National Art Board is Arraigned for Neglect of West: Gallery Advisory Council Taken to Task by Vancouver Man." Mortimer-Lamb, the "Vancouver man," was described as being "familiar with his subject to the point of being an authority." In particular, he took exception to costs being incurred by the BC Art League when it borrowed elements of the national patrimony. "A struggling and financially embarrassed local art society is called upon to pay heavy express charges both ways, not to mention insurance," on these "not very superior works" that the National Gallery had seen fit to loan to the league.[12] His comments were reprinted in the Montreal *Gazette* and were taken up in editorials in the Winnipeg *Tribune*, the Edmonton *Journal*, and the Ottawa *Journal*, and provoked a lengthy reply from Eric Brown. "There never was any intention of making the National Gallery into a permanent national supply of free art," Brown snorted, "however much Mr. Lamb of Vancouver thinks that this is the right of anyone claiming it."[13]

On another matter, Mortimer-Lamb wrote to the Vancouver *Province* on October 23, 1923, regarding the suggestion that the BC Art League form a civic art collection and that they begin it by buying a "Cavalier and Roundhead" period costume piece by a painter named Bundy. "Not Bundy," Mortimer-Lamb fumed, "an English academician of very ordinary attainments." He suggested instead a collection that, he said, would one day be priceless, including paintings by distinguished Canadian contemporary artists, and he named J.W. Morrice, Tom Thomson, A.Y. Jackson, and J.E.H. MacDonald. Showing some leadership, he put up one hundred dollars to start the fund for the purchase of Canadian

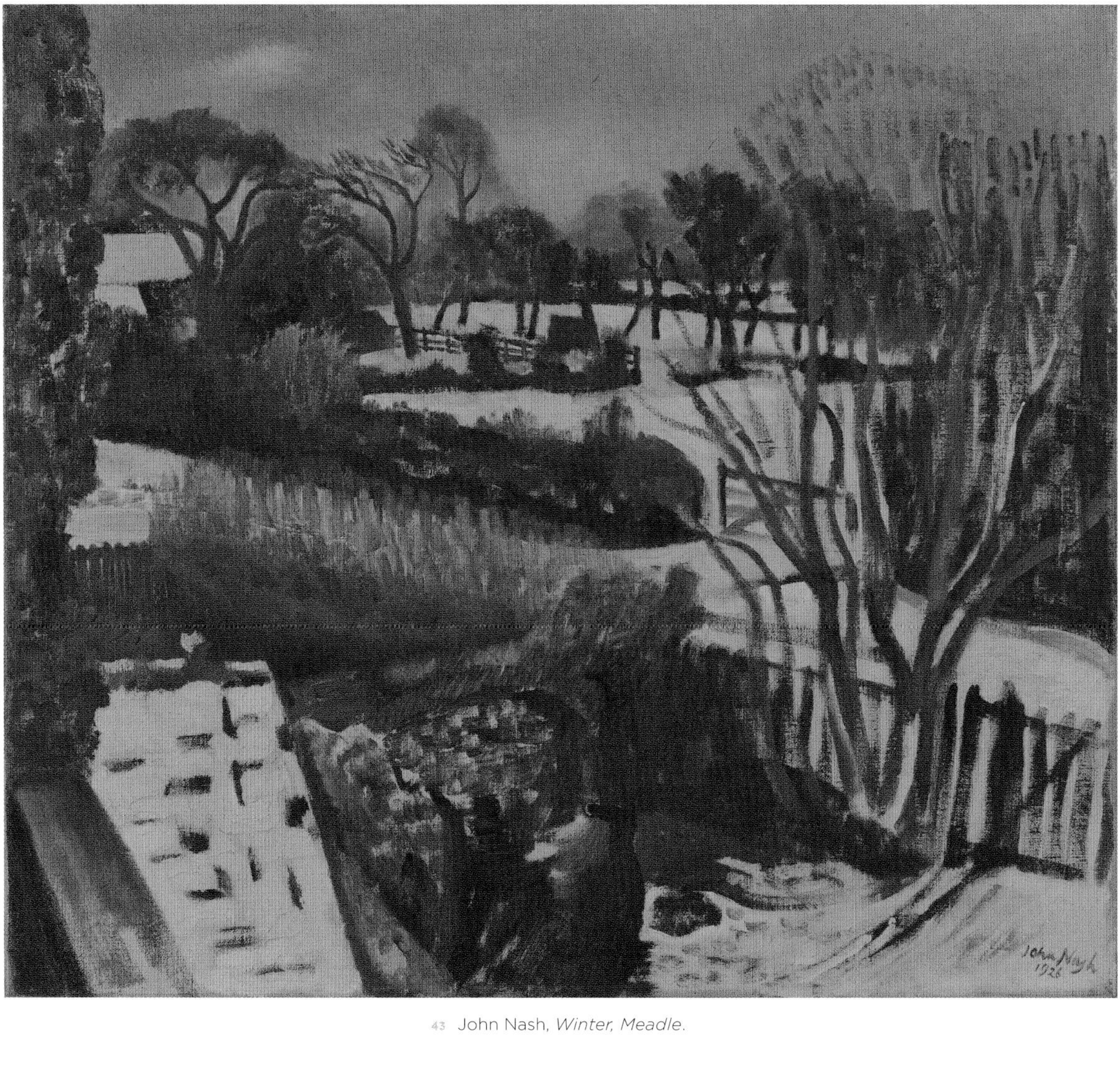

43 John Nash, *Winter, Meadle*.

paintings for the collection.[14] Regrettably, his advice was ignored. Even as late as May 24, 1931, the Vancouver *Sun* reported that Charles H. Scott was on a buying trip for the new Vancouver Art Gallery. From Bury, Lancashire, Scott wrote that "London opened our buying campaign . . . I am safe in saying that Vancouver is going to have the best collection of British art in Canada."[15]

Not that Mortimer-Lamb was opposed to British art. He had earlier corresponded with Frank Brangwyn, a brilliant etcher and lithographer, and acquired a number of his prints; he opened communication with John Nash and around 1923 bought two of Nash's attractive oils. These and many other fine examples of art from his homeland are now in the collection of the Art Gallery of Greater Victoria. However, he believed that a national or civic collection should pay attention to its own constituents first.

During this time Mortimer-Lamb built a little house across the road from his Rayside farm, to forestall anyone else doing so, and took in a tenant. According to Molly, this man had seven or eight children and could not come up with the rent. This was unacceptable to her father and may have played a part in the family's selling out and moving to the Kerrisdale area of Vancouver. Of course, the city of Vancouver was growing quickly and becoming more interesting to art lovers. The BC Art League now had its own exhibition rooms and was dedicated to establishing a civic art gallery and art school; as a result, the Vancouver School of Decorative and Applied Arts (now Emily Carr University of Art + Design) was founded in 1925.

In 1926, Mortimer-Lamb purchased a very appealing two-acre estate in Kerrisdale, at 1075 West 54th Avenue. The grounds had been laid out by an early settler, a Welshman who had worked to achieve an environment reminiscent of "the old country." Mortimer-Lamb fell in love with it at first sight and was enchanted by its winding roadway, large lawn, and many flower beds. It was graced with well-placed flowering trees and shrubs, now reaching maturity. There were two houses on the site, one with eight rooms and the other a smaller lodge at the entrance. For this he paid $20,000, and he enjoyed it for the next twenty years. As well as a Gravenstein apple tree, he planted cherries, chestnuts, pears, and a vegetable garden, and there was a barn where he kept a cow and a donkey. The stone terrace in front led down to flower gardens and a tennis court. As ever, Mary Williams was in charge of the home and garden, entertaining groups of friends who came on the weekend to play tennis. Molly remembered that "Mum would have made a huge tea—eclairs, cakes, sandwiches, a big jug of milk, and a bigger teapot of Nabob orange pekoe tea."[16]

Mary and Mortimer-Lamb continued to lead somewhat separate lives, and Molly's recollection provides a telling example of their different tastes. "My father had a collection of valuable Oriental pots and vases, and one from the Ming dynasty was particularly rare. It was pure white and stood on three legs. My mother loved the vases, but always wanted to fill them with flowers or branches of apple or cherry blossoms, which bothered my father."[17]

At this time, Mortimer-Lamb set up the Pictorial Photography section at the North West Provincial Exhibition in New Westminster; after the event he was thanked for his "extreme kindness and assistance" in a letter from the Committee for Pictorial Photography and Fine Art, of which John Vanderpant was the chairman.[18] Earlier, Mortimer-Lamb had been first an exhibitor and then a judge at this annual exhibition. Vanderpant and Mortimer-Lamb evidently felt an immediate kinship:

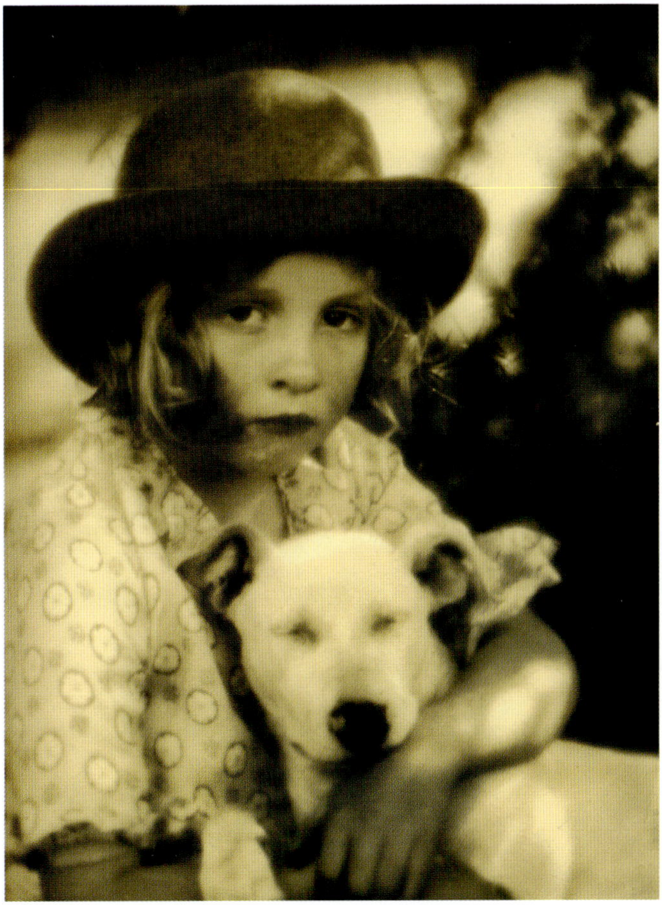

44 Mortimer-Lamb, *Molly and her dog*.

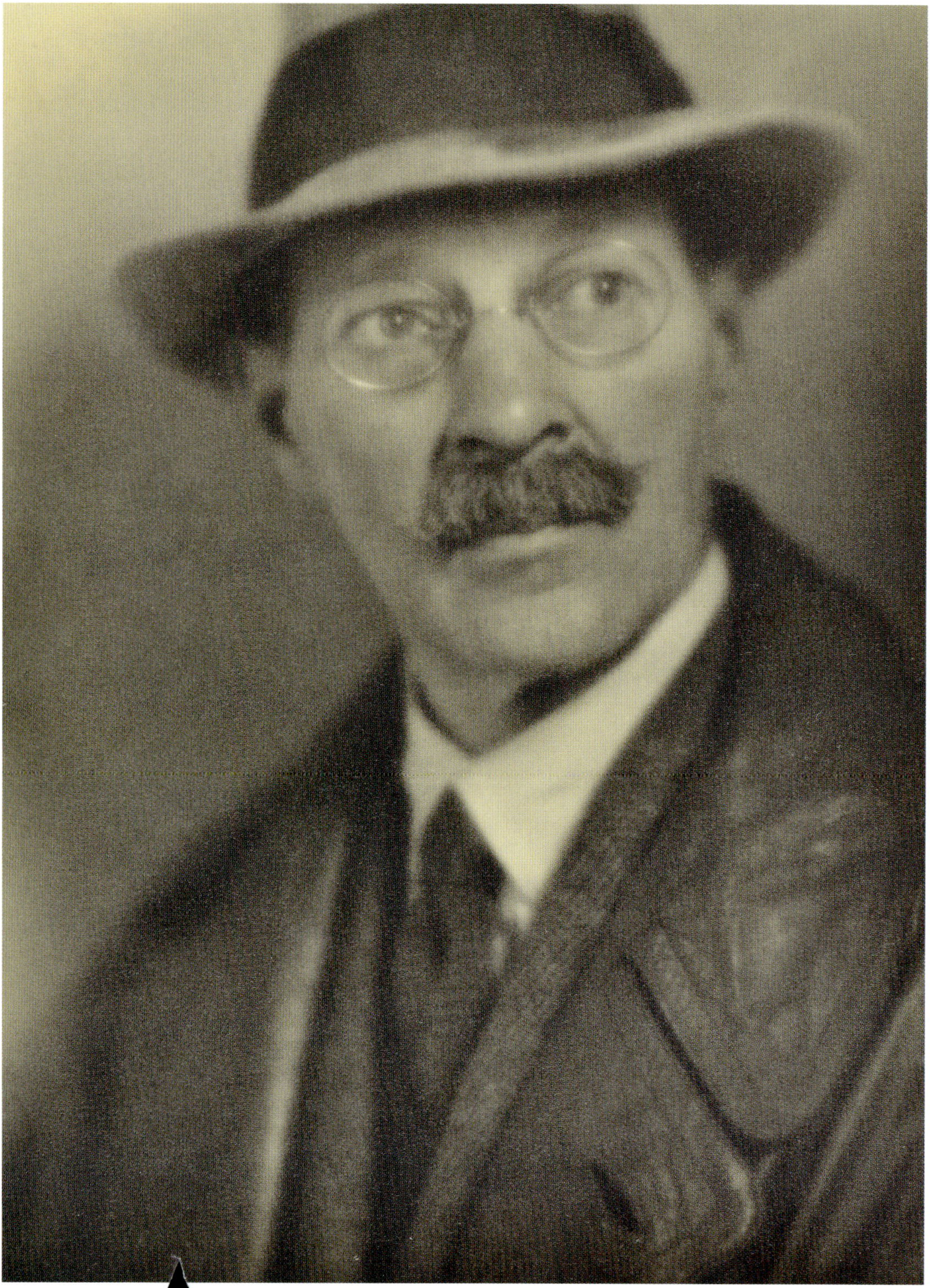

45 John Vanderpant, *Harold Mortimer-Lamb.*

both were talented photographers and keen arts advocates. Vanderpant's daughters recalled that "someone" suggested that their father move his business to the larger city of Vancouver. That someone was Mortimer-Lamb, and the two men formed a partnership with the intention of operating a photography studio and art gallery.[19]

In a letter to Arthur Lismer in January 1926, Mortimer-Lamb wrote that "my friend [Vanderpant] is an exceptionally good photographer and expects to earn his livelihood by that means, as we don't anticipate that art sales will support a business. Personally I do not expect to make any money out of it, but it will give me a new interest and perhaps I may have an opportunity to do some useful work in the interests of art here." He went on to ask for help from Lismer, himself a member of the Group of Seven: "Could you arrange to send us a small exhibition of the work of the Group—one example of each member would serve."[20]

The Vanderpant Galleries, as the enterprise was named, offered an important venue for art in the city of Vancouver. Vanderpant's skill as a photographer and the influence of the older man with the growing art circle in Vancouver and across the country seemed sure to attract a clientele. Mortimer-Lamb rented the second floor of a building at 1216 Robson Street for their partnership, signing on for a period of three years at a rental of eighty-one dollars per annum. He undertook to equip the photographic studio and to provide from his own collection the art and antiques with which to decorate and stock the gallery; in return he was to "have first claim on rentals due and interest at 7% on money so invested, out of the income of the firm," as profits permitted. Vanderpant was to supply whatever photographic equipment he could and, like Mortimer-Lamb, he would be reimbursed from the partnership's profits. Moreover, Vanderpant was to have "second claim on a salary of $200 per month out of the income of the firm."[21] After deducting expenses, they agreed to divide equally the balance of the net profits.

As noted, Mortimer-Lamb looked on the venture as an opportunity to add a new interest to his life; he would be content if Vanderpant could earn a salary for himself and the galleries could provide an outlet for the Group of Seven on the Pacific coast. In a later letter to Lismer, written on March 8, 1926, he once again asked if "until we are in a position to buy outright, do you think it would be possible to arrange that we be sent a few canvases by yourself, [A.Y.] Jackson, [J.E.H.] MacDonald, and perhaps [Clarence] Gagnon and [A.H.] Robinson on consignment?"[22]

Photos from the time show an elegantly appointed salon decorated with Georgian furniture and Persian carpets and hung with elements of Mortimer-Lamb's art collection. Toward the rear was a room adaptable to the purposes of a photographic studio in which memorable portraits of A.Y. Jackson, Eric Brown, Fred Varley, and Vera Weatherbie were taken. A smart little pamphlet was printed to mark the opening, listing oil paintings, watercolours, and etchings. Many of these belonged to the art collection Mortimer-Lamb had created when he was living in Montreal.

Of course, representative photographs by Vanderpant and Mortimer-Lamb were prominently displayed. "The Vanderpant Galleries," the pamphlet noted, "specialize in Photographic Portraiture and Pictorial Photography of Homes and Gardens."

This enterprise was evidently modelled on Stieglitz's gallery at 291 Fifth Avenue in New York. Like 291, Vanderpant Galleries was set up to recognize and promote the interrelationship of innovative trends in painting and photography. Everything seemed perfectly arranged for

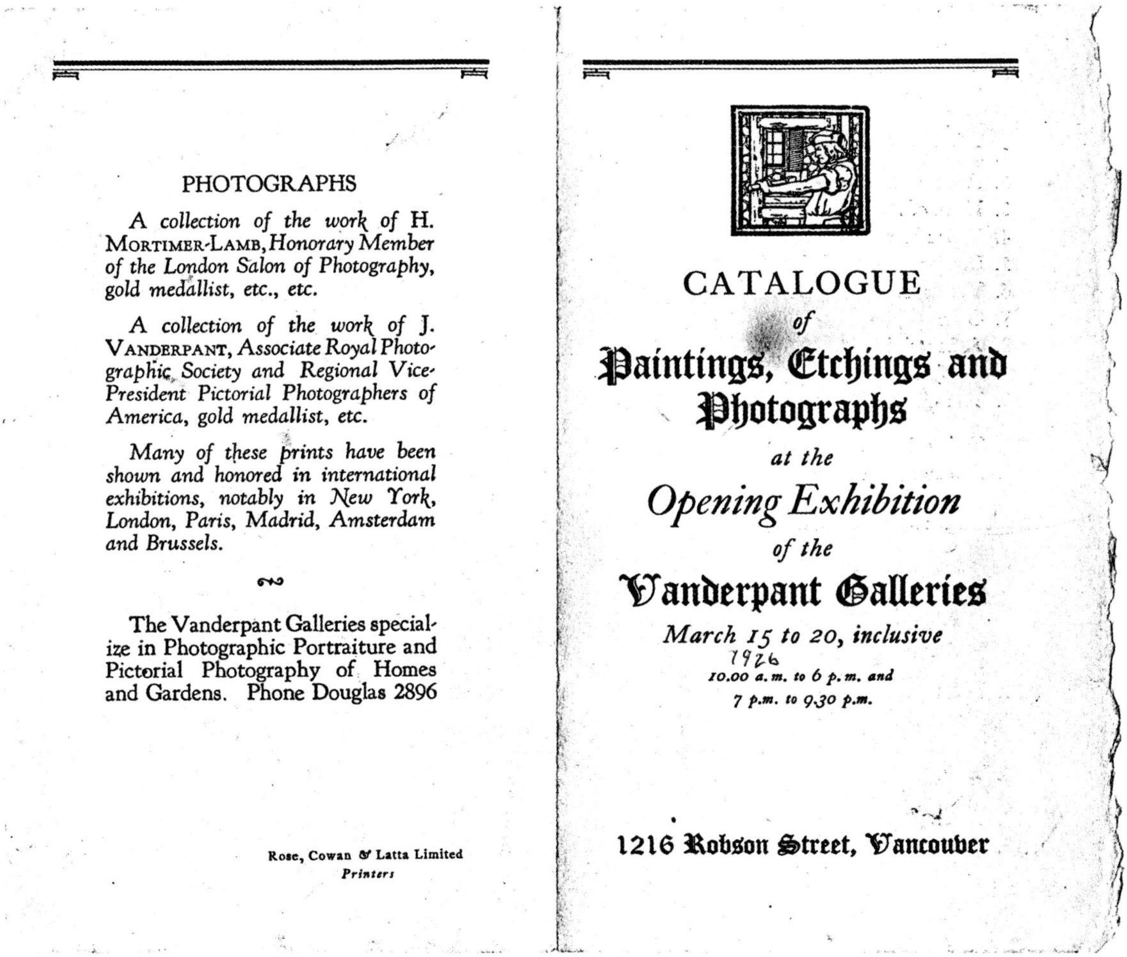

PHOTOGRAPHS

*A collection of the work of H.* MORTIMER-LAMB, *Honorary Member of the London Salon of Photography, gold medallist, etc., etc.*

*A collection of the work of J.* VANDERPANT, *Associate Royal Photographic Society and Regional Vice-President Pictorial Photographers of America, gold medallist, etc.*

*Many of these prints have been shown and honored in international exhibitions, notably in New York, London, Paris, Madrid, Amsterdam and Brussels.*

The Vanderpant Galleries specialize in Photographic Portraiture and Pictorial Photography of Homes and Gardens. Phone Douglas 2896

Rose, Cowan & Latta Limited
*Printers*

CATALOGUE

*of*

**Paintings, Etchings and Photographs**

*at the*

*Opening Exhibition*

*of the*

**Vanderpant Galleries**

*March 15 to 20, inclusive*

1926

*10.00 a.m. to 6 p.m. and*
*7 p.m. to 9.30 p.m.*

**1216 Robson Street, Vancouver**

46 Catalogue from the opening of Vanderpant Galleries.

success, but, while it is possible that some modern paintings and a few antiques were sold, instead of recouping his original investment, Mortimer-Lamb lost money with every passing month. He tried to remain optimistic, but three months after the opening he reported to Lismer that the business "has proved so far a 'frost.' I hoped that it would at least make enough to pay the overhead but instead of that it has become a heavy monthly charge—sufficiently so to cause me a great deal of worry. Nevertheless, I shall have to manage somehow to carry the thing on until the end of the year in anticipation of the Xmas business being profitable enough to recoup my losses." By July he admitted that he had lost more than a thousand dollars, though he felt that he and his partner had "stirred up lots of interest and are doing useful missionary work."[23]

Vanderpant kept his New Westminster studio going during that first year and commuted to Vancouver two or three days a week, but he became increasingly frustrated. Apparently Mortimer-Lamb insisted on doing all the camera work, leaving Vanderpant to do all the developing and printing, and by March 1927 the partnership had ended. At that point Vanderpant opted to take over the business and the building's lease. He also kept some of Mortimer-Lamb's furnishings—a Chippendale table and chairs, a Georgian bookcase, and a Chinese cabinet and screen, among other things—which were paid for slowly over the ensuing years. Artworks were left to be sold on consignment, and many years passed before Mortimer-Lamb was repaid the money he had invested. This was a sort of subsidy he provided to the young photographer and his family. The two treated each other "with the courtesy of gentlemen," but their friendship was over.[24]

The end of the partnership was not the end of the Vanderpant

Galleries, which continued to be a focal point of the city's art activities. Under the management of John Vanderpant and his family, the galleries provided musical evenings and spirited discussions, involving, among others, the staff and students of the Vancouver School of Decorative and Applied Arts. Vanderpant left behind the outdated soft focus of Pictorial photography, embraced the clean, cool forms of Modernism, and made his mark as a photographer.

Vancouver's art school was to become an engrossing part of Mortimer-Lamb's life. In his correspondence with Arthur Lismer, principal of Toronto's Ontario College of Art, he asked Lismer to consider taking a teaching role at the new school then about to open in Vancouver. Lismer had plenty to do in his current position but, in a letter of August 10, 1925, recommended one of the teachers working with him in Toronto, Frederick Varley. "Varley would be likely to put some go into it," Lismer exclaimed. "Varley is a great teacher . . . he creates a fine, forceful atmosphere—and he can draw—has a good technical sense—could develop Commercial Art—and he needs a change, and a new environment."[25] Mortimer-Lamb was already aware of Varley, whose work had come with the travelling shows from the National Gallery. He had written about Varley's *Sunflower Girl* portrait in the Vancouver *Province* after seeing it in 1922, and it was probably through his encouragement that Varley was offered a job at the school.

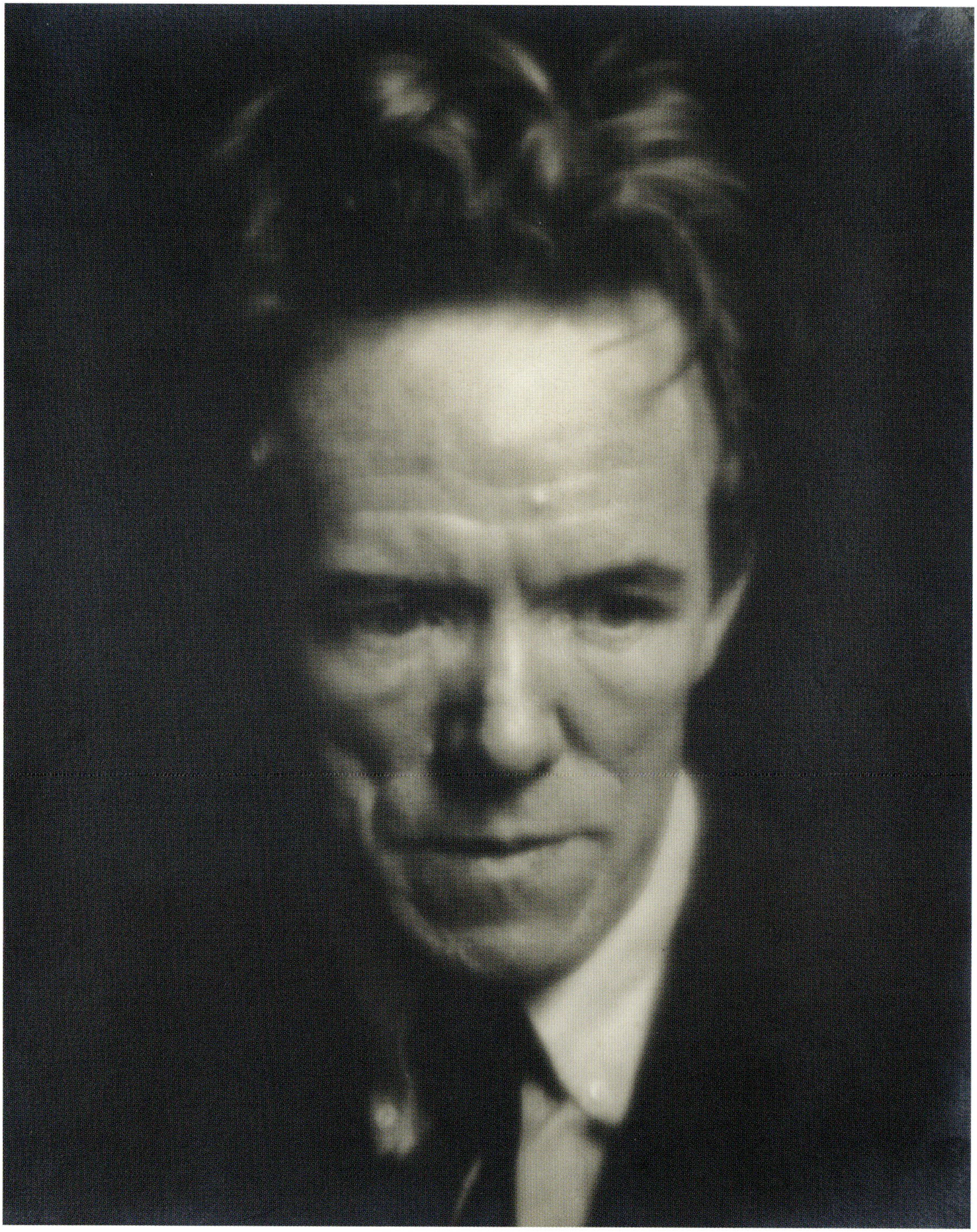

47 Mortimer-Lamb, *Frederick Horsman Varley*.

CHAPTER FOUR

# Fred Varley in Vancouver

At this point, the life of Harold Mortimer-Lamb changed focus. He was fifty-five years old, productively employed in the mining industry, and living in a lovely home; the last of his children was almost grown. His twin goals of establishing an art school and a civic gallery in Vancouver were coming to fruition and he had effectively retired as an artistic photographer. The Modernist painters he championed, the Group of Seven, had gained significant recognition and were on the point of disbanding as a group. For the next few years he continued quietly along his steady course, and his influence became a powerful catalyst for the lives and careers of two important Canadian artists, Frederick Varley and Vera Weatherbie.

Fred Varley's ten years in Vancouver were probably the high point of his artistic career. Mortimer-Lamb, in his discreet way, had been instrumental in bringing Varley to the west and was his primary patron here. The two formed a respectful friendship that endured even after Varley returned to Ontario, and though Mortimer-Lamb remained in the background, Varley's years in Vancouver were constantly underscored

48 John Vanderpant, *Vera as the Virgin Mary*.

by his presence. Earlier, the scenes he had painted on Georgian Bay in Ontario were influenced by his fellow members of the Group of Seven, while in British Columbia he painted the mountains in a unique way, a combination of the Group of Seven plein air style and his interpretation of misty Chinese landscapes. When he set to work on a pair of portraits of a young and beautiful student from the art school, they were driven by a passion unseen in his earlier commissions.

Vera Weatherbie's relationship with Varley, as his student, his model, and then his lover, has never been fully disclosed. Mortimer-Lamb was quietly aware of her from the first and she went on to become an essential figure in his life. This is an appropriate place to untangle the threads that bound these three together and to tell the story of Varley and Vera and Mortimer-Lamb in its correct sequence.

Varley, a native of Sheffield in the north of England, was living in Toronto in 1926 and was ready for a move. With a wife and four children to support, he was burdened with debt and suffering from what he considered to be too little recognition for his work. The newly opened Vanderpant Galleries was keen to provide a venue to show his paintings, which met with the ready encouragement of Mortimer-Lamb. The job in Vancouver offered Varley new fields to roam through in a vast and attractive landscape. Hired as head of drawing, painting, and composition at the year-old Vancouver School of Decorative and Applied Arts, he joined a community of energetic, inquisitive, and empathetic souls. Foremost among them was a Scot, J.W.G. Macdonald, who had also arrived in Vancouver that year to become head of design at the school. Macdonald later wrote that Varley "laid the cornerstone of imaginative and creative painting in BC."[1]

Students in Varley's first class at the school included B.C. Binning,

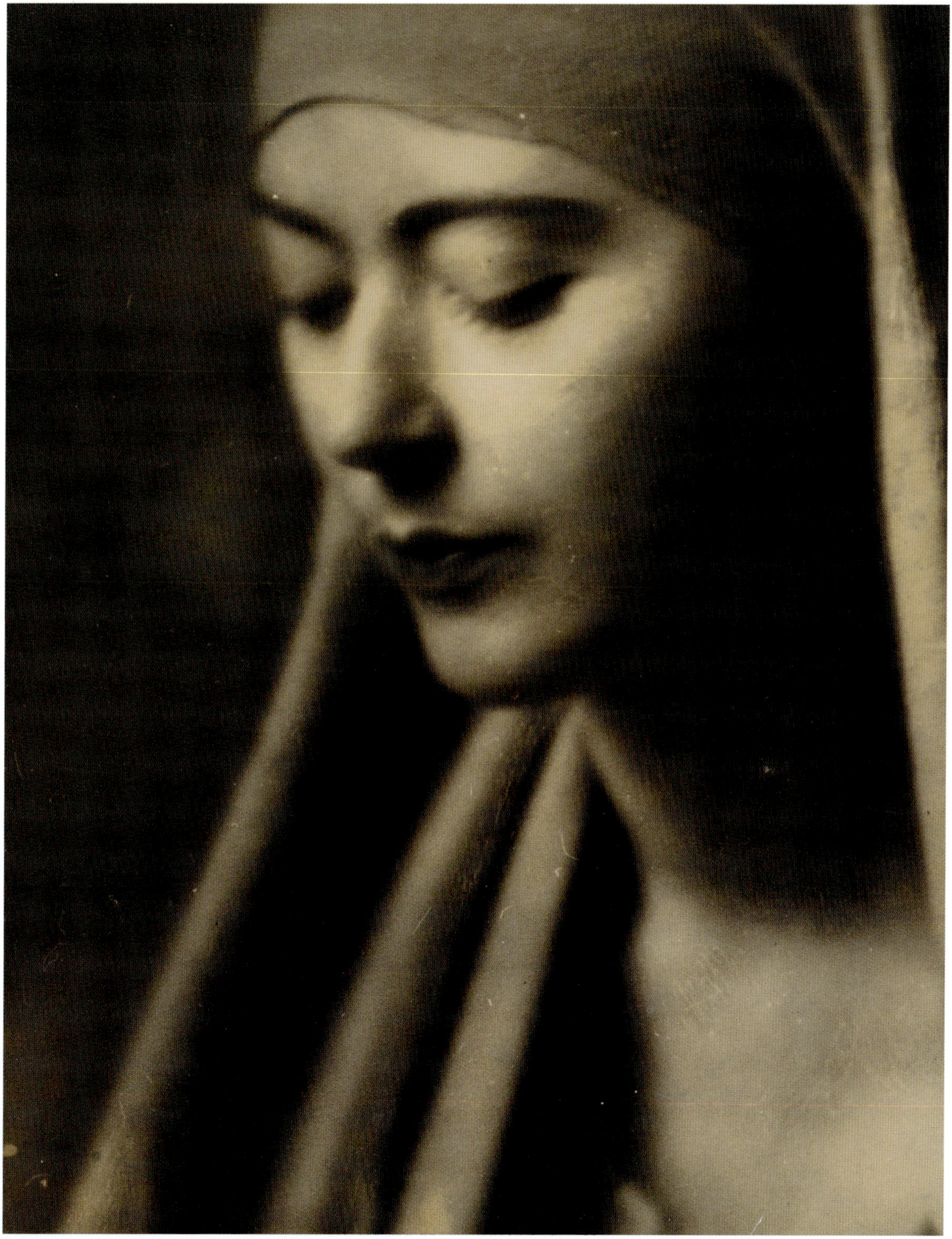

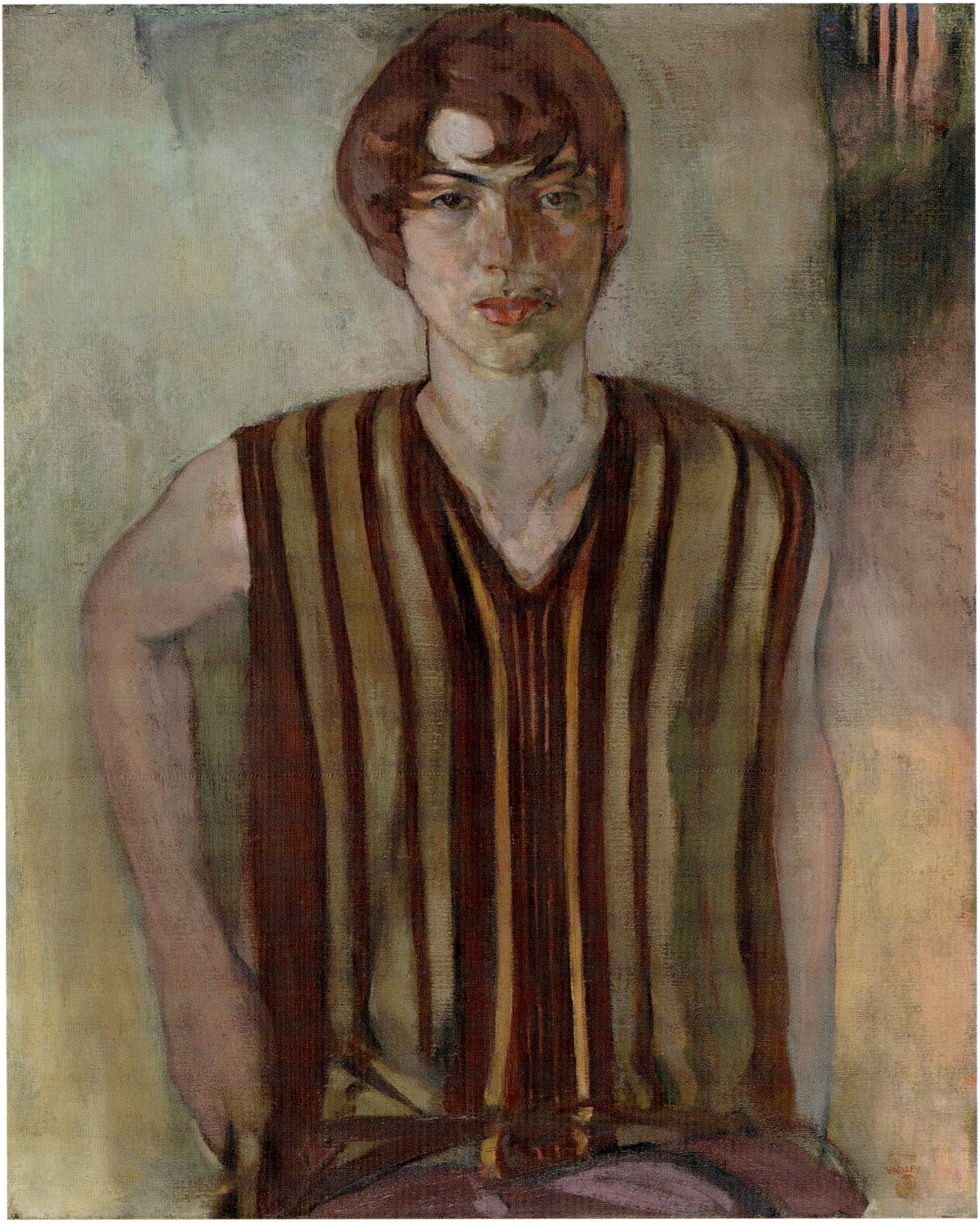

49 F.H. Varley, *Vera*.

Philip Surrey, Orville Fisher, and Fred Amess, who all went on to distinguished careers as professional artists. These were great times at the school, and after a day at their easels, students and teachers socialized together downtown. When Varley returned late in the evening to his wife and children at their boathouse home on the tide line at Jericho Beach, he was apt to stay up most of the night cooking and playing the piano. If he could fit it in between school terms, he would take a week off and hike up into the Garibaldi Ranges north of Vancouver with his new friends. As the years went by, he spent less and less time with his family. He had a downtown studio, which he rented with Macdonald, in a huge old house at 1087 Bute Street called The Parakantas.

Vera Weatherbie was born in 1910 in Vancouver and attended Britannia Secondary School. Her photo album presents a picture of a comfortable home life in the Strathcona neighbourhood, near Chinatown in Vancouver's East End. Her parents were Presbyterian, Molly Lamb Bobak recalled. "They were terribly strict, not at all progressive, fiercely moral."[2] Somehow Vera persuaded them to let her attend the new art school in its first year, 1926. In her second year Varley became her drawing teacher, and sometimes she joined the students who gathered to swim and sing and play badminton after school at his home at Jericho Beach. In 1928, her final year as an undergraduate, Vera was given the role of the Virgin Mary in the school's Christmas production, an old English "miracle play" titled *The Christmas Pageant of the Holy Grail*. John Vanderpant was in the audience and he was so struck by her appearance that he asked her to come to his studio, where he took some photographs of her dressed in her simple stage costume. The images he made are perfectly poised on the cusp between Pictorialism and Modernism and became the most significant photographs

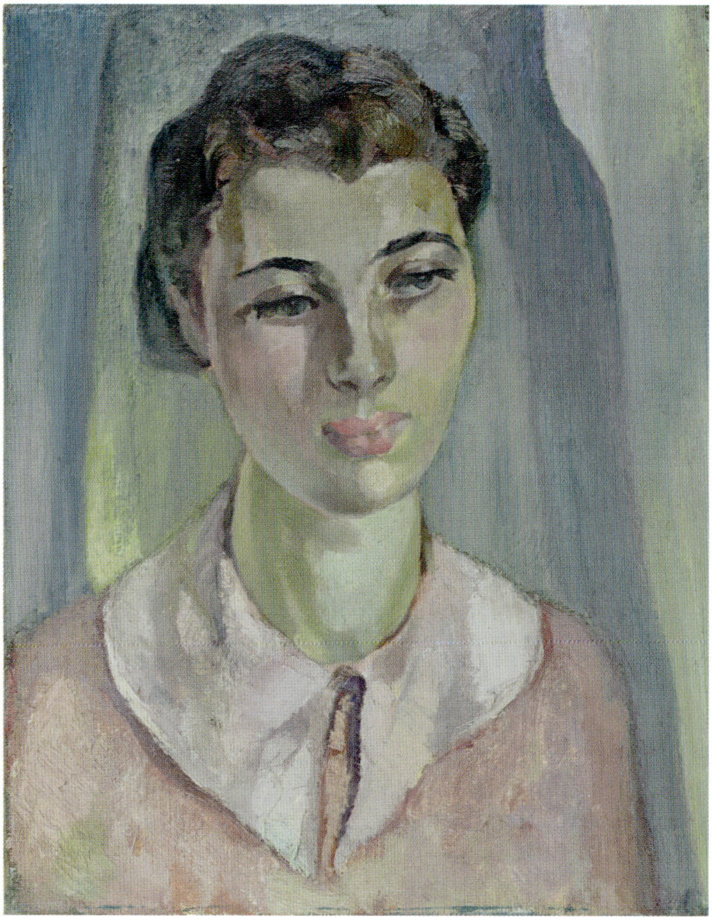

50 Vera Weatherbie, *Self Portrait*.

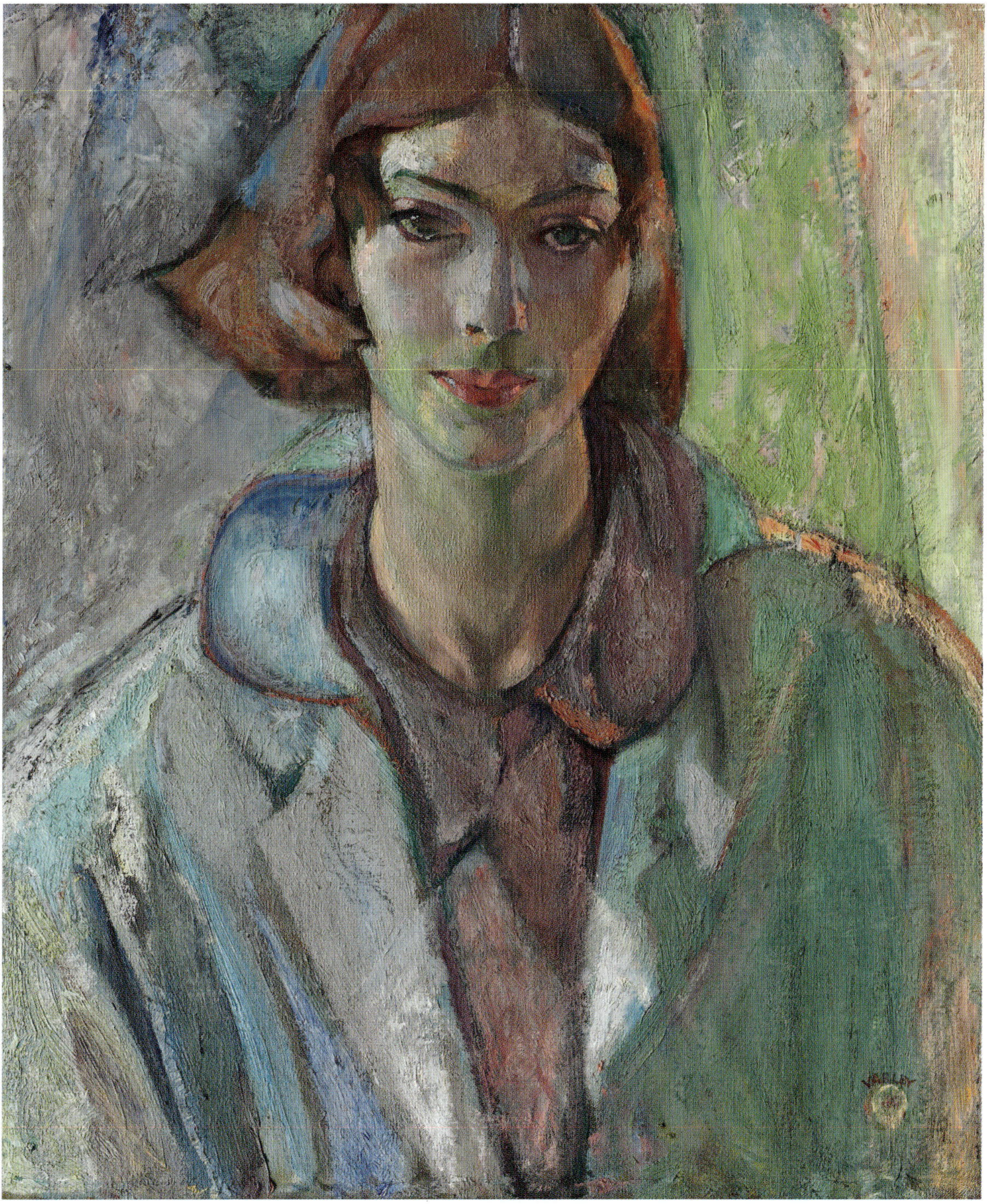

51 F.H. Varley, *Vera*.

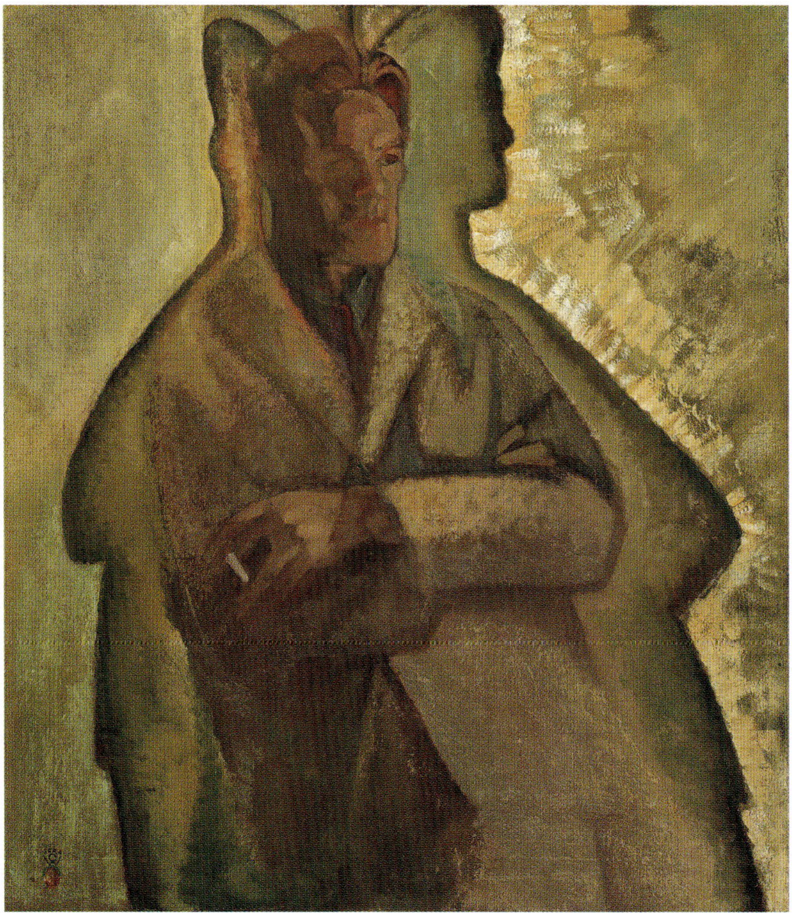

52 Vera Weatherbie, *Portrait of F.H. Varley*.

from Vancouver during that period. Different versions of this soulful image of Vera, both from directly in front and in part profile, are preserved among Mortimer-Lamb's papers and are held in the collections of the Art Gallery of Greater Victoria and the Vancouver Art Gallery.

After graduating from the art school in 1929, Vera continued with a postgraduate year. Following their teachers' example, some of her girlfriends took a studio in The Parakantas building; Vera and a fellow student, Irene Hoffar, rented one too. It was in The Parakantas that she first posed for Varley, who painted her with bobbed hair and a striped blouse. "She was shy and beautiful," Molly recalled, "and moved with a grace that made me think of a Japanese tea ceremony. They say Varley was the sort of teacher you either totally followed or totally rejected. Vera was one of the followers."[3] The painting, known as *Vera* (1929), subsequently won the Willingdon Prize, Canada's top award for painting, when it was exhibited at the National Gallery in 1930 and it became part of that gallery's collection. Varley at the time was forty-nine years old and Vera nineteen.

Building on the success of this first portrait, Varley painted another picture of her; *Vera* (1930) is one of the most highly regarded of all Canadian portraits. The overtones of a malachite green are said to evoke Vera's spiritual nature; complementary tones of violet represent her aesthetic qualities; yellows and pinks add to the mysterious harmony. Vera's hint of a smile suggests a warm sensuality as she gazes at the artist—and the observers—through her captivating eyes. Molly wrote that Vera "was tiny-boned and had almond-shaped eyes and a delicately pursed mouth."[4] There seemed to be something Asian about her facial features. This painting was treasured from the first and was eventually presented

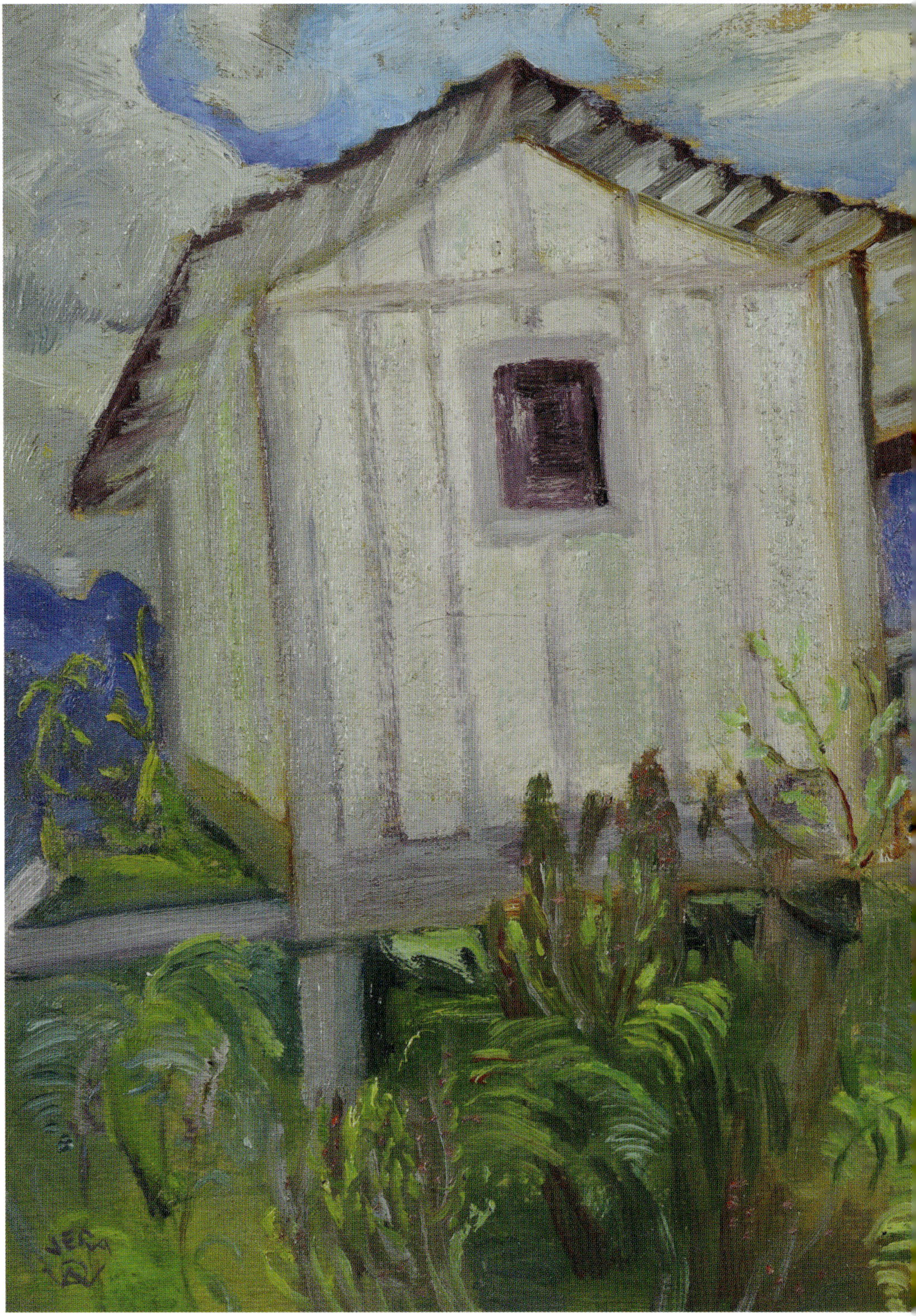

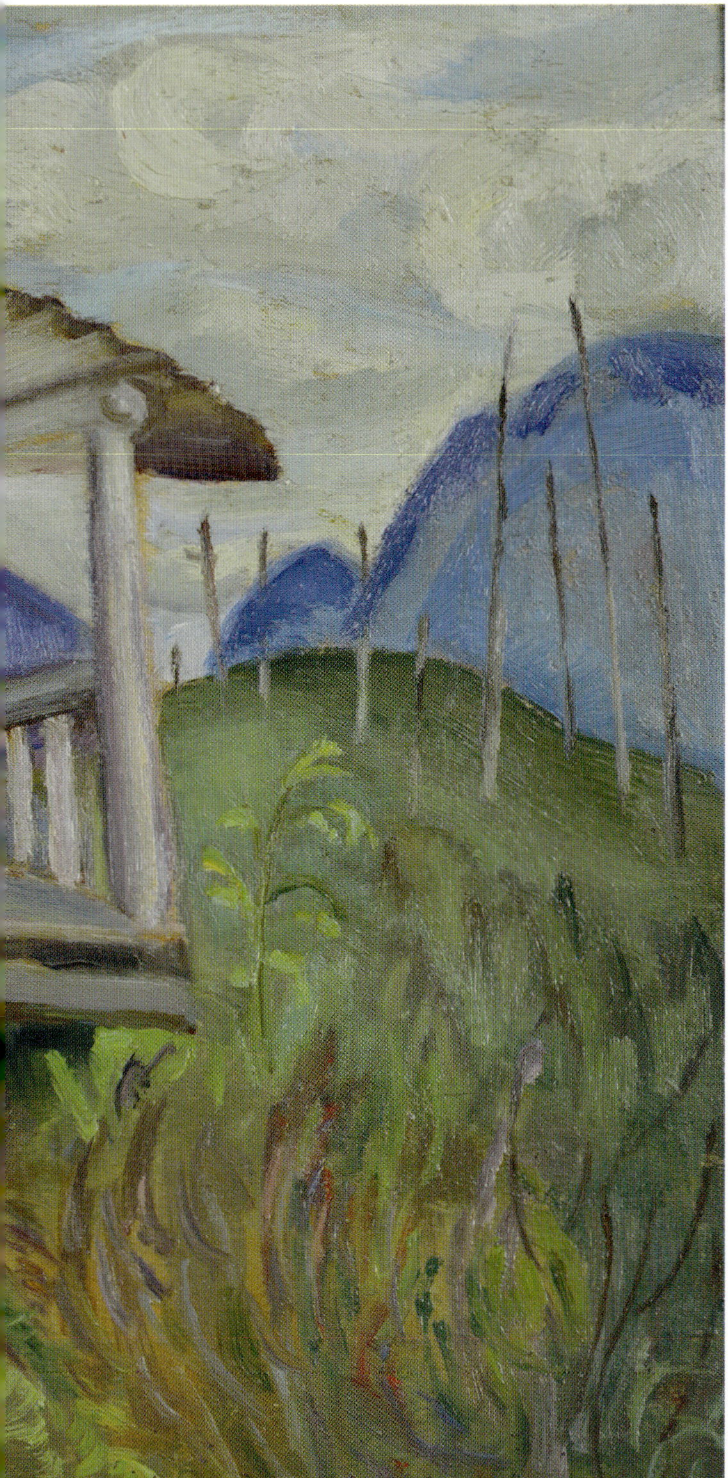

53 Vera Weatherbie, *Solitude*.

to Canada's National Gallery in 1968 by Vincent Massey. Later, when it was reproduced as a postage stamp, Vera became a national icon.

Varley credited Vera with the unique colour sense he adapted to create his best works of this period. Clearly she was more than just a model to him. At the time he was portraying her, she painted her *Portrait of F.H. Varley* (*circa* 1930). Advanced in composition and suffused with the same sort of spiritual tone that would become Varley's trademark, it now belongs to the Vancouver Art Gallery. With constant practice and Varley's encouragement, Vera's talent continued to grow. In recognition of this she was awarded the J. Fyfe-Smith Travelling Scholarship by the Vancouver School of Decorative and Applied Arts in 1930, and this enabled her to spend six months studying at the Royal Academy in London. She sailed to England from Montreal with her friend and studio mate, Irene Hoffar, in September 1931, and they shared a flat in Chelsea. In addition to her studies, Vera was charged by Varley with the task of promoting his career among the contacts he had left behind when he was last there in 1919, but his hopes on this account were not realized. The correspondence between Varley and Vera at this time offers the best evidence of the level of intimacy that had been established between them.

In a letter dated October 9, 1931, he referred to her as his "dearest" and "darling." Referring to her comments about the cool weather, he replied, "You tell me you have invested in woolen undies. Can I imagine them? . . . Your beauty needs not accoutrements, not even woolen." In closing he begged, "Look in the glass dear and kiss yourself goodnight for me. Yours, Fred X. That X," he went on, "is a kiss on the end. It is tremulous and throbs its way right across space—and makes an invisible chain—catch hold and send some more back."[5] It is probably safe to

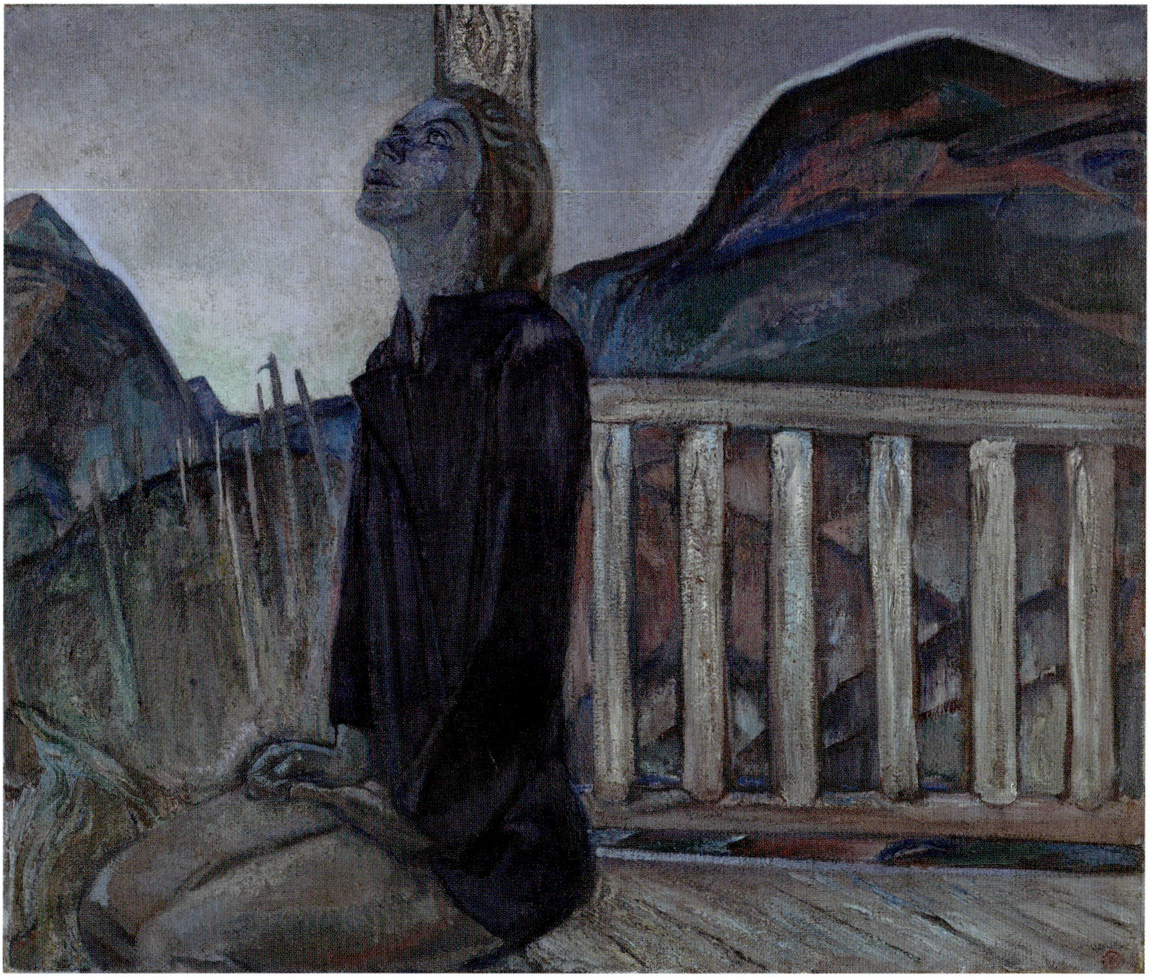

54 F.H. Varley, *Dharana*.

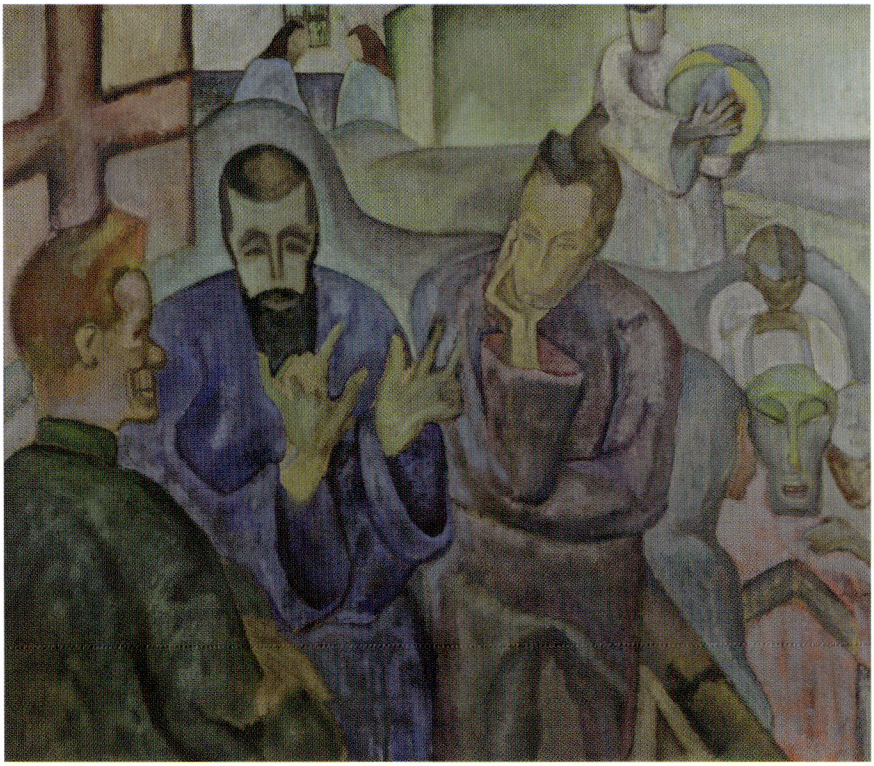

55 Vera Weatherbie, *Varley, Tauber, Macdonald*.

assume that what had taken place between them recently in Vancouver was both passionate and physical.

Upon her return from London in the spring of 1932, Vera shared a studio in Vancouver, this one on Granville Street near Dunsmuir, with Irene Hoffar and Margaret Carter. Mortimer-Lamb stayed in the background, but in his quiet way, he made things possible for the young woman. He bought Vera's portrait of Margaret Carter, which he later donated to the Vancouver Art Gallery, and seemed to be taking a proprietary interest in the well-being of these recent graduates.

When not teaching at the Vancouver School of Decorative and Applied Arts or working in his studio, Varley, with Vera, began exploring the watershed of Lynn Canyon. This is a steep and scenic wilderness in North Vancouver, easily accessible then by a short ferry trip across the harbour followed by a ride up the mountain on a streetcar. One afternoon in 1932 they were walking along a pipeline road that ran up the valley and stopped to sketch at an abandoned forest ranger's cabin. Paintings of the cabin by both artists exist, painted that day on location; there is also a watercolour by Varley of Vera sitting on the porch.

These images evolved into a landmark painting by Varley. Titled *Dharana* (1932), it is a view of a young woman in a mountain valley, lost in some sort of spiritual transport. This was a peak moment in Canadian art, and the painting is a record of a truly transcendent experience: Vera channelling the universe as witnessed by her lover, the premier portrait painter of the age. Varley later explained that Dharana is a Buddhist level of contemplation at which man reaches oneness with nature. This painting seems to be a summation of everything—model, mood, location—that was important to him at the time, embodied in the person of Vera.

The atmosphere was serene in Lynn Canyon, but down in Vancouver change was in the air. Some of the employees of the Vancouver School of Art (formerly the Vancouver School of Decorative and Applied Arts) were given notice that their salaries would be cut and their hours reduced. Protest proved futile and at the end of the spring term in 1933, many of the staff, with the support of at least half of the student body, left to organize a school of their own. They took over a former car dealership and service garage at 1233–39 West Georgia Street, where, in September, they opened the British Columbia College of Art. Attracted by the breakaway nature of the endeavour and the charismatic leadership of the teachers, 234 students joined up for a full program of study including painting, drawing, commercial and theatre arts, design, clay modelling, and colour theory. Vera, Beatrice Lennie, and Margaret Williams, all former students of Varley, were employed as assistants. They got off to an enthusiastic start and that winter put on the Ben Jonson play *Volpone*, with masks and music. Spirits ran high and the administration proposed a summer school in Garibaldi Park.

The Garibaldi summer venture never materialized, but Varley found his own getaway. In the summer of 1934 he came upon a house for rent on Rice Lake Road in Lynn Canyon. It was a two-storey summer home that lacked many creature comforts but did have a piano. Varley took this as a sign that it was meant to be his, and he rented it as his home away from home.

Many paintings that later became part of the Mortimer-Lamb bequest show the view from this house: a little bridge crossing the rushing waters of Lynn Creek in the foreground, backed by fresh second-growth timber and the remains of a recent forest fire. Overtopping all was the snow-capped Mount Seymour. Amazingly, this wilderness, trailing wisps of mist like

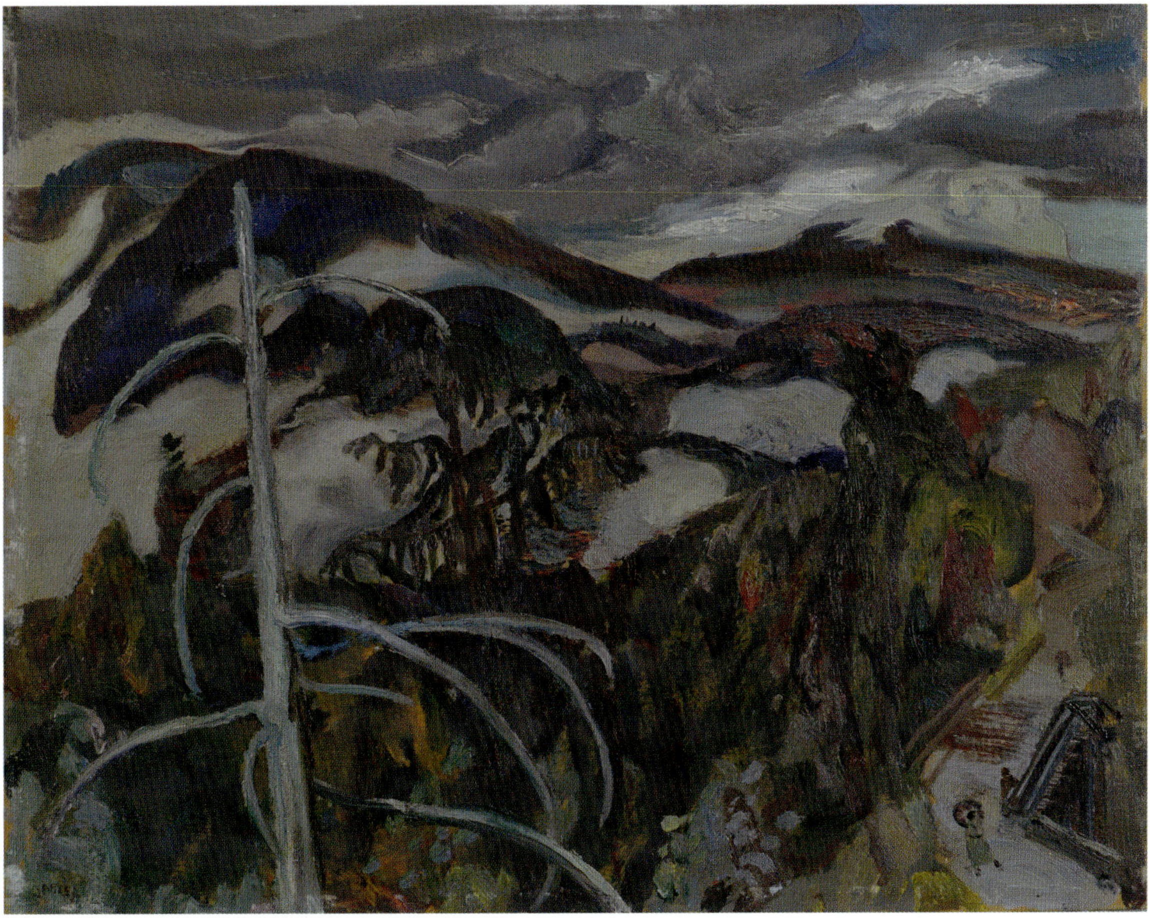

56 F.H. Varley, *Weather, Lynn Valley, B.C.*

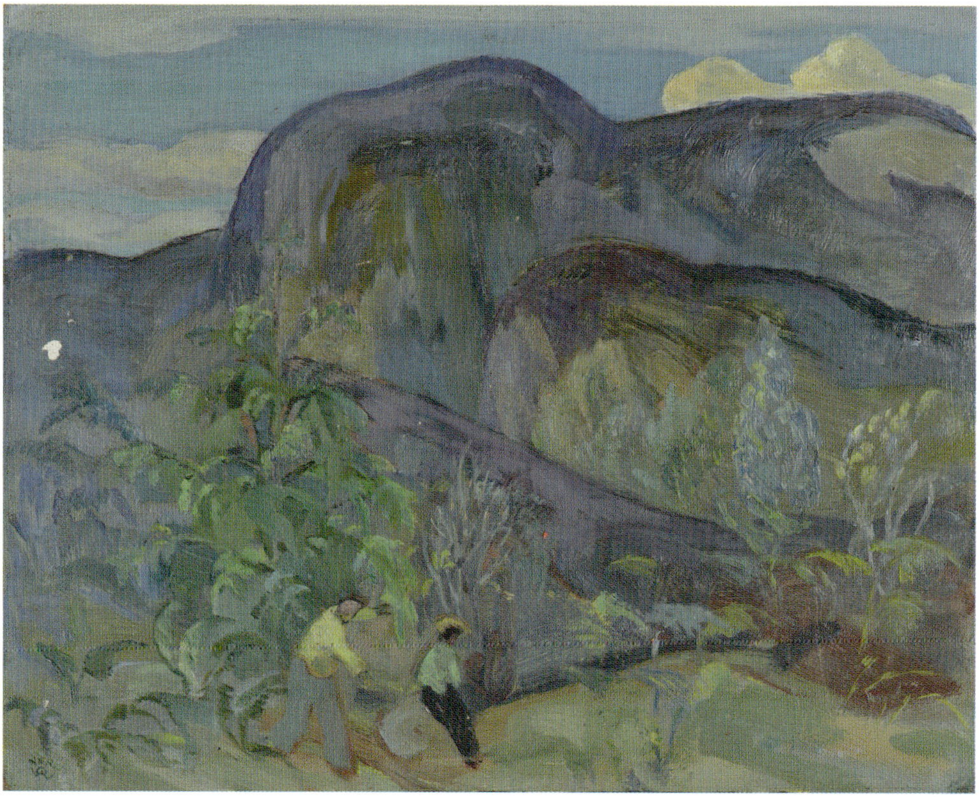

57 Vera Weatherbie, *Untitled (landscape with two figures).*

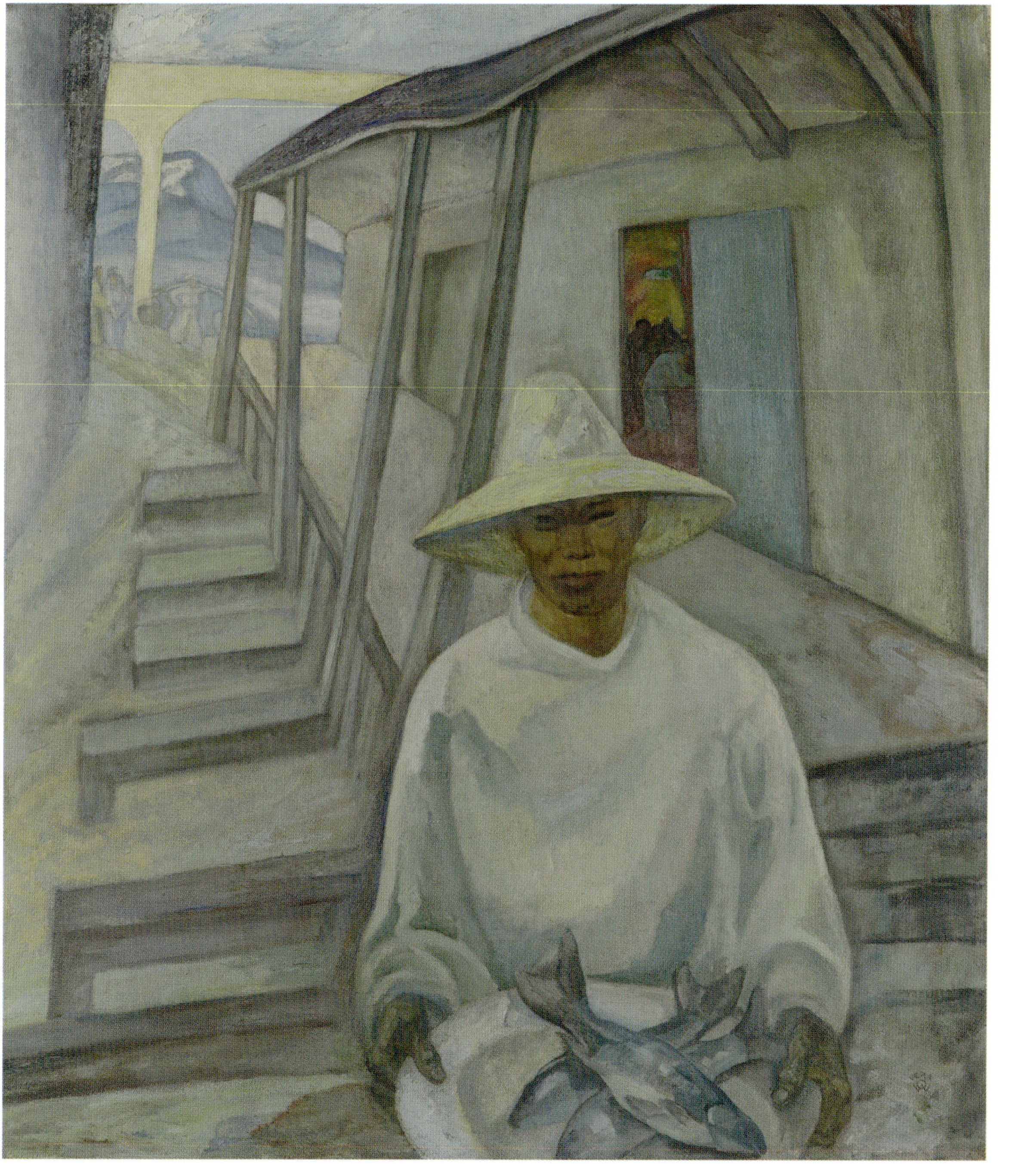

58 Vera Weatherbie, *My-E-En*.

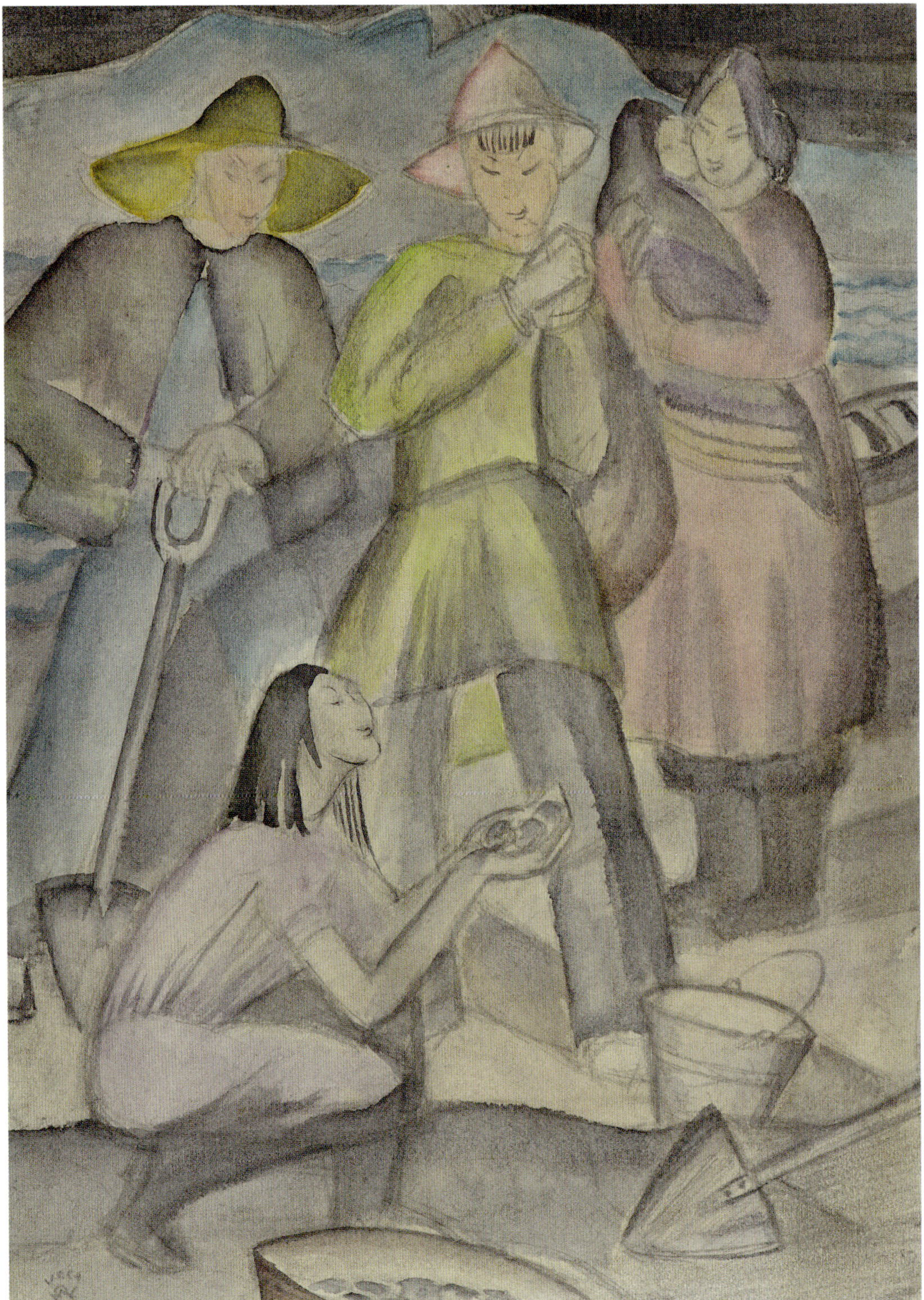

59 Vera Weatherbie, *Clam Diggers*.

a Chinese scroll, was just forty-five minutes from downtown Vancouver. Varley left his family down below to struggle on without him and eventually moved up to Lynn Canyon full time. Vera did not actually move in with him, but she was a frequent visitor. During November of that year, in the midst of the economic depression, Varley was operated on for a mastoid infection, and Vera's patient nursing was crucial to his recovery.

Varley's wife, Maud, and their children—three boys and a girl—had earlier that year been evicted from the house at Jericho when they couldn't pay the rent, and during the series of evictions that followed, they lost their furniture too. Maud eventually moved to North Vancouver, where rent was cheaper, though she had scarcely enough money to feed the children. While Varley gave his family little thought and less money, he single-mindedly pursued his artistic calling in the company of the young woman who was his model and muse, the source of his inspiration as a painter. Vera may have been tormented by mixed emotions at this time, but she never wrote down her feelings.

Working in painting studios both in Lynn Canyon and in downtown Vancouver, Vera was teaching Varley about colour and much else. Her career was on the rise. Her large canvas titled *My-E-En* was featured on the cover of the November 1934 issue of the Vancouver Art Gallery's *Bulletin* and had been awarded the Beatrice Stone Medal at the gallery's annual show that year. It shows a Chinese fish peddler by a tenement on the shores of Burrard Inlet. The North Shore mountains looming in the distance were the background of both her painting and her life just then. In a letter he sent her to in 1939, Varley acknowledged that "I learnt more of Art, true Art in those years than at any other period—you taught me."[6] Much later, in an interview in *Maclean's* magazine, he called her "the greatest single influence on my life."[7] What she taught him is made specific in a National Film Board production from 1953 in which it was explained that Vera taught Varley about auras: vibrations that surround all people, revealing the true state of their emotions and spirit. These vibrations are depicted as colour by those spiritually ready to receive them.[8]

While spirituality and vibrations were certainly interesting, down on the material plane things could not continue heedlessly while the Depression lingered on. The BC College of Art lasted only two years, as the romantic enthusiasm that brought it into being so quickly was not sufficient to guide the fortunes of a serious institution of higher learning. With no sustaining economic base, no political support, and not much governing structure, it could not compete with the Vancouver School of Art during those hard times. By the summer of 1935 the fledgling school was finished.

During this period, in the mid-1930s, Mortimer-Lamb was approaching retirement age and was less involved with the day-to-day activities of the mining institute. Within the art world his role was also changing. As a sensible manager and administrator volunteering with the BC Art League, he had been active in the genesis of the Vancouver School of Decorative and Applied Arts. Now, with time to get away, he found himself joining the day-to-day activities of the art students. In the summer of 1935 he went with fifty students and artist-teachers from the art school on a summer sketching trip to Savary Island.

Savary is a low-lying island in the Strait of Georgia north of Powell River, about 160 kilometres from Vancouver. The trip was led by Charles H. Scott, principal of the school, and he was accompanied by Ross Lort, E.J. Hughes, Fred Amess, Peter Aspell, B.C. Binning, and many other young artists. They all stayed at the Royal Savary Hotel on Indian Point and each day spread out

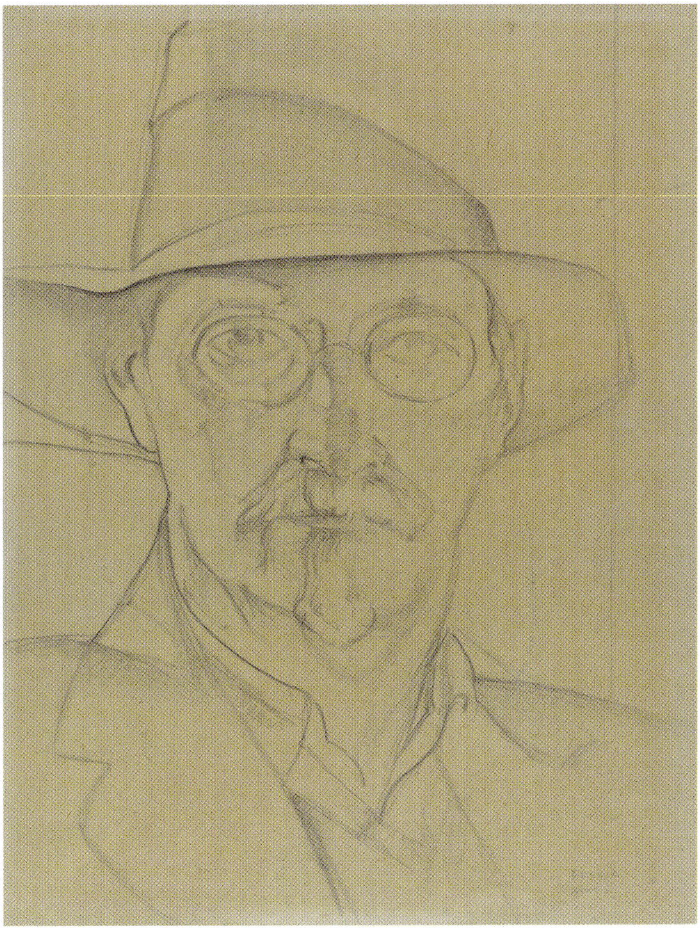

60 Fred Amess, *H. Mortimer Lamb, Esq.*

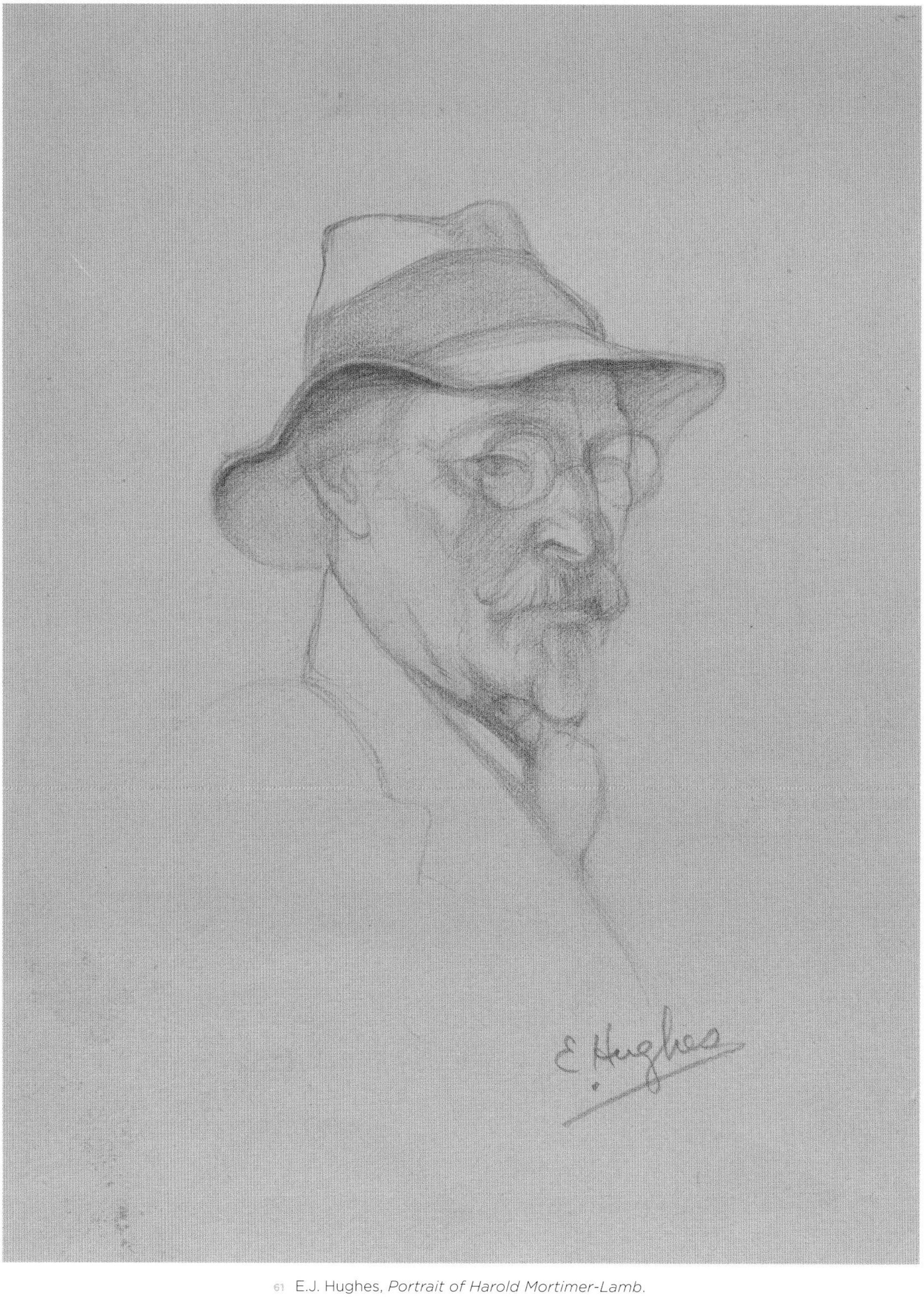


61 E.J. Hughes, *Portrait of Harold Mortimer-Lamb.*

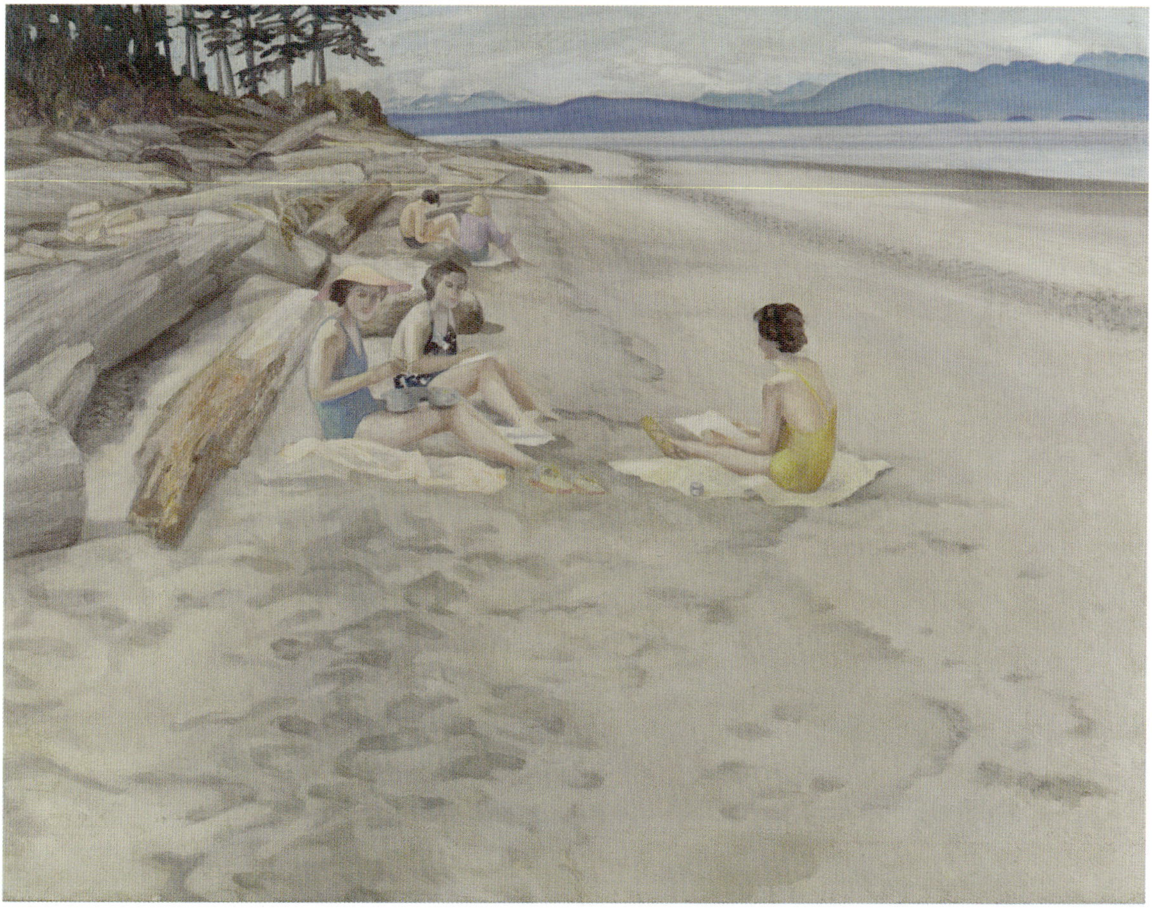

62 Fred Amess, *Beach Scene, Savary Island.*

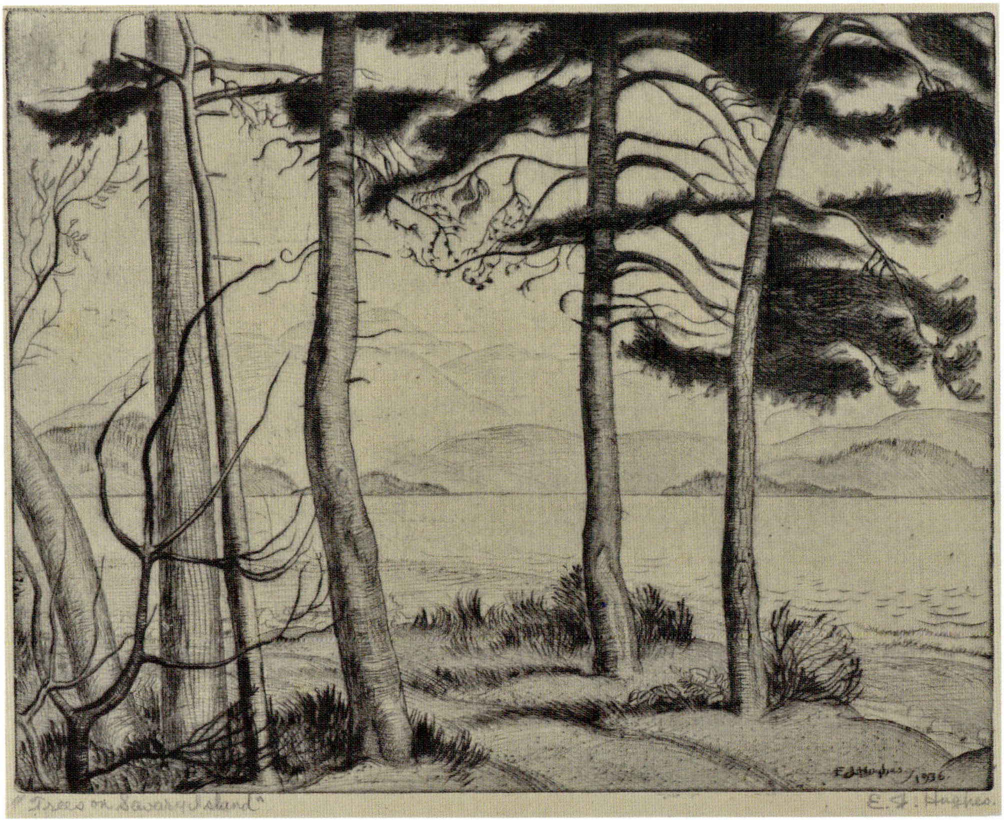


63 E.J. Hughes, *Trees on Savary Island*.

across the island to swim, play golf, picnic, and paint. To judge by the artwork produced, this must have been a true summer idyll. Mortimer-Lamb posed in his fedora for a number of young artists who sketched him in pencil—perhaps all of them at the same time—and he took quite a few casual snapshots, enjoying the inspiration of this sympathetic group. During the two weeks on the island he also had some impromptu painting lessons from Amess, a Varley student who later became the principal of the Vancouver School of Art. It appears that Mortimer-Lamb's interest in painting, which had lain dormant in him since his time with Laura Muntz almost twenty-five years earlier, was beginning to emerge.

Mortimer-Lamb brought home some interesting souvenirs from this trip, including three drawings of him by students Binning, Hughes, and Amess. Later, Mortimer-Lamb purchased the most highly developed of the pictures produced on the Savary trip, a large oil by Amess that depicts students on the beach. All these works now belong to the Art Gallery of Greater Victoria. In addition, he acquired a rare early etching by Hughes, titled *Trees on Savary Island*. This very group of trees, backing the beach and framing the view out into the strait, appears in photos from Mortimer-Lamb's family album.

Back in Vancouver, things were unravelling for Varley. With the closure of the BC College of Art he was jobless and penniless. His alcoholism and philandering had brought him to an impasse, and his affair with Vera was coming to an end. Varley wrote to Mortimer-Lamb, who had been keeping an eye on the dissolute artist, "[B]y this time, I suppose you will sum me up as having no use for women apart from releasing the activity of the male—m. m. m.—ph!"[9] There may be some truth in his self-evaluation. Vera remained his heart's ideal, but she had cooled toward Varley and never returned to his side. Reacting to the situation, in December 1935 she escaped to Seattle to stay with her brother for a while.

Without his model, Varley was saddened, and without a salary, he was destitute. To help him out, Mortimer-Lamb and John Vanderpant each commissioned Varley to paint them. There is an intensity to his portrait of Mortimer-Lamb that bespeaks a frank understanding between the two men. It is imbued with the "spiritual" colour scheme with hints of malachite green and violet, which show Vera's influence. The painting, which is indeed a superb characterization, was given to the Vancouver Art Gallery in 1941 by Mortimer-Lamb. Both Mortimer-Lamb and Vanderpant wrote letters in 1935 to Harry McCurry at the National Gallery proposing an escape for the beleaguered artist. They were agreed that if he could stop drinking, get a bit of financial support, and meet some patrons, things would be different. The idea was accepted by McCurry, and Varley's sale of his self-portrait to the National Gallery provided him with the money to make the trip to Ottawa. He had reason to be grateful that his friends had influence in high places.

Varley took the train to Ottawa in April and was commissioned to paint the chairman of the board of trustees of the National Gallery, H.S. Southam. Varley was put up at the Chateau Laurier while he undertook the painting. He was also given his paint and canvas and, in a situation inconceivable in today's museological atmosphere, was provided with one of the gallery's exhibition halls as his own studio. However, within a short time he managed to offend everyone with his late hours and smoking in the gallery. Throughout this stay he wrote to Mortimer-Lamb, keeping him apprised of his opinions, most of them acerbic, about the potential patrons he was meeting in Ottawa and the

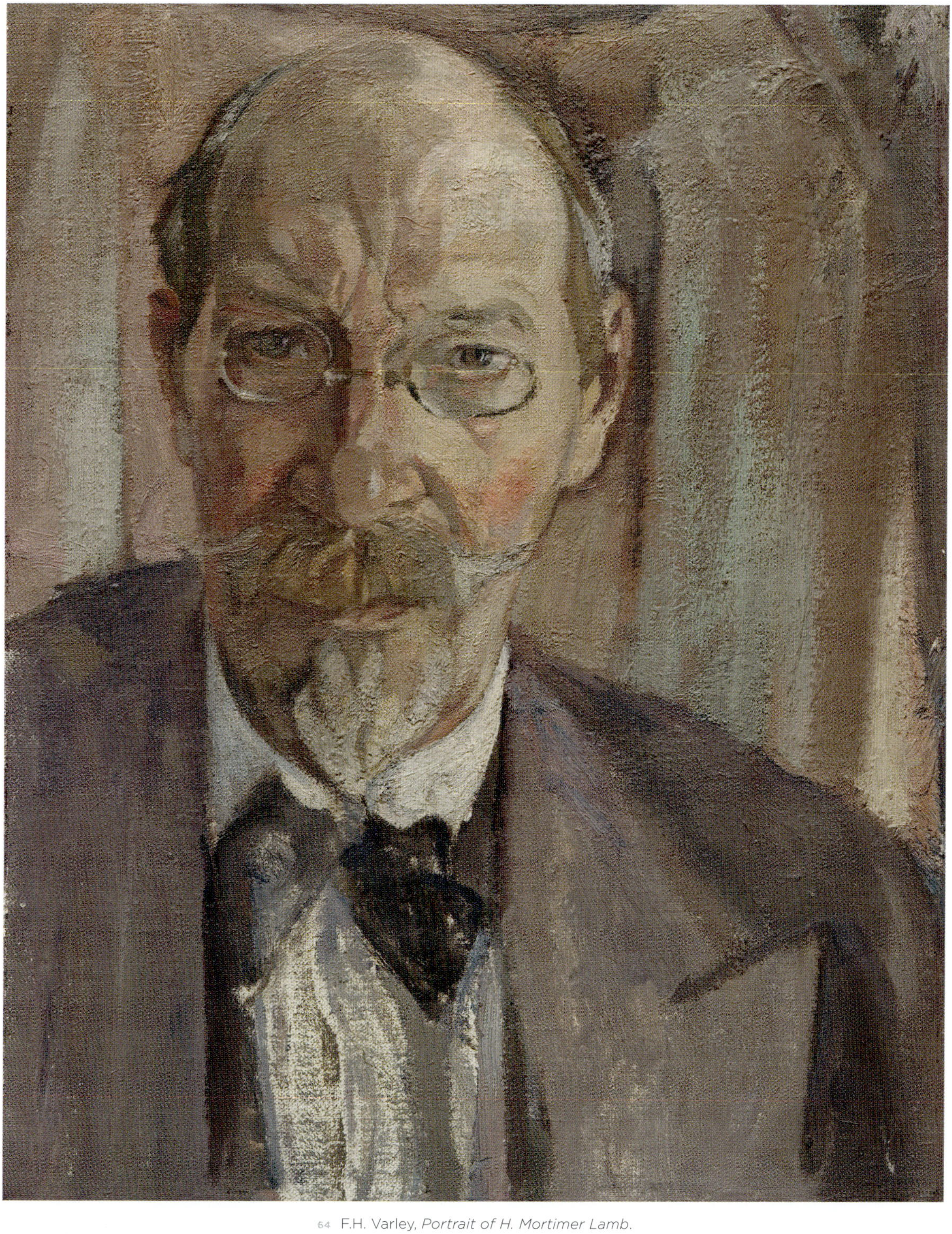

64 F.H. Varley, *Portrait of H. Mortimer Lamb.*

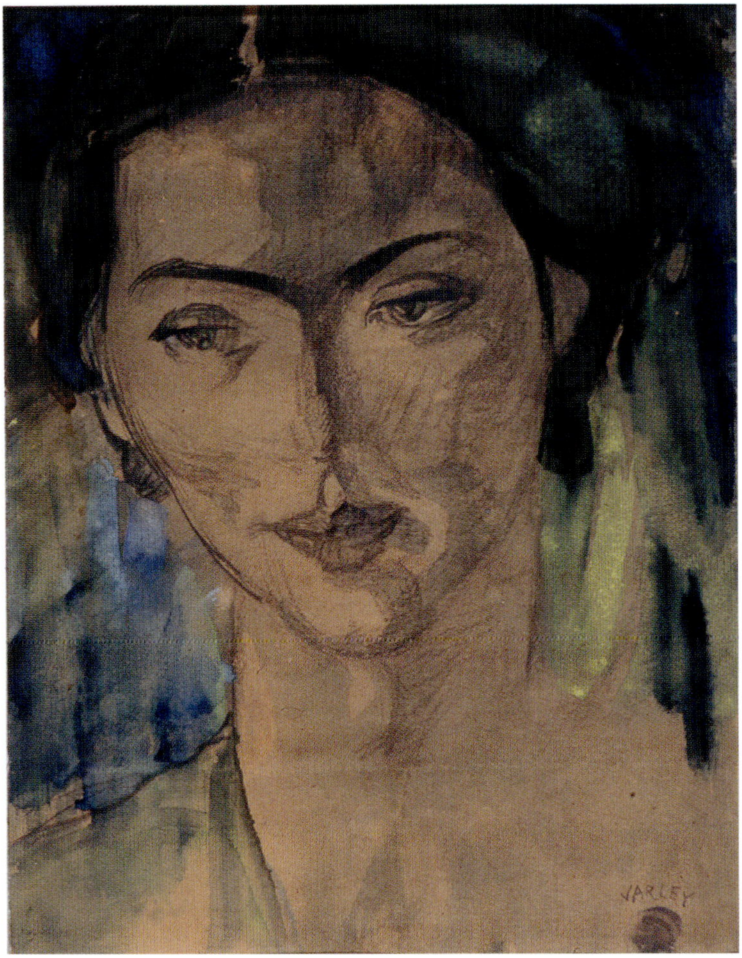


65 F.H. Varley, *Vera*.

activities of the members of the former Group of Seven. In July of that year Varley was asked to vacate the premises.

In late summer 1936 he took what was left of the money he had received for the commission and returned to the west, hoping to resume his happy existence in Lynn Canyon and to renew his relationship with Vera, who had recently returned from Seattle. Mortimer-Lamb had been patiently paying the rent on the Lynn house to secure it for him, but things did not go as Varley had hoped.

When Varley met Vera on his return, he created a moody pencil sketch of her, tinted with watercolour, which he gave her as a gift. In it she appears as a mature woman, her thoughts turned inward. Before the end of September that year she had booked herself passage on the *Empress of Britain* and sailed for Yokohama. It was time for her to get out of town. Her itinerary for this trip is not clear, but she stayed away for a number of months.

Varley also looked for an exit. He persuaded Maud to move into the house at Lynn to hold it for his later use, and by early October he was back in Ottawa. There he continued to complain that his would-be sponsors and patrons were "arrogant, narrow-minded, selfish and self-important."[10] After the fiasco with the Southam commission, Varley busied himself with a huge, symbolic self-portrait titled *Liberation*. It depicts a striding figure breaking free from shackles, with an unleashed energy like Christ emerging from the tomb. To Varley's despair, this magnum opus was not accepted for the Royal Academy's annual show in London. Settling further into the sentimental embrace of his thoughts and imagination, he got to work on a "memory picture" called *Night Ferry, Vancouver*. The ferry he depicted was the boat that, in his dreams, would take him to his love nest at Lynn Canyon. The lone artist is seen standing on an upper deck near an erect flagpole, while on the deck below two lovers commune in front of the seething whirlpool that is the boat's wake. This painting was submitted to but not accepted for an exhibition at the Art Gallery of Toronto.

In a mood of deepening melancholy in his studio in Ottawa, Varley set to work on another painting from his memory and imagination. This one, titled *Mirror of Thought*, showed the view from the house at Lynn Canyon. Mountains loom over the valley that had been his Eden, and two lovers dally, joined in conversation on the bridge. The artist is in an upper room, hopelessly remote from them. He presents himself caught close up in a shaving mirror with a cigarette dangling from his lip, appearing crucified against the crossbars of the window frame. The mood is foreboding. This powerful statement was his last gift to Vera; in it he depicted himself looking longingly at the woman who was no longer willing to share his life. Like so much else that documents this fabulous and doomed romance, *Mirror of Thought* became part of the bequest of Mortimer-Lamb and Vera.

Varley made a final trip to the coast in August 1937. There he found Maud and the children living in the Lynn Canyon house, for which Mortimer-Lamb was still paying the rent. Later that year she received an unexpected inheritance from an aunt and was able to buy it outright. On this trip to Vancouver, within a day of his arrival, Varley was discovered by Maud in a movie theatre with Vera. That was the end of his relationship with both Maud and Vera. A modest exhibition of his sketches, with photos by Vanderpant of some of his work, took place, but even the sale of forty items did not provide the artist with funds for long. Then one of his paintings was rejected by the *Northwest Artists* exhibition in Seattle. A broken man, he accepted money for a ticket back to Ottawa from one of his former students. He got on the train and never saw the coast again.

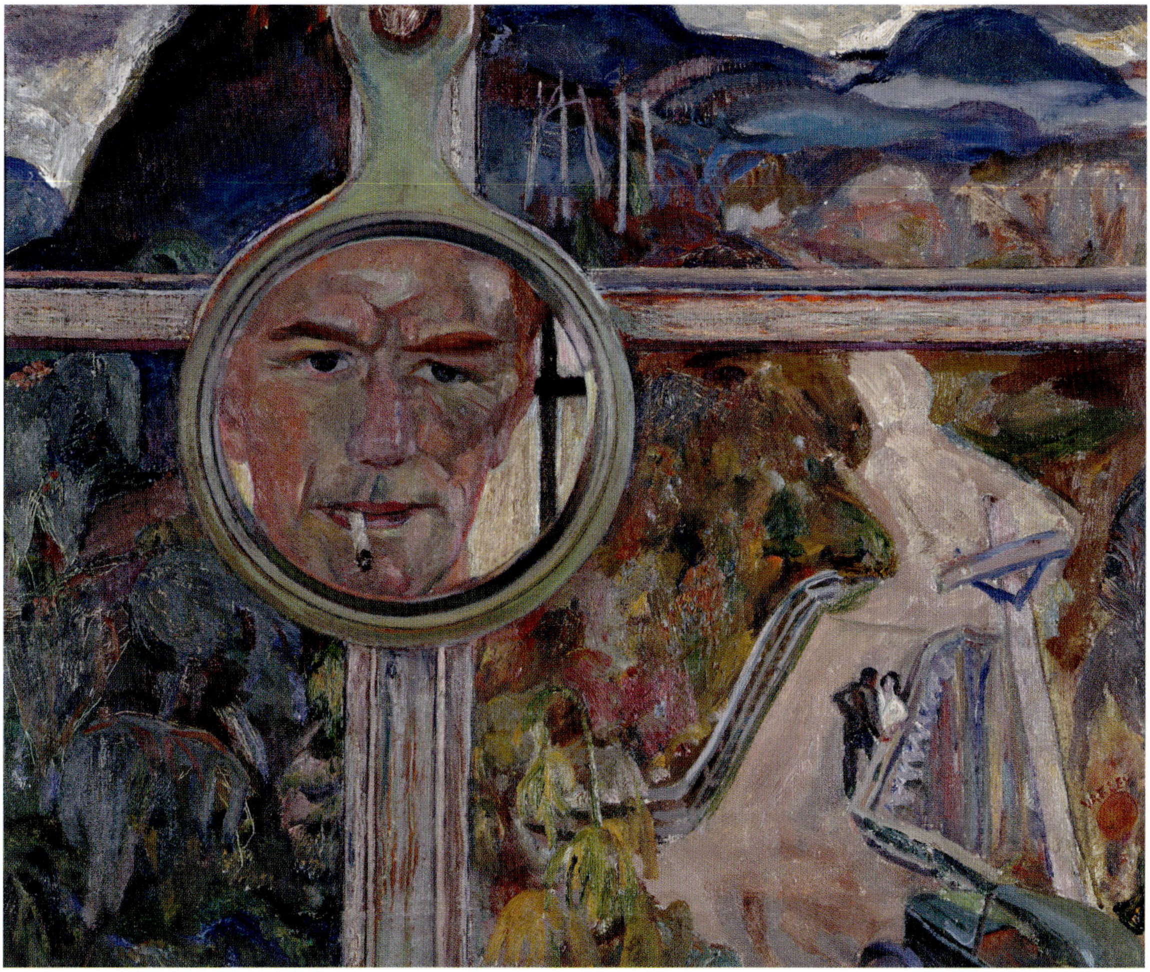

66 F.H. Varley, *Mirror of Thought*.

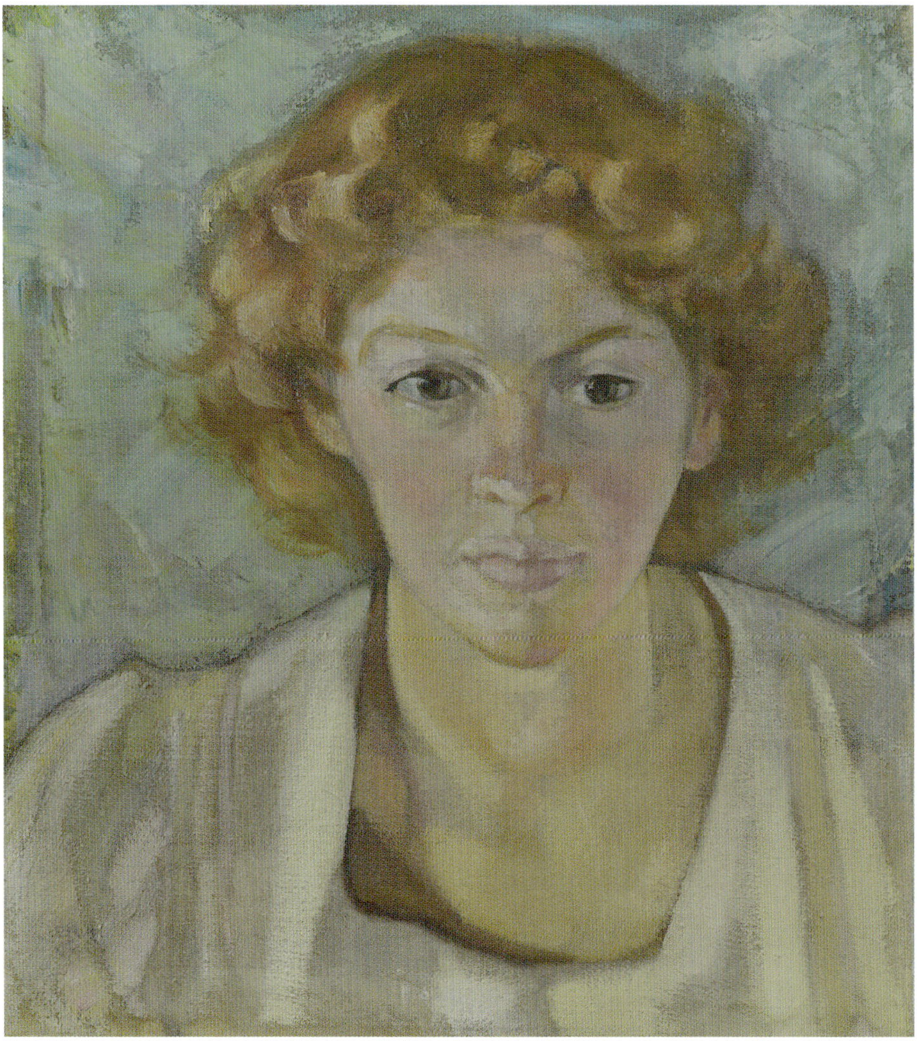

67 Vera Weatherbie, *Portrait of Molly*.

CHAPTER FIVE

# Harold and Vera

During Fred Varley's tumultuous years in Vancouver, Mortimer-Lamb's life seemed calm by comparison. He carefully cultivated the gardens of his delightful home on 54th Avenue, along with Mary Williams, who enjoyed her own social circle there. Molly had grown up on the grounds with her older brother Willoughby, and she later wrote, "My mother did all the work. We had a cow, and there was weeding to do. She entertained like you wouldn't believe. Her tennis partners would come out on Sunday on the streetcar in their whites. We had to roll the court and cut the grass. We had pit bull terriers. There was always tea, and saucers of milk from the cow."[1]

While Mortimer-Lamb continued his executive activities with the mining institute, he also promoted BC's artists on the national stage. An illustrated article under his name appeared in *Saturday Night* magazine on December 9, 1932, regarding what he called the first "All British Columbia Exhibition" at the new Vancouver Art Gallery. The exhibit included the work of 160 artists, and the story featured photographs of Charles H. Scott's

68 Mortimer-Lamb, *Molly painting.*

scene of art students titled *Alfresco*, J.W.G. Macdonald's *The Black Tusk, Garibaldi Park, BC*, and Charles Marega's marble bust of Bernard McEvoy. Mortimer-Lamb followed up this story in subsequent issues of *Saturday Night* with important articles dedicated to Emily Carr in 1933 and to Vera Weatherbie in 1934.

Mortimer-Lamb also gave unstintingly of his time to the Vancouver Art Gallery. A card-carrying member even before the gallery opened, he was elected to its first board of directors. By the time of the gallery's opening, the unprecedented sum of $100,000 had already been committed by several businessmen for the purchase of works of art. The money was spent under the direction of the major benefactor, H.A. Stone, and not a single Canadian work of art was acquired—most were British academic artists of the nineteenth and early twentieth century. An opportunity to rectify this situation came in 1931 when the gallery hosted an "all-Canadian exhibition."

Mortimer-Lamb was one of four members of the acquisition committee at the time, and they purchased paintings by James W. Morrice, H. Mabel May, and A.Y. Jackson. Writing in the Vancouver *Province*, he asked, "Who would have believed, five years ago, that a responsible body of citizens acting for a civic gallery would deliberately have acquired for its permanent collection an A.Y. Jackson?"[2] Jackson himself noted in his autobiography that it was "shocking to read the Vancouver papers, all trying to outdo each other in condemning the exhibition, and the letters to the press were almost venomous."[3] Mortimer-Lamb wrote that the "laughter" of the Vancouver critics was somewhat late. "It is merely an echo of the cachinnations, now stilled, in Toronto and Montreal of nearly a quarter of a century ago. Nevertheless the interest that has been

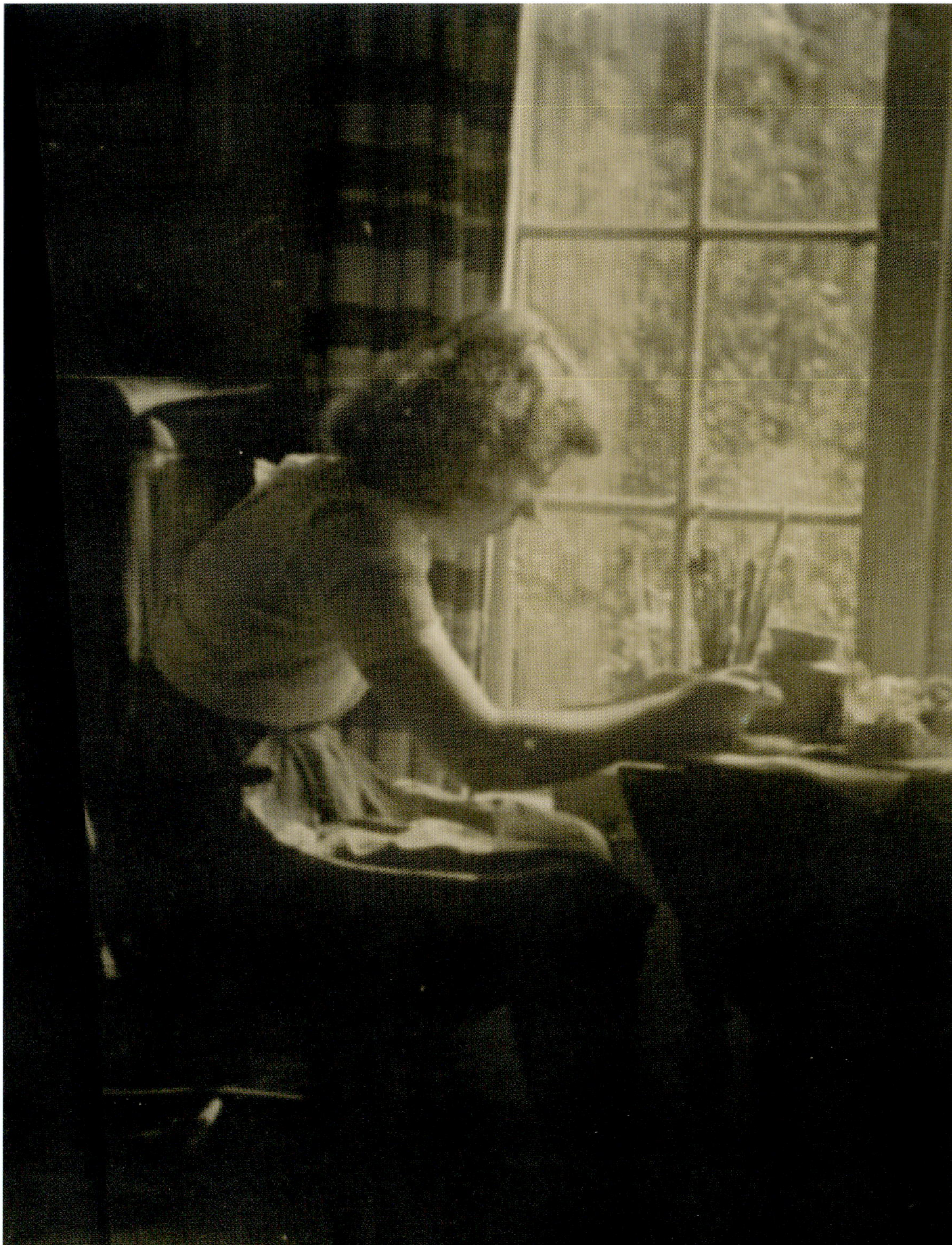

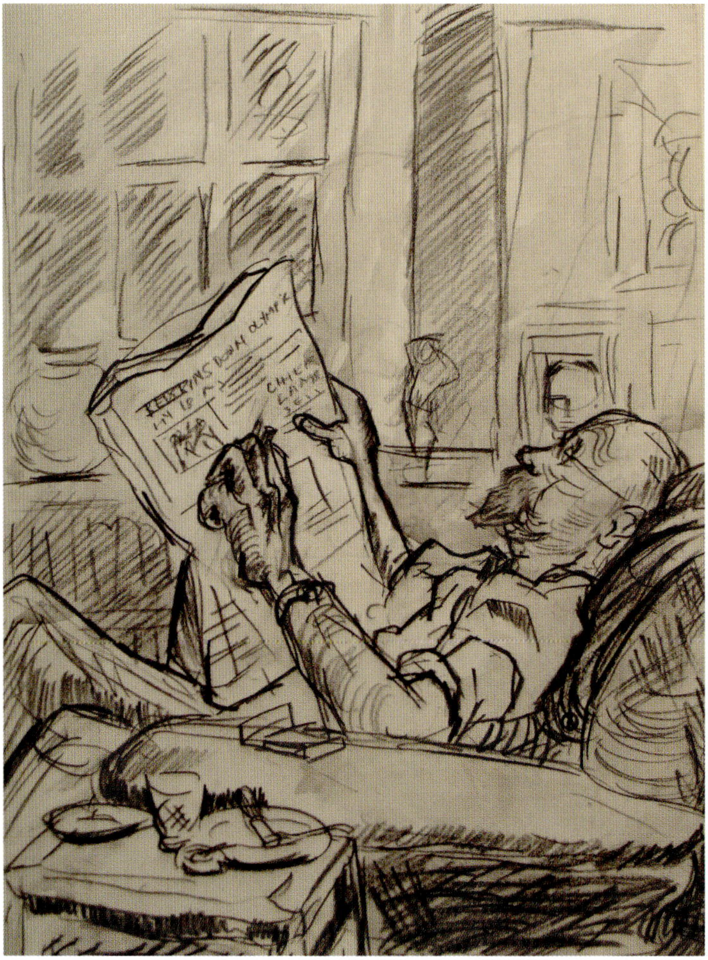

69 Jack Shadbolt, *Mortimer-Lamb at home.*

created is a healthy sign. In time perhaps Vancouver may even become an art centre."[4]

Mortimer-Lamb had acquired relatively little art for himself during the years since his move to Vancouver and almost all of it was created by his friends. In addition to the portrait of himself by Varley, he purchased a fine oil of Howe Sound by J.W.G. Macdonald as well as paintings by Vera Weatherbie and her friend Irene Hoffar. He also acquired a Charlie James totem pole about 127 centimetres tall and dug up some stone objects on his Kerrisdale property. He donated these artifacts to local museums and, as was his habit, followed up to evaluate the reception of his gifts. From the provincial museum in Victoria, Frank Kermode wrote a belated letter to thank him for the stone paint dish found in Burnaby and hoped he would consider his decision to withdraw the gift. Apparently, when Mortimer-Lamb had visited the museum the staff couldn't find it immediately, but he decided to let them keep it when later they discovered that it was on display.[5]

Mortimer-Lamb's support of Vera had been considerable over the years, and now she often visited the family's household in Kerrisdale. "I never asked her anything about that time," Molly wrote in her memoir, "but I know Vancouver society was very hard on her, especially after Varley left to go east. She must have felt very much alone then, but Dad remained a friend and admirer of her work and even supplied her with a studio and materials during the late 1930's."[6] As before, he continued to pay the rent on her Bute Street studio, apparently asking nothing in return.

Perhaps it was as a quid pro quo that in 1938 Vera painted the charming portrait of Molly exhibited in the *BC Artists Annual Show* that year at the Vancouver Art Gallery. It may be Vera's most accomplished portrait, though Molly wrote in her memoir that she never felt the painting looked much like her. "I was a plumpish kid then with untidy hair, peasant clothes, sad moods, dizzy heights, big eating sessions, but Vera painted me quietly with no flying ribbons."[7] The introspective mood the picture captures may be more reflective of Vera's state of mind than Molly's, for after Varley's departure she was enjoying peace and stability. Soon after the canvas was finished Mortimer-Lamb sent it to Harry McCurry at the National Gallery for consideration, but it was returned.

Molly, though just seventeen, was granted special permission for early enrollment at the Vancouver School of Art. She studied there for the next three years, and found the young Jack Shadbolt to be a particularly inspiring teacher. Before long, Shadbolt also visited Kerrisdale and painted Molly, though his casual watercolour sketch is considerably less charming than Vera's studied oil. "Shadbolt often came out to our house right after school," Molly recalled. "As soon as we got to our house he would begin to draw everything and everyone—my brother Abby, Emma the dog, Dad's teapot with pears around it. His energy was amazing."[8] Shadbolt's drawing of the teapot depicts part of the silver service that the German industrialists had presented to Mortimer-Lamb on his trip to Dresden in 1909. A sketchbook from about 1940 was recently discovered among the Mortimer-Lamb Papers and includes a number of drawings of those times in Kerrisdale, in particular studies by Shadbolt of Vera and Mortimer-Lamb.

In his later years Mortimer-Lamb took up painting again. Shadbolt affectionately recalled watching him standing to paint in his garden. With his hat, smock, and beard he apparently looked like the aged Cezanne, frowning in concentration while Beethoven and Mozart floated out from

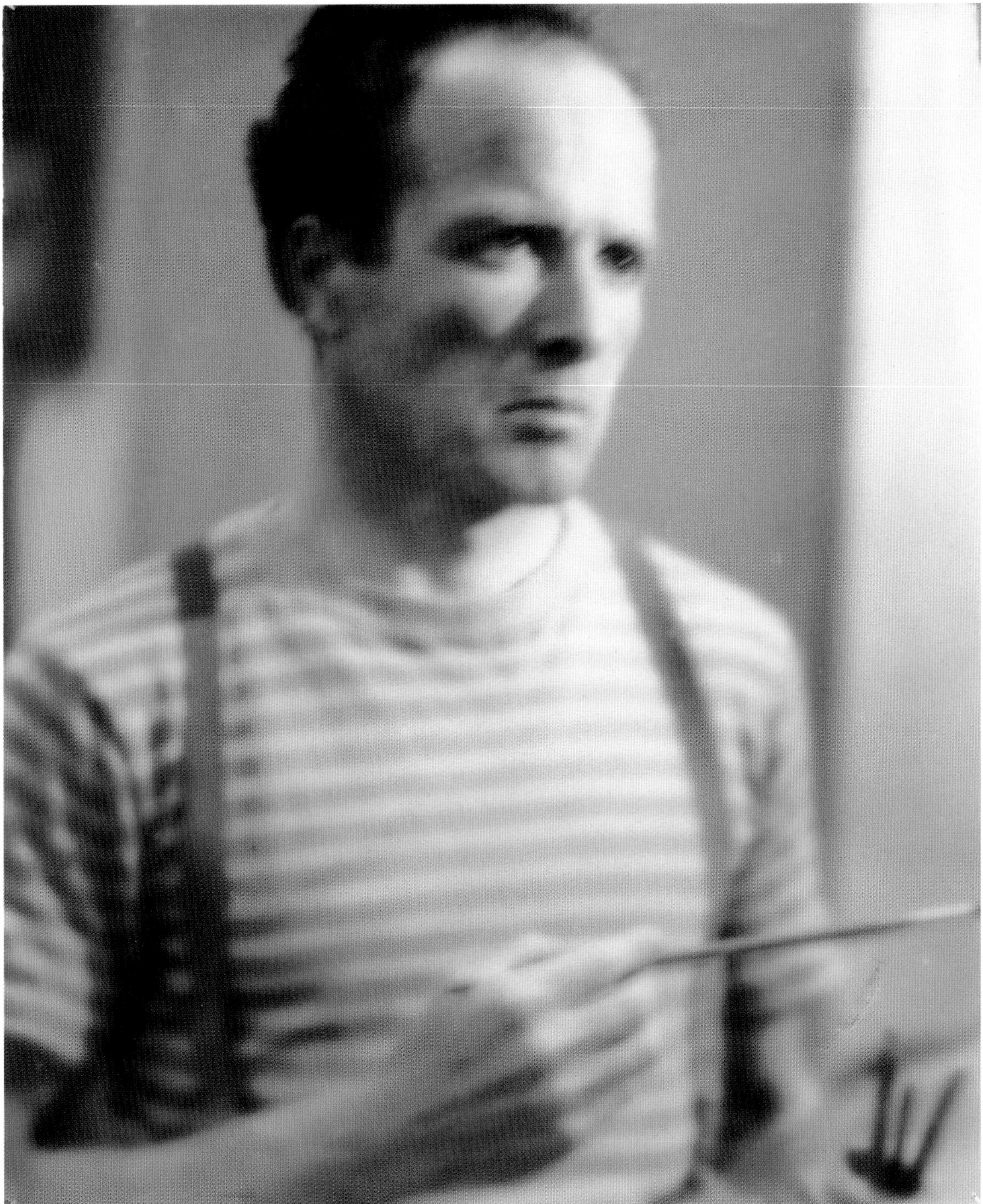

70 Mortimer-Lamb, *The Communist* (Jack Shadbolt).

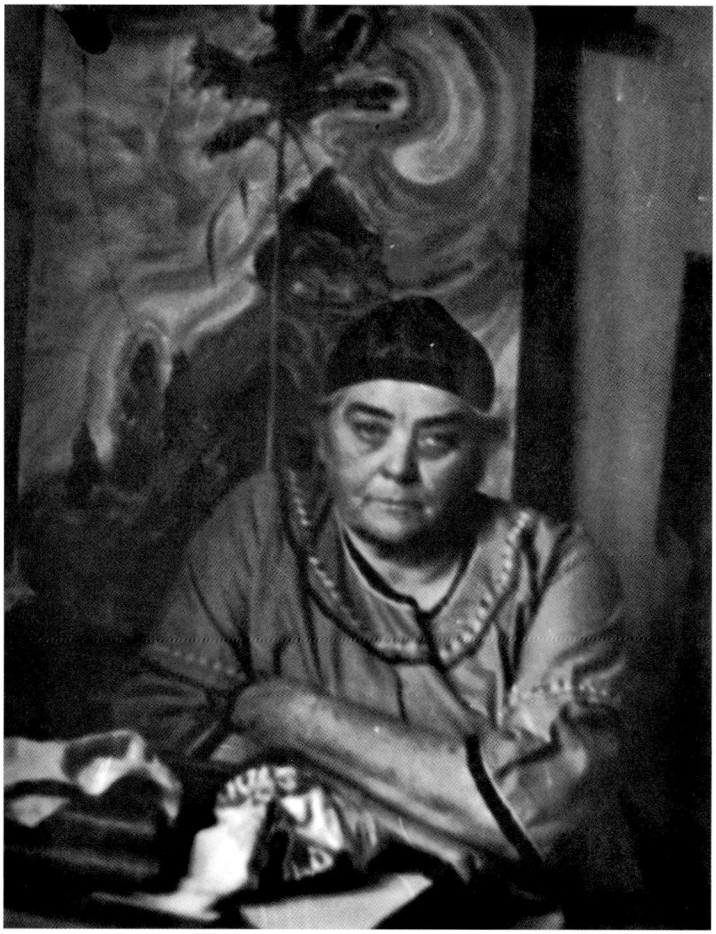

71 Mortimer-Lamb, *Emily Carr in her studio*, cropped version printed by Mortimer-Lamb.

the gramophone in his studio. Mary was usually close at hand with tea and fresh-baked bread, and the whole had "a feeling of an enclosed world."[9] The household was a haven for visiting artists, and his family photo albums indicate that Mortimer-Lamb and Mary hosted a succession of garden fetes and costume parties. Snapshots record boisterous fun in an interior pleasantly cluttered with Buddhist statues, Chinese carpets, and paintings by Mortimer-Lamb's associates. When not in a party mode, Mortimer-Lamb, in his late sixties, could be quite withdrawn, working away in his studio and only seen at mealtimes. He seemed to enjoy this role as a man in the background, a facilitator.

Bringing his own energy to this artistic milieu, Jack Shadbolt painted a mural for Mortimer-Lamb's new studio, his "music room." Charles H. Scott officiated at the first showing of the large painting, the title of which was *Emperor Lamb and the Lions*. Molly remembered that "when it was unveiled, Dad hated it. The mural had a Chinese theme, with Mum a big nude Buddha and Dad a mean-looking mandarin." Molly was depicted as a monkey. "I forget the rest but Dad didn't find it funny and it ended up in the barn."[10] Shadbolt then painted another mural for him, this one now part of the collection of the Fine Arts Gallery of the University of British Columbia. A still life on a vast scale, it was painted in 1940 on two canvas panels, in total about five metres across, and was much less controversial in theme. His willingness to try again shows that Shadbolt and Mortimer-Lamb must have appreciated each other's company. Though no longer as active with his camera as he once was, Mortimer-Lamb made a studied photograph of the younger artist with a paintbrush in his hand, using a soft-focus style in the Pictorialist mode. In keeping with the self-dramatizing nature for which Shadbolt was remembered, the image was titled *The Communist*.

72 Mortimer-Lamb, *Emily Carr in her studio*, modern print from original negative.

During this period Mortimer-Lamb also made his unforgettable portrait of Emily Carr, considered to be the finest photograph of the brilliant artist. Carr is shown in her studio, surrounded by stacks of canvases, with an Indian basket on the table beside her. She wears her typical homemade smock and hairnet, with the powerful canvas of trees and sky, *Sunshine and Tumult* (1939), surging in the background. Her look of penetrating determination sums up this artist, who struggled for many years to express the profound experience of her life on the west coast. Mortimer-Lamb made closely cropped prints from this negative and one was used, without permission or any credit to him, on the back cover of *Growing Pains*, Carr's autobiography, which was published posthumously in 1946. The original negative of this image, which shows considerably more of the context of her studio, has recently come into the collection of the Vancouver Art Gallery.

Mortimer-Lamb had not exhibited with The Linked Ring or the London Salon since 1926, but he kept up his connection with the group and was considered a senior member. In 1938 he was inducted as an Honorary Fellow of the Royal Photographic Society of Great Britain and was asked to send them a self-portrait. At their request, in 1945 he donated a further six pictures to the society. Later, he concluded his association with them by adding four more prints to their collection of his work, some dating as far back as 1912. In 1956 he was named a life member, and the society continues to preserve these prints in its archives in Bath, England.

Once again war was raging across Europe, and its effects were felt halfway around the world. In Kerrisdale, Mary and Mortimer-Lamb hosted a steady stream of expatriates from England, who stayed with

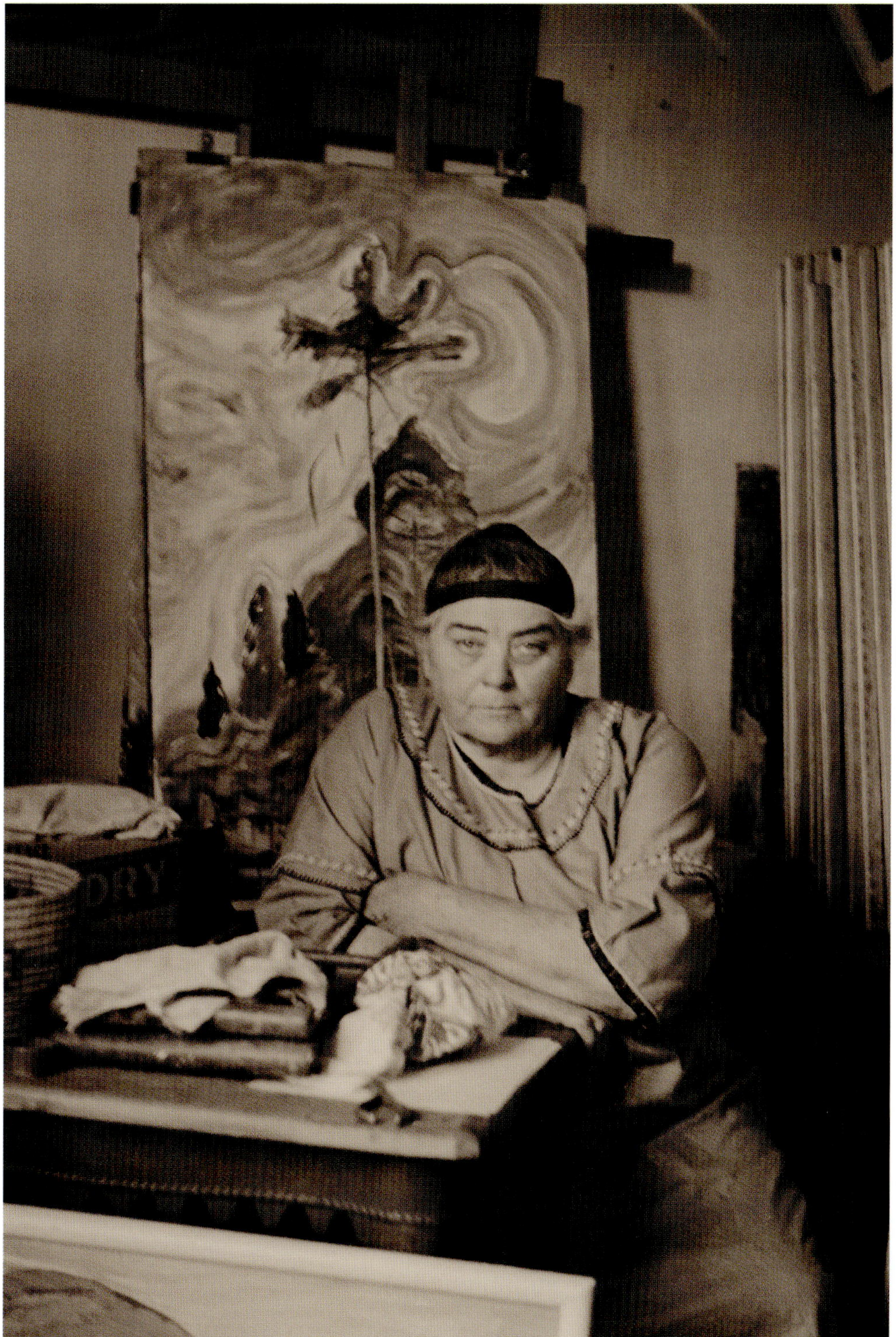
DRY

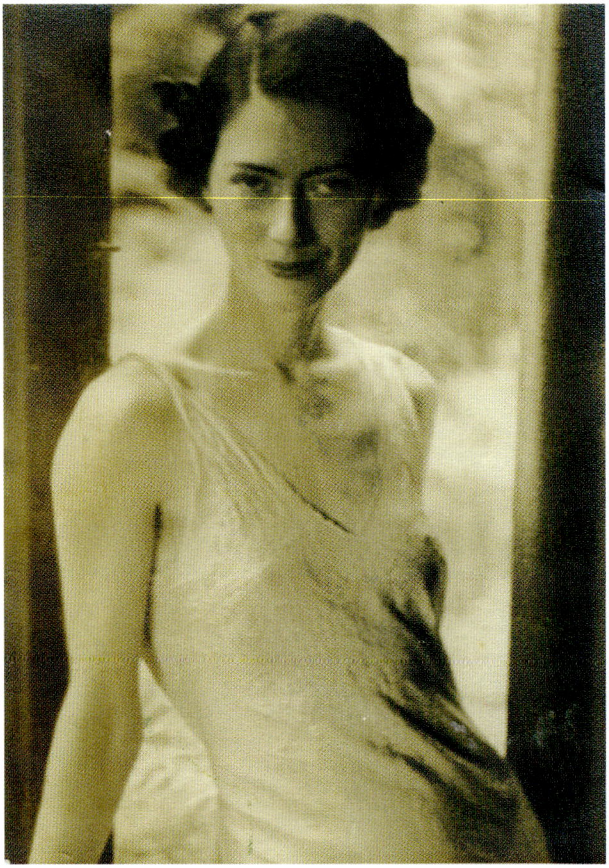

73 Mortimer-Lamb, *Vera*.

them. He ate lunch with them on Sundays, but most of the time the elderly artist could be found in the studio wing on the far side of the house where he found solitude for his meditating, listening to the music of Gabriel Faure, and painting. There was one visitor who was particularly welcome. Pamela Diamond, the daughter of British critic and artist Roger Fry, came with her three children. While the two daughters went to private school in Victoria, Pamela and her youngest, a son named Roger, moved in with the Mortimer-Lamb household. Molly shared her candid memories: "Roger was bright and precocious. Pamela was modern, and Roger was allowed to be natural in his habits. That's the first thing that put Dad off—the kid would fart in his studio. But he loved Pamela. They talked about art and she allowed him to hang her Renoir portrait above his fireplace."[11] When the Diamond family returned to England, they left as a gift for their gracious host a fully realized oil painting by Bloomsbury artist Duncan Grant, titled *Study for a Ballet Scene*.

After a long life in the shadows of the household, Kate Lamb had passed away in 1939. Though Kate had married Mortimer-Lamb and lived with him since 1896, her death went unmentioned in his papers. By this time, their four surviving children were grown and on their own. The youngest son, Willoughby, was an ordained priest of the Church of England, married and living in his parish in England. Mary Williams's days as housekeeper were drawing to a close and Mortimer-Lamb, now a widower, was at long last free to remarry. In fact, he asked for Mary's hand, but she refused him. Despite their many years together, and the parentage of their daughter Molly, theirs was not a love match. Instead, to repay her for her kindness he bought her a waterfront property of about forty acres, a summer resort called Arbutus Point, on Galiano Island, overlooking Active Pass. After she moved there, she ran it as a holiday camp and lived a life of rural happiness for many years.

With her departure imminent, Mary urged Mortimer-Lamb to propose marriage to someone else. He apparently thought this an excellent idea and invited his first prospect, Grace Melvin, to join him for lunch at the Hotel Georgia. Melvin, whom he had known for almost twenty years, was a teacher at the Vancouver School of Art and the sister-in-law of Charles H. Scott, the principal. "That evening, when he came jerking up the drive in his Austin 10," Molly wrote, "Mum could hardly wait to hear the news. I remember him tugging his goatee and giving a nervous laugh." Melvin had also refused him. Undaunted, Mary suggested he try again, and she mentioned young Vera Weatherbie. "At first," Molly continued, "he couldn't conceive of her accepting him. They were friends, but so far apart in age."[12]

Almost immediately Mortimer-Lamb proposed to Vera, during lunch at the Hotel Georgia, and she readily accepted. They were married on May 4, 1942. She was just thirty years old and he was almost seventy. "Many no doubt were critical of the marriage because of the considerable disparity in age," Mortimer-Lamb reflected in his "Reminiscences" twenty years later.[13]

Molly wrote a first-person account of the marriage of her father and Vera, a vital chapter in a remarkable love story. At the age of twenty-two, Molly was working at Yellow Point Lodge near Nanaimo on Vancouver Island during the summer of 1942. Early in May she took a day off from her job at the lodge.

I went down to Nanaimo, took the [steamship] *Princess Elaine* down to Vancouver, then the old Number 17 streetcar. Up our drive in the dusk, the sun was sending its last dappled patches of cool light through the lovely Lombardy poplar trees outside the back door. When I tried the door it was locked. Mum never locked the door, and I knew something was up. I saw that a kitchen window was open so I climbed up it and let myself in . . . It was dark and I must have made quite a commotion because I'd hardly jumped to the floor when Dad appeared, coming slowly through the hall with another figure close behind him.

"Dad," I said, "you have shaved off your beard!"

"Moll," he said, "I was married today."

"To Miss Melvin?" I blurted out.

"No," said a small voice behind Dad. "To me. Do you mind?"

It was Vera.

We hugged each other and had a little talk, and I went up to my old bedroom and cried. Not because of the marriage but because our old life was over. As for Dad and Vera, that was the beginning of a long and happy life together.[14]

At the age of seventy, Mortimer-Lamb was on the threshold of a marvellous new life. He prepared for the change by disposing of elements of his art collection, making his most significant donation to the Vancouver Art Gallery. He gave them three paintings by Arthur Lismer and two by Frederick Varley, two oil sketches by A.Y. Jackson, a drypoint by Paul

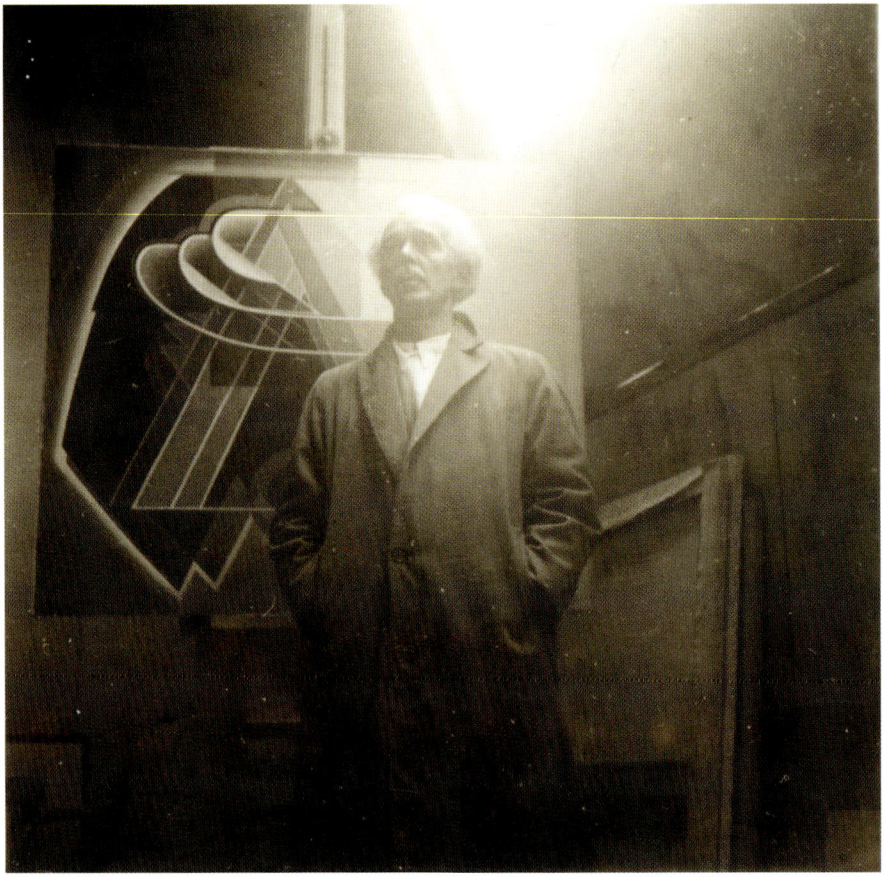

74 Mortimer-Lamb, *Lawren Harris in his studio.*

Goranson, and a folio of drawings in reproduction by the Group of Seven. He also began negotiations to dispose of *Gypsy Head* (1919), an important oil by Varley that he had purchased at what he felt was a very low price some ten years previously. The sale was eventually arranged with the National Gallery in 1943, with the understanding that Varley would share in the proceeds.

Mortimer-Lamb continued to lighten the load of his responsibilities. Shortly after his marriage to Vera he sold the property on 54th Avenue and bought a thirty-three-year-old house on an acre at 4648 Belmont Avenue in Point Grey. On the south side of one of Vancouver's most prestigious streets, it had a splendid view of the North Shore mountains and Howe Sound. He later wrote that he got it for "the ridiculous price of $7,000. In the boom of 1911 the land alone, unimproved, had sold for $70,000."[15] Now it boasted a lovely home, extremely well built, of generous proportions with a living room over thirty feet long. His gardening instincts delighted in the Japanese cherry trees, rhododendrons, azaleas, lilacs, japonica, fish pond built of stone, and tennis court. In all, it presented an air of comfort and gracious living.

A further advantage of this new home was that Lawren Harris, essentially the founder of the Group of Seven, lived with his wife, Bess, nearby at 4760 Belmont. The Harrises had burned their bridges socially in Toronto in 1934, when they left their respective spouses and together moved to the United States. They had been living in a progressive artists' community in New Mexico, but, due to wartime restrictions about taking money out of Canada, they were unable to stay south of the border. In 1941 they took up residence in Vancouver, and their lovely home soon became central to Vancouver's progressive art scene.

75 Mortimer-Lamb, *A.Y. Jackson and Vera in the garden.*

The salons and musical evenings they hosted at 4760 Belmont continued what had taken place at the Vanderpant Galleries in previous years. Recently, among Mortimer-Lamb's papers a number of small photographic studies of Harris have come to light. These show Harris standing by his easel, in some with his painting titled *Abstract #7* (1939) and in others with an oil of *Mount Ann Alice* (*circa* 1941).

Jim Varley, son of the artist, has written that his father was "very bitter" when he found out about the marriage of Vera and Mortimer-Lamb.[16] He suggested that Mortimer-Lamb's efforts to resettle Varley in eastern Canada had some ulterior motive—that he wanted Varley out of the way so he could steal Vera and marry her himself. The facts indicate that this was never the case. Mortimer-Lamb's efforts on Varley's behalf were clearly made to help the painter break the cycle of despair that had plagued him, and the idea that Mortimer-Lamb might marry Vera came at the suggestion of Mary. The final proof that there was no bitterness between them comes from Varley's own continuing correspondence with Mortimer-Lamb and Vera, which is on file at the Art Gallery of Alberta in Edmonton. In 1939 Varley concluded one of his chatty notes to Vera with this salutation: "Best love to you Vera. Remember me to the many, including H. Mortimer . . . remember me kindly to H. Mortimer—I wrote to him a week ago." In a letter of 1941 Varley mentions that he had recently sent five paintings to Mortimer-Lamb, who had purchased one. And in 1943, after their wedding, he asked Vera to "give my affectionate greeting to H.M."[17]

Varley remained grateful to the now-married couple throughout his life. Despite trips west as far as Kootenay Lake in the interior of BC, he never returned to the coast, yet he continued to think fondly of his old friends. In 1946, in a letter to Vera, he wrote, "Pass this on to my old

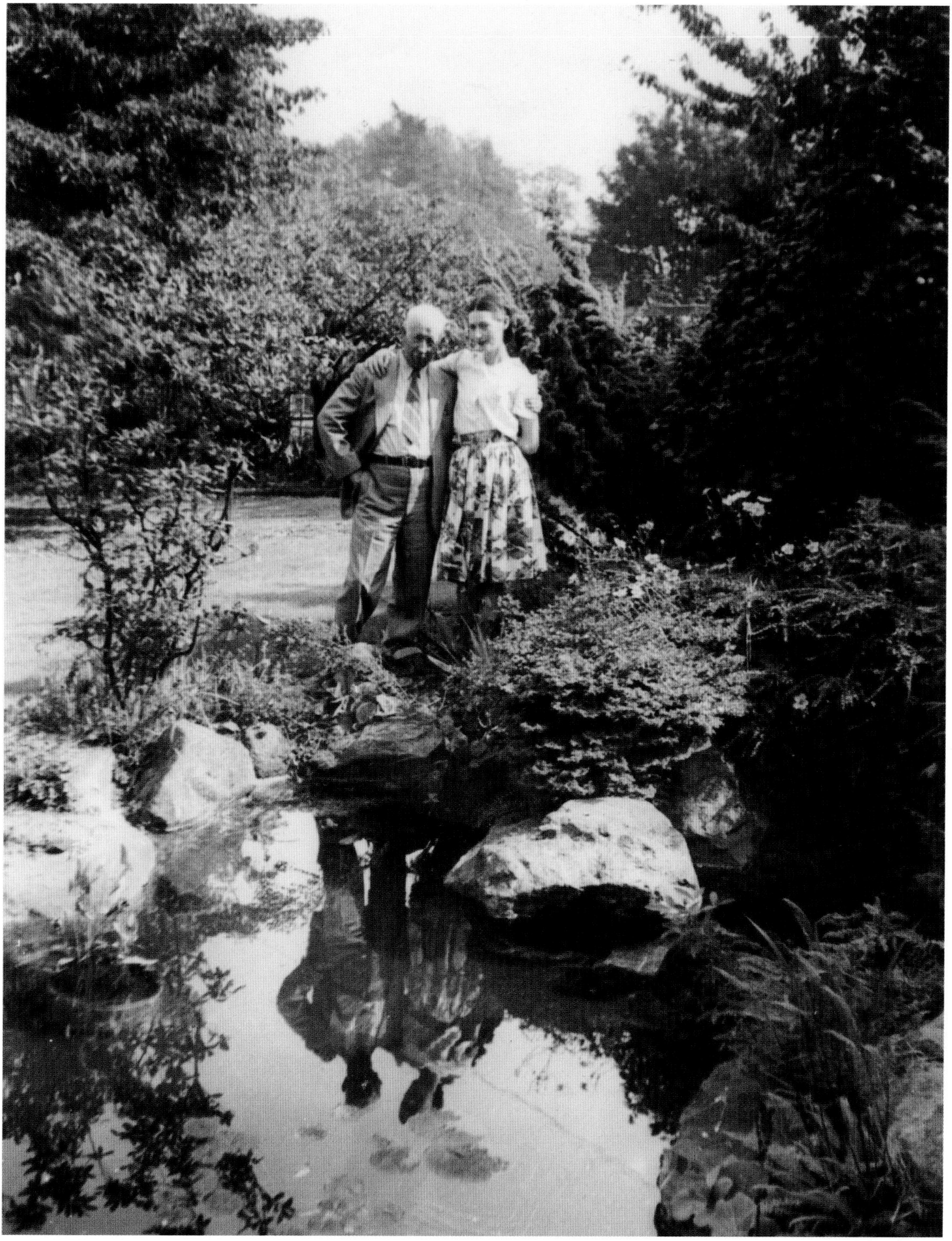

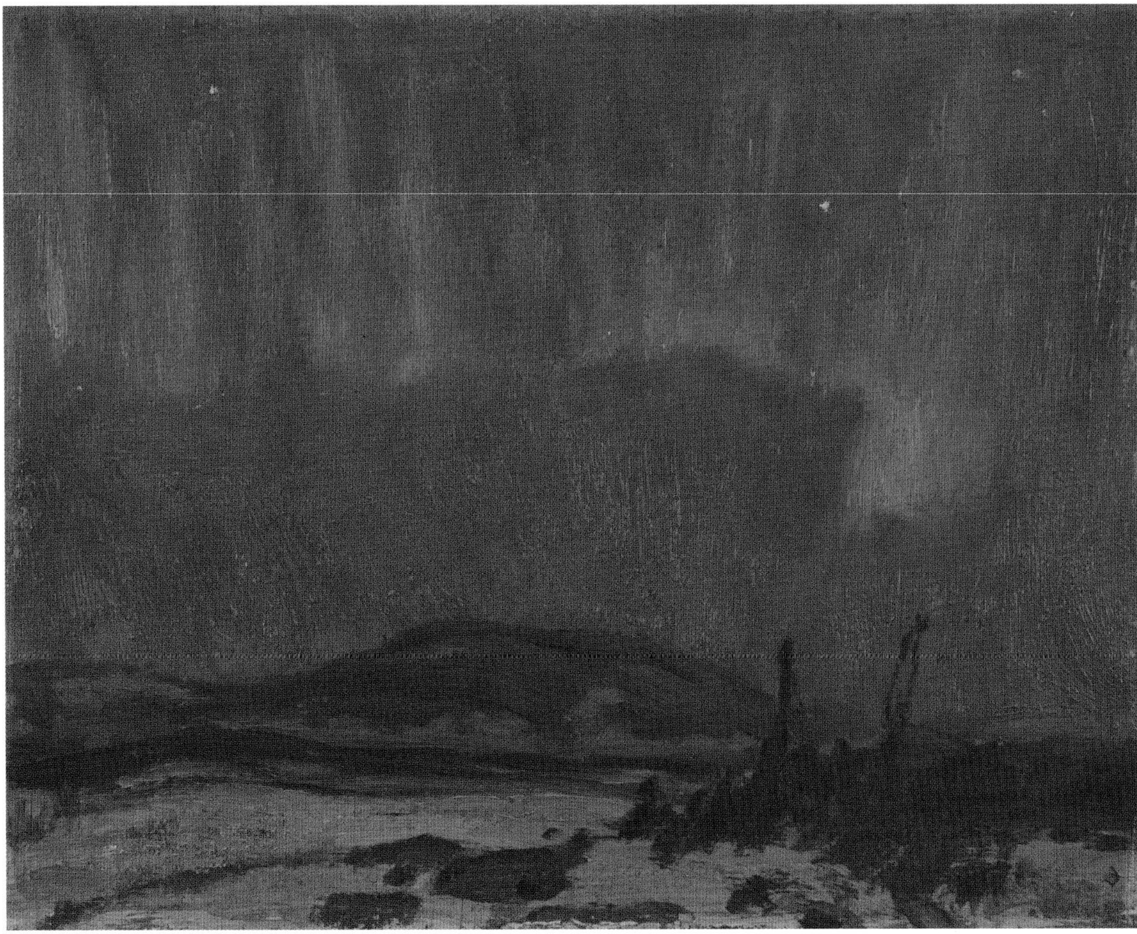

76 A.Y. Jackson, *Northern Lights*.

friend Mortimer for my impression is that he is so completely happy and I want to say hello to him too. HM: why don't you write to me. I said there ain't no such completeness, but you are adventurous and being so I feel very near to understanding you as there are not many who remain and retain the kid spirit. 'Those whom the gods love' etc. I wish I could see you—both of you—wonderful isn't it? I could leave here tonight and have breakfast with you in the morning."[18] No bitterness there, but perhaps a trace of sadness at the loss he had brought upon himself.

Approaching the age of seventy-five, Mortimer-Lamb formally retired from the Mining Association of British Columbia. In a lengthy tribute to him in the *Canadian Mining Journal* of March 1946, R.C. Rowe recalled that Mortimer-Lamb "may entertain you with a lecture on painting, or deluge you with Bach, or he may pound you with an argument and drive you into a corner with cold practical logic which will leave you without a leg to stand on, or an argument to clothe your naked soul. All in all he is a gentleman in ways and a man of parts, and we predict that he will have a wonderful time in retirement, for he, above all the men we know, has learned how to spend time with an eye to its greatest value."[19] Here was a true picture of the man, a unique character to discover among a group of mining engineers.

Out on Point Grey, life could scarcely have been sweeter. From his garden he could look out over Burrard Inlet. He took pride in his five adult children, savoured the pleasure of the company of his young, devoted, and beautiful wife, and enjoyed esteem in his community. In 1945 he was asked by the Vancouver Parks Board to judge an art show in Stanley Park, and Barbara Swann of the Art Gallery of Toronto

77 Mortimer-Lamb, *Vera in a print dress.*

corresponded with him regarding her research into Emily Carr. He made fresh additions to his art collection and, through a renewed correspondence with Arthur Lismer, arranged the purchase of his lovely little painting *McGregor Bay*. A.Y. Jackson continued to correspond and visit and was photographed in the garden with both Vera and Mortimer-Lamb. In 1946 his painting *Northern Lights*, an oil sketch from his time as a war artist on the Alaska Highway during the Second World War, entered the Mortimer-Lamb collection.

At that time Mortimer-Lamb made significant donations to the Vancouver Museum, including a terra cotta image from Costa Rica and a fragment of a twelfth-century jar from Persia. His large model totem pole, carved by Charlie James in 1917, was also included in this eclectic donation, to which many other pieces were added in 1957. A painting by Jack Shadbolt titled *Indian Totems* was given to the growing collection of the University of British Columbia Library.

And he was returning to his study of painting with a new vigour. In 1945 Mortimer-Lamb enrolled in a correspondence course with the Ralph M. Pearson Design Workshop in Nyack, New York, but its "mail-in critique service" offered nothing of value to a man of his experience. Then he enrolled in courses at the Vancouver School of Art, where he must have been their oldest student. B.C. Binning, who had been a student of the school and was subsequently a teacher there, wrote an unsolicited letter of encouragement dated January 22, 1946, in which he noted that "yesterday Jack [Shadbolt] hung up your tempera compositions at school and I had a good look at them—let me say, & honestly, it has been a long while since I have had such a thrill—how on earth do you get that colour—& the arrangements??—I told Jack I should take

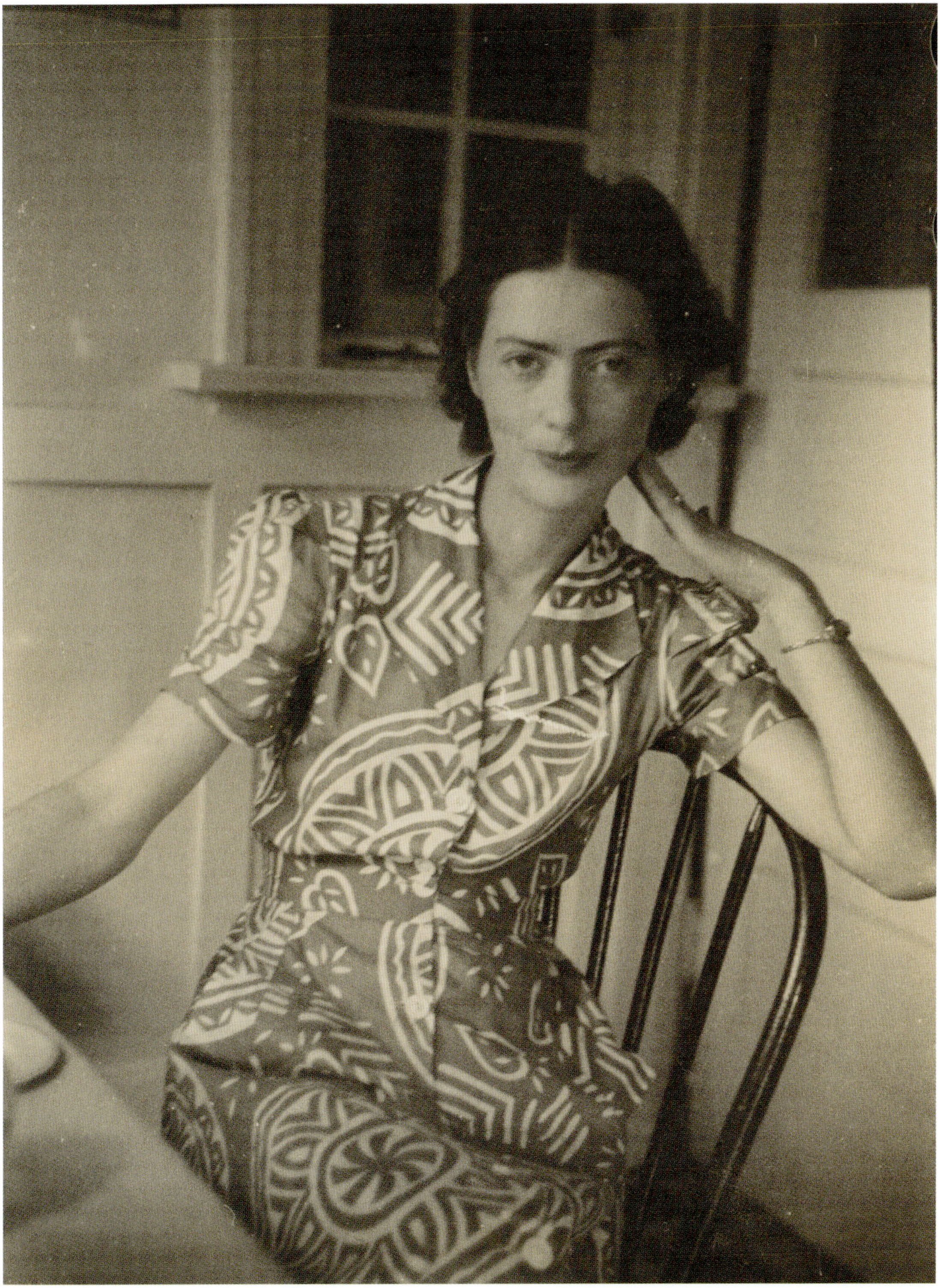

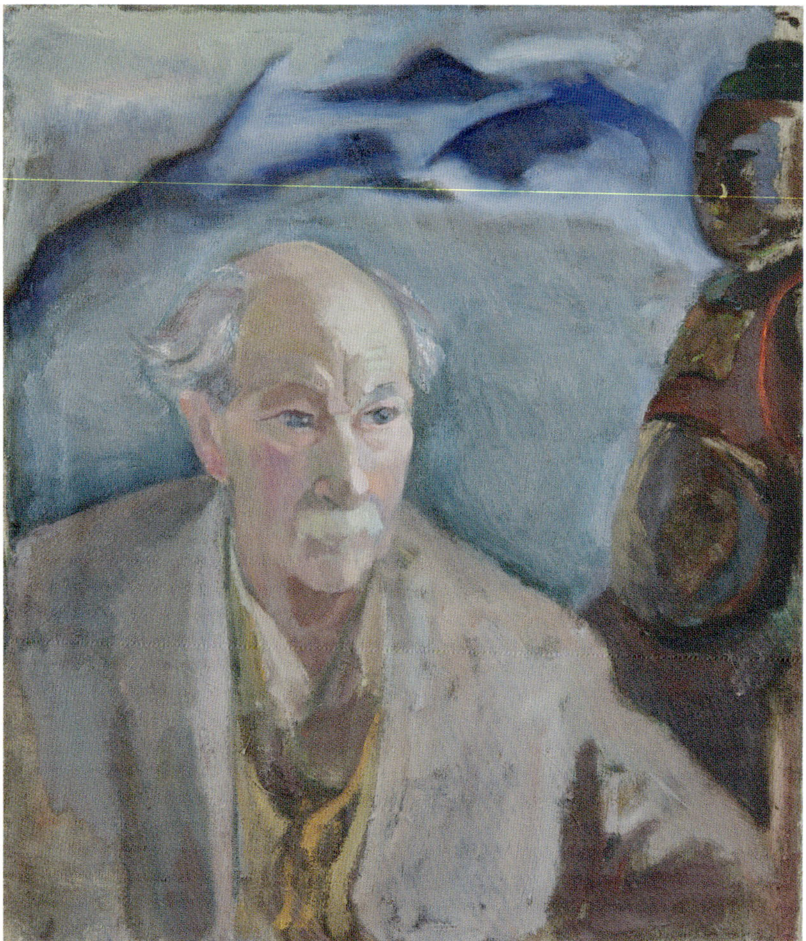

78 Vera Weatherbie, *Portrait of Harold Mortimer Lamb.*

lessons from you . . ."[20] Those who dismiss Mortimer-Lamb's paintings as the work of an elderly amateur would do well to consider the informed opinions of excellent artists and teachers such as Binning, who found much to approve of and admire in his work.

Perhaps some of Mortimer-Lamb's inspiration was coming from Vera. Molly, who had graduated from the Vancouver School of Art some years previously and was gaining national recognition as a war artist, saw life on Belmont Avenue first-hand. "After my father married Vera, she looked after him like a little Japanese handmaiden. She waited on him hand and foot. He kept telling her she should paint, sunflowers and things, but she just wanted to follow him around. In fact, she used to encourage him to paint."[21] While very few paintings can be attributed to Vera during this period, she did exhibit in the *BC Artists Annual Show* at the Vancouver Art Gallery in 1944, 1945, and 1949. A portrait of the elderly Mortimer-Lamb, recently donated to the Art Gallery of Greater Victoria, may be the last painting from her hand.

As Vera's production dwindled and ceased, Mortimer-Lamb devoted more and more time to painting. Again, Molly is the witness: "From that time on, Dad never stopped painting his joyful gardens and fantasies. He would put a canvas on his easel, sit in his armchair, chain-smoke, contemplate for some time, then walk to the canvas and nervously put a dab of paint somewhere he felt it belonged—sometimes even a series of small strokes. No, not strokes—nervous dabs. Painting became his chief pleasure and his great love."[22]

Among those who immediately grasped the unique qualities of Mortimer-Lamb's paintings was Doris Shadbolt, wife of the painter Jack Shadbolt and a long-time curator of the Vancouver Art Gallery.

She sang his praises in an article in *Canadian Art* magazine in 1947, titled "Painter of an Intimate World." It would be hard to gainsay her evaluation: "Every so often one comes upon a rare pure painter, whose work makes no broad or forceful statement, displays no startling technique, discovers no unusual form, adds no tremendous weight to an old tradition nor sets the direction for a new, but is of true and singing beauty. Harold Mortimer-Lamb is surely such a painter. The character of his personality would perhaps be best characterized by the word *joy*—joy in the intimate world around him." Shadbolt went on to observe that "under the spell of this personality, the most ordinary scene . . . emerges with the magic of a childhood dream."[23]

A few years later Mortimer-Lamb and Vera moved to a new home on Capitol Hill, the northwest slope of Burnaby Mountain. Beginning in 1950, their new address was 450 North Hythe Street. "When I moved to Burnaby," Mortimer-Lamb explained, "I did so in part because the taxes were considerably lower [than in Point Grey]. Succession duty tax amounts almost to confiscation."[24] In fact, there were many other things to attract him to his new hilltop home, not the least of which was a vast panoramic view west down Burrard Inlet, beyond Second Narrows Bridge to the city of Vancouver. In addition to the new house, he bought the adjoining lot and planted many trees—hemlock, spruce, vine maple, dogwood—which combined with a thick, second-growth hedge below the site. He added a new studio for himself and settled down "to try to express in paint my love of colour and light and to grow flowers."[25]

In Molly's recollection, the two shared a delightful existence. "Vera used to tease him. She loved being a woman and he was the husband. It was charming, really. It wasn't a bad thing at all. The two of them would

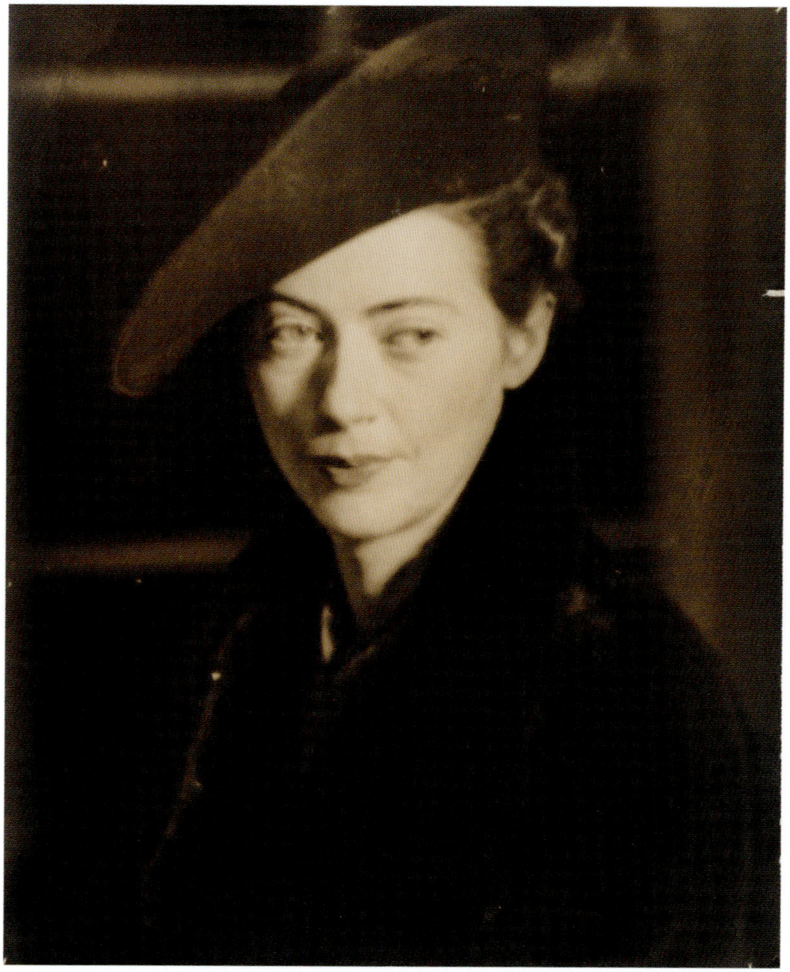

79 Mortimer-Lamb, *Vera wearing a hat.*

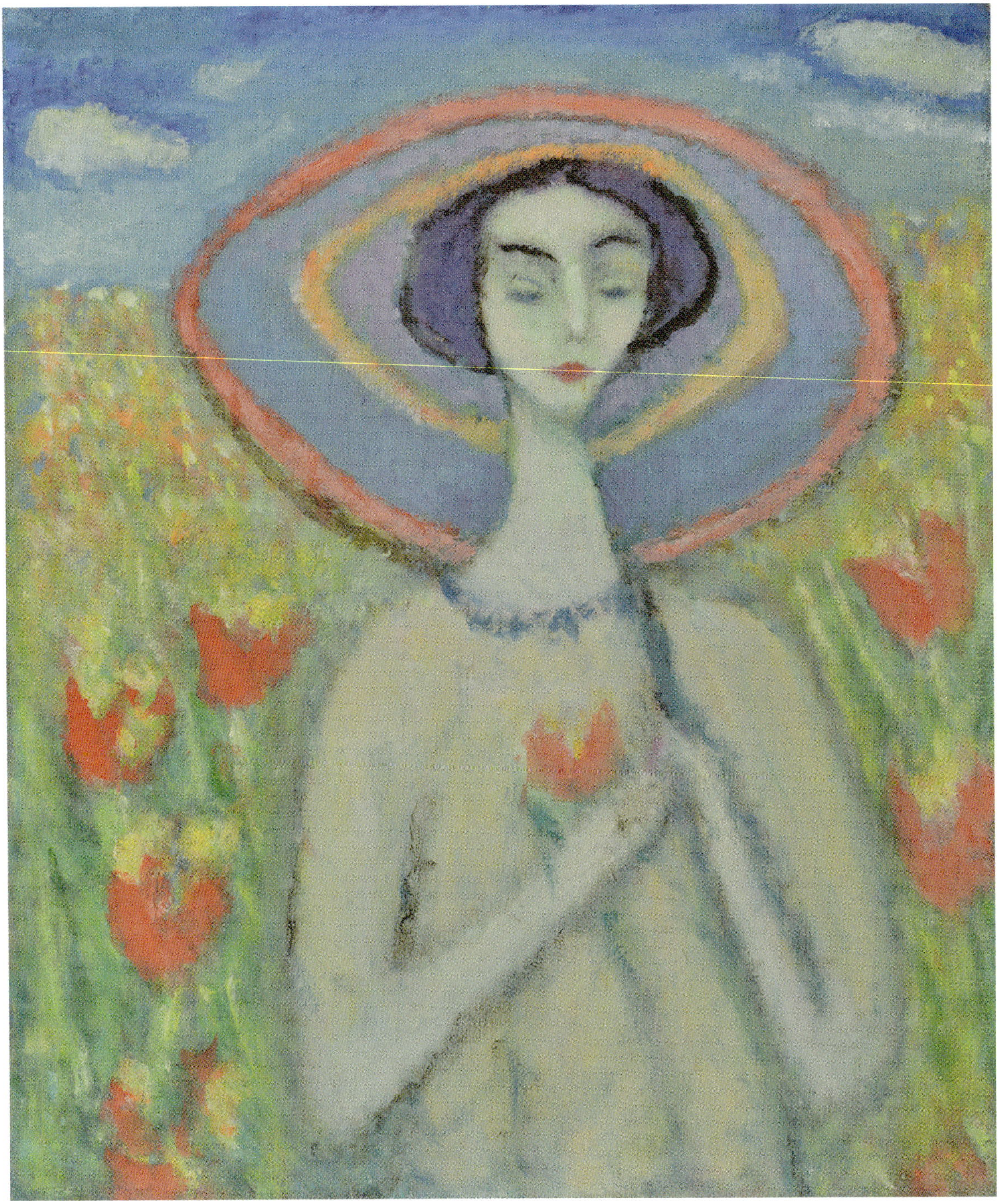

80 Mortimer-Lamb, *Girl with Tulips*.

go off to the Salvation Army and dress up in cheap coats. And laugh, and laugh! That was her life from then on, housekeeping for him. And, you know, they were the happiest twenty-five years of my dad's life."[26]

Around 1960, Mortimer-Lamb, approaching ninety years of age, took pen in shaking hand and set down his impressions of this May-December relationship. His own words offer a unique description of married life and his admiration for the woman who shared it with him. Here is what he wrote in his "Reminiscences" under the heading "Vera":

> We were married on May 4, 1942 . . . Many no doubt were critical of the marriage because of the considerable disparity in age. She was only thirty—I on the verge of seventy. But at the time neither of us regarded this to be of primary import, though each doubtless regretted that it existed. What to me at least was of major importance was that as the French would say we were sympathetic. That is to say we shared much in common, our tastes as near as could be were identical. Our love of Art and nature, of a quiet and peaceful existence, of gardening and in the production of fine specimen flowers, of roses in particular.
>
> Neither of us had social ambitions or aspirations. In fact we both are poor mixers, slow to invite friendship and this is a sad defect in character or disposition, for which neither of us had cause to boast. It breeds resentment and unpopularity, which may be ignored but nevertheless is uncomfortable and often disconcerting.
>
> We are now in our twenty-second year of harmonious and

happy married life unmarred by any regrettable or disturbing incident. Few marriages can equal that record. In the beginning our marriage was based on friendship. Naturally passion was never a motivating cause. The friendship has deepened and cemented as has affection—in my case—by appreciation and admiration as I came to realize Vera's manifold talents and capabilities.

She is, as I have already said, often to my apprehension, and despite my protests and arguments for the desirability for a moderation of her activities, a near indefatigable woman, but will tackle anything usually with success, from correcting ill-fitting dentures, to plumbing. She is incidentally an admirable house-keeper, an excellent cook, an expert seamstress, even to making me a dressing gown that was the admiration of the nurses when I was in hospital, and she not only combines the skill and abilities of a home decorator, but continues to practice her art as a painter of originality and vision. Lately since I have become a chronic invalid she has been to me a devoted nurse. I owe her very much.[27]

Jack and Doris Shadbolt were close neighbours on Capitol Hill in Burnaby and found many ways to show their enthusiasm for Mortimer-Lamb. A significant exhibition of his work at the Vancouver Art Gallery in June 1952, curated by Jack Shadbolt, was billed as "the thousandth exhibition" in the gallery's history. It had three parts, presenting elements of Mortimer-Lamb's photography, art collection, and painting. Shadbolt wrote in his introduction to the photography section of the

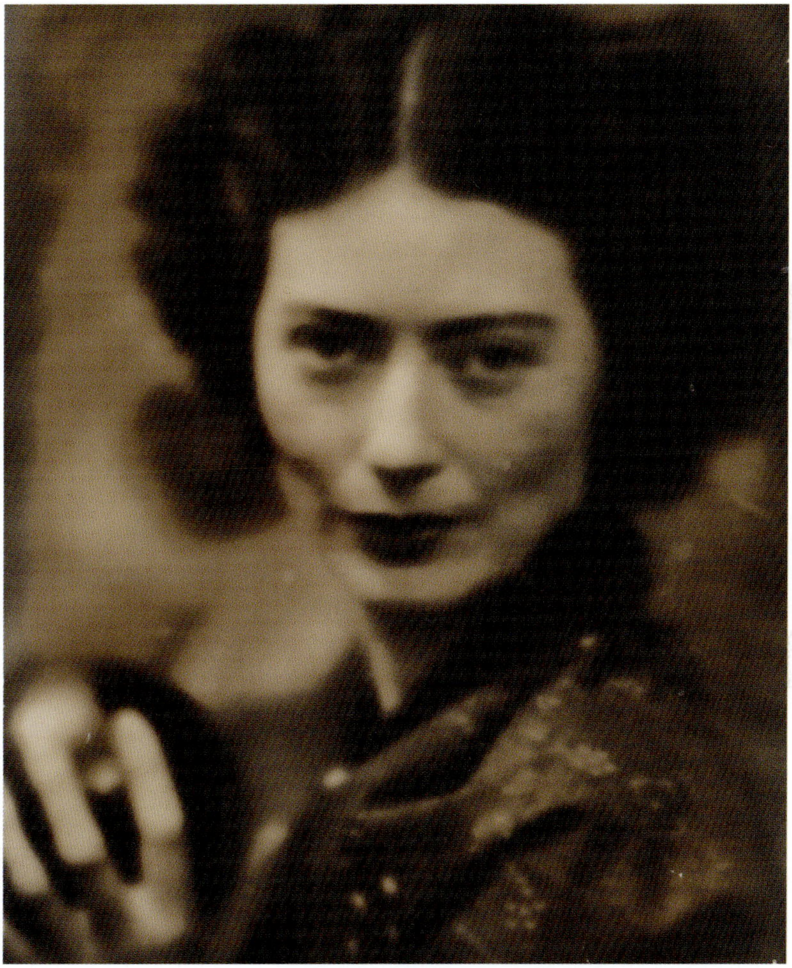

81 Mortimer-Lamb, *Vera with a glass globe.*

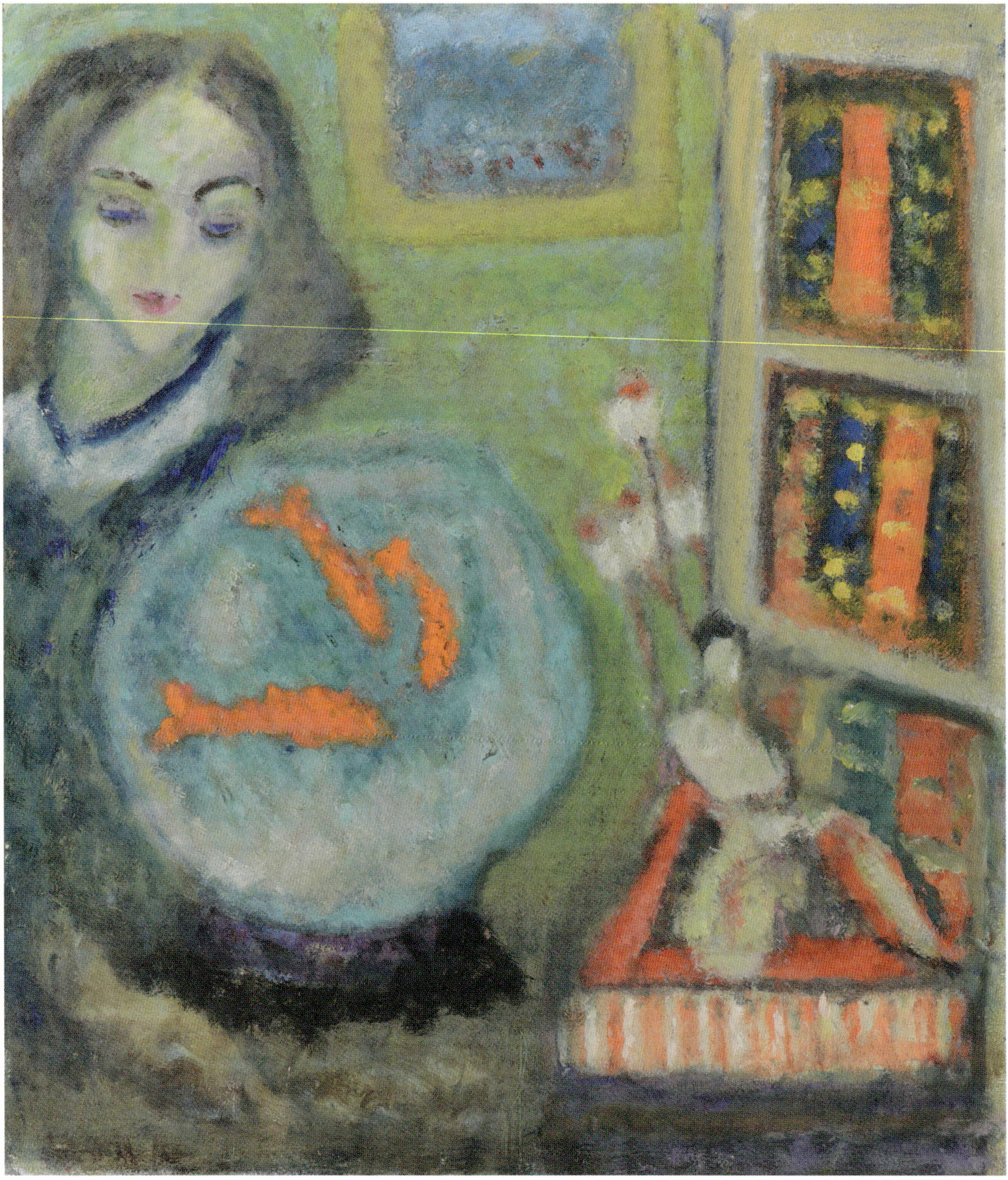

82 Mortimer-Lamb, *Vera and the Goldfish.*

show, "Mr. Lamb's portrait studies are superbly sensitive and his figure and landscape themes the essence of poetry." In reference to his paintings, Shadbolt said that "it required the greatest persuasion to accomplish this showing of his pictures since he paints for his own pleasure . . . Painted always out of the joy and fullness of his own experience, they sing with light and colour."[28]

The lovely home on Burnaby Mountain from which these paintings emerged was merry and bright, with a fire in the grate and a fat canary chirping in the sunny window. Art books and Persian carpets, along with the large and eclectic art collection, brought in the world. The paintings of Mortimer-Lamb make a wonderful record of the time he spent with his charming companion. Colin Graham was familiar with that world and, in a short catalogue for an exhibit of Mortimer-Lamb's paintings in 1978, wrote that "instead of dry, self-conscious experiments of a tired ex-critic, we find a fresh and naïve sensibility full of dream-like poetry . . . The best of his paintings are intuitive, living poetry, visions of an ideal world suffused with tremulous vibrating colour and a radiant light."[29]

Considering the long trajectory of Mortimer-Lamb's life and work, his paintings can be seen as a continuation of the Pictorialist sensibility. Their subject matter is usually simple, daily reality with a touch of symbolism. The paint is applied with an infinity of tiny dabs of colour, resulting in a soft, diffuse focus. In his time, his paintings were most often compared with those of Pierre Bonnard, the Post-Impressionist painter of the Nabi group who made a virtue of staying at home with his beloved wife, the muse and subject of his work. While praise for his painting was not lacking, Mortimer-Lamb always insisted that his skill in drawing was not up to that of a second-year art student, and because of this handicap he would never really go beyond the status of an inspired amateur.

The Mortimer-Lamb Papers, and particularly his late personal photographs, show that he remained a Pictorialist at heart, registering not the actual facts but their essence, as he had previously explained. By about 1930, John Vanderpant had moved on to embrace the eccentric perspective and abstract formal patterns of the Neue Sachlichkeit (New Objectivity) movement, working in the realm of "straight photography" and reportage without darkroom manipulation, while Mortimer-Lamb quietly continued in his preferred manner. For his own pleasure he created loving portraits of Vera, infused with the emotional charge that made the apparently outdated Pictorialism so effective. She posed for pensive pictures against a dark background, sometimes with statues from Mortimer-Lamb's art collection as a telling counterpoint. She was seen with a large glass globe; she sat for him wearing a fashionable hat and fur coat, a smock, or an attractive sundress. More than once he captured her in a quiet moment as she attended to her sewing.

As the years went by, Mortimer-Lamb found satisfaction in locating new homes for pieces of art from his collection. In 1952 he donated a painting by Vancouver's Don Jarvis and a canvas by the French painter Adolphe Hervier to the Vancouver Art Gallery, and a few weeks later added a work by the principal of the Vancouver School of Art, Fred Amess. A particularly welcome gift was the lovely oil titled *Hepaticas* (1936) by Canadian David Milne. An ancient temple carving from Japan went to the Museum of Anthropology at the University of British Columbia, and in 1954 he made his first contribution to the Art Gallery of Greater Victoria. This was a print of his 1904 photograph of Victoria artist Sophie Pemberton, and the gift reflects his growing friendship with Colin Graham, founding curator of the Victoria gallery. During the 1950s Mortimer-Lamb continued to purchase art. A travelling exhibition of British art came to the Vancouver Art Gallery from the British Arts Council in 1955, and he arranged to buy a painting by Keith Vaughan from the show. He made a gift of that oil, *Oyster Fishermen* (1948), to the Vancouver Art Gallery. Later, in 1957, he entered into correspondence with Anne Redpath of Edinburgh, considered the foremost Scottish painter of her day. This resulted in his purchase of *The Alabaster Lamp* (1958), which he immediately donated to the Vancouver Art Gallery, and of two further oils, which he left to the Art Gallery of Greater Victoria.

The Vancouver Art Gallery honoured Mortimer-Lamb by including both photographs and paintings by him in its 1958 exhibition *One Hundred Years of B.C. Art*. Robert Hume, the curator, wrote to Mortimer-Lamb to point out that he was the only artist to be represented in both the historical and the contemporary sections of the show. Photographs by Mortimer-Lamb included his portraits of Fred Varley, George Arliss, Ross Lort, and Emily Carr. The municipality of Burnaby, to mark the same centennial, sponsored an exhibition of twelve paintings by Mortimer-Lamb, in addition to a group show featuring thirty other artists and a small display of Emily Carr's work. The show took place in the new Burnaby Municipal Hall.

Doris Shadbolt gave an interview on CBC Radio at that time and made many pertinent observations about Mortimer-Lamb's paintings. "His genius, if you want to call it that, is in the fact that he has discovered the absolutely proper and right way to convey this vision of joy," she noted, "and for him the element by which he conveys it is almost pure colour."[30] At the conclusion

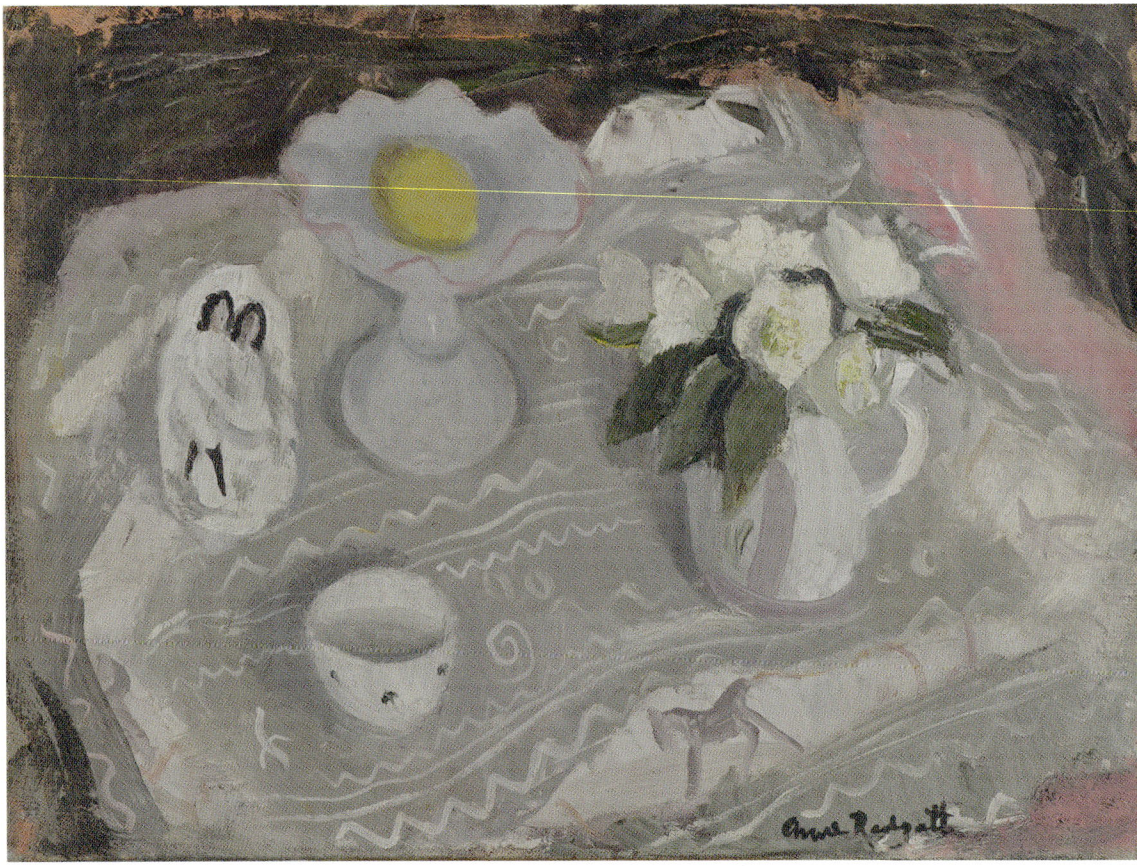

83 Anne Redpath, *Still Life with Two Figures.*

of the Burnaby show, Mortimer-Lamb presented one of his paintings to the Burnaby Municipal Hall, and Vera presented one of hers, with the hope that this would inspire the formation of a municipal art collection.

Another project of the 1958 centennial had larger implications. In 1952, around the time he was hired as curator of the Art Gallery of Greater Victoria, Colin Graham visited the Shadbolts in Burnaby. The visit was purely social, but as he got up to go, they told him of a remarkable man living just a few houses away and suggested that he visit Harold Mortimer-Lamb. Graham did so and struck up a friendship. "Harold Mortimer-Lamb, Vera and I seemed very much to be on the same wavelength," Graham wrote, "and I used to look forward keenly to visiting them whenever I could spare the time."[31] Soon, Mortimer-Lamb began offering gifts for the Victoria gallery's collection.

Molly went further. "He loved Colin Graham," she said. "He was so sympathetic. And Victoria was the first place Dadda had lived in the west—it was much dearer to him than Vancouver."[32] He had made his first photographs in Victoria in the 1890s and there, in 1904, he discovered art through his meeting with Sophie Pemberton. In fact, Pemberton had returned to Victoria in her old age and lived there until her death in 1958. The Victoria gallery was established in an old Queen Anne-style mansion on Moss Street, just a few blocks from tree-lined Pemberton Road, where Mortimer-Lamb had lived from 1900 to 1905; endowing the art gallery in his old neighbourhood was a return to his roots.

The new gallery in Victoria enjoyed considerable community support from the start, but its collection could not grow, for the tinderbox mansion that housed the gallery had no safe storage space. Moreover, without a modern gallery facility, exhibitions of valuable artwork on loan from the National Gallery and elsewhere, such as Mortimer-Lamb had long championed, could not be arranged. Between them, Graham and Mortimer-Lamb realized that a major donation of artworks of considerable value and prestige would inspire the community to build what they referred to as a "fireproof wing" as an adjunct to the old building.

In the March-April gallery bulletin, Graham announced that Mortimer-Lamb had given Victoria two gifts, to encourage the gallery to build a suitable place to store them: a fine drawing in charcoal and watercolour of Vera by Varley (1936) and a vivacious scene of shipping by the Proto-Impressionist Eugène Boudin, titled *The Harbour of Fécamp*. The Boudin was one of the prizes of his collection, purchased when Mortimer-Lamb was under the influence of the wealthy and knowledgeable Montreal collector George Drummond. When the gifts were made to the gallery, Graham wrote to Mortimer-Lamb that "the Board of Directors and I have something of the feeling of a second Christmas . . . Nothing like this has happened to us before. Your offers have given us tremendous stimulus and encouragement."[33] By the end of 1957, construction of the fireproof wing had been taken on as the gallery's centennial project, a move that was celebrated by the arrival in Victoria of further gifts from Burnaby.

Mortimer-Lamb's next donations to Victoria included a superb Varley panel—perhaps the best of all his Lynn Canyon landscapes—titled *Weather, Lynn Valley, B.C.*, as well as two other portraits by him. Another member of the Group of Seven was represented with the presentation of the gallery's first painting by A.Y. Jackson, *Northern Lights* (1943). The gift of the small oil *The Ploughman* by Homer Watson was considered an exceptional piece of luck by the delighted Graham. In total, Mortimer-Lamb gave twenty-six artworks to the new gallery during 1957.

Over the years the gifts kept coming. While their value as individual works of art was at times considerable, the paintings have had a larger significance in that they furthered an appreciation of Canadian painting in this far western outpost. In fact, what Mortimer-Lamb chose to collect, and thus to donate, shaped the collection policies of the Art Gallery of Greater Victoria from that point until the present. First, he was interested in Canadian art, especially that of the west coast, and he actively supported contemporary local artists. Second, he gathered representative examples of European art, especially British, with a strong emphasis on printmaking. Third, he enjoyed decorative arts such as Delftware, pewter, silver, furniture, and glass. And, finally, he had a broad interest in the arts of Asia, including Japanese paintings, tea wares, and prints, Chinese scrolls and porcelain, and statuary of a religious nature from Japan, China, Thailand, and Tibet. It was these gifts that set the course of the Victoria collection of Oriental art, a collection that is now world-renowned and, in many categories, certainly the best in Canada.

In his old age, Mortimer-Lamb was respected by younger artists. Writing from Menton in the south of France in 1957, Jack Shadbolt mentioned that the Val de Carei reminded him of a place in Victoria, up on the rocks of Gonzales Hill looking down over the Chinese cemetery. Like Mortimer-Lamb, Shadbolt had spent his early years in Victoria and knew he would recognize the reference. Moreover, Shadbolt felt that, as he continued with his painting, he was closer to Mortimer-Lamb in spirit. In a letter, he offered a profound testimonial to the man whom he had admired for twenty years.

"I have always felt, as you know, that you had the inner secret," Shadbolt wrote. "I consider you, of all the people I have met, the nearest in

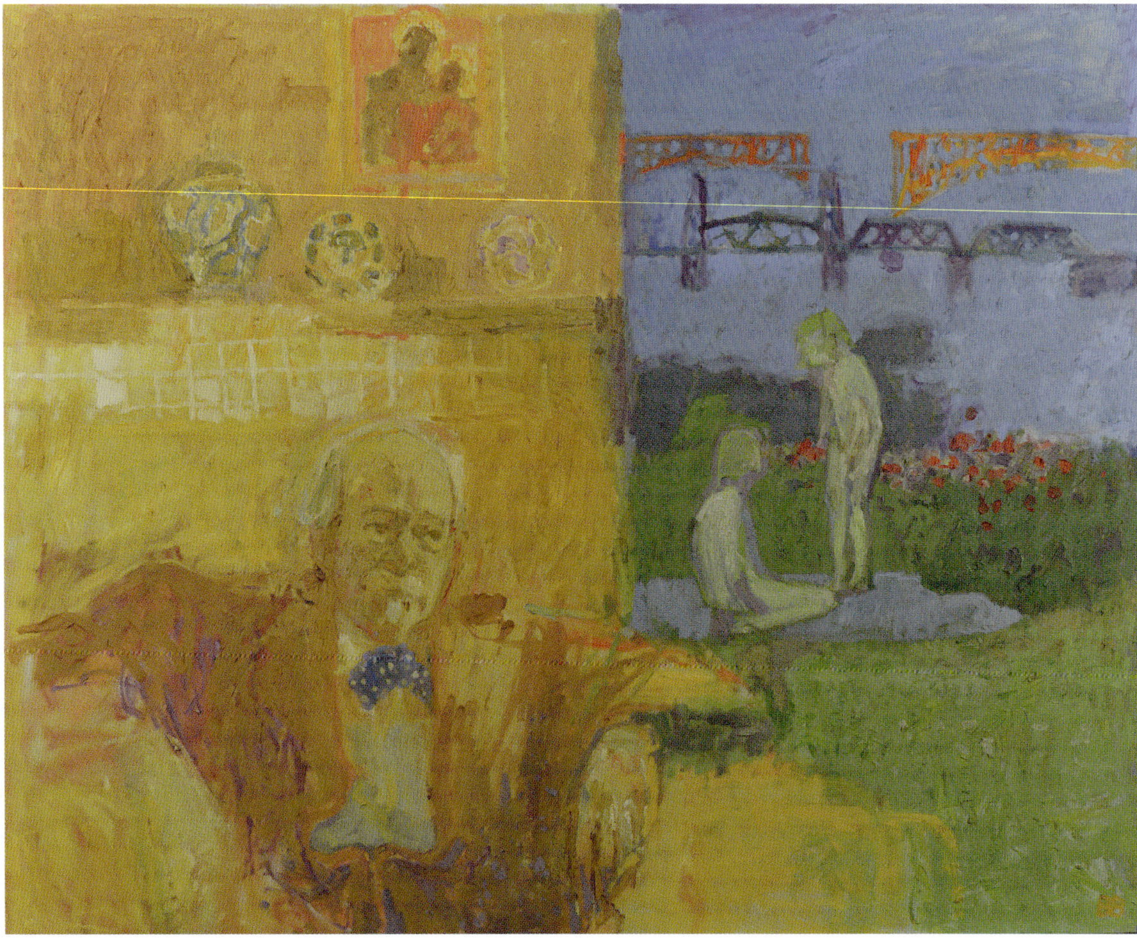

84 Bruno Bobak, *Portrait of H. Mortimer-Lamb.*

temperament to a true creative artist—you might have been a Bonnard. You compose in a totally unorthodox way, you sink yourself into the experience and you have an uncanny power of evocation born out of sheer love of the things you paint . . . Your work has been a good teacher to me; and I am glad I have been able to repay you a little by having unfailing confidence in it even when you had little yourself."[34]

Throughout the 1960s, life slowed for the elderly Mortimer-Lamb, as might be expected for a man over ninety. A.Y. Jackson kept up their correspondence until the end, reporting that the Studio Building, his long-time home base in Toronto, had been sold. In a card sent just before Christmas in 1962, Jackson recalled the newspaper column to which Mortimer-Lamb had responded so long before when, in 1913, he first supported the young painter. "Big eulogy in the Toronto *Star*," Jackson noted. The former critic S. Morgan-Powell had died. "If anyone dug up his printings on Art it would show he was one hundred percent wrong."[35] Posterity has proved that Mortimer-Lamb's opinions were almost infallibly right.

Joe Plaskett, who grew up in nearby New Westminster, came by the hilltop home on Burnaby Mountain and painted Mortimer-Lamb's portrait. It is a simple and straightforward rendering, compared to the one Bruno Bobak created. Bobak, whose art education took place in Vancouver, had married Molly Lamb after they had each completed their war service, and he and Molly frequently visited Mortimer-Lamb. He painted a large and deeply thoughtful portrait of Mortimer-Lamb, easily identified by his goatee and his spotted bow tie, seated in a comfortable chair. Above him, on a mantelpiece, are Delftware plates and a Greek icon of the Virgin and Child, all of which were later bequeathed to the Art Gallery of Greater

Victoria. Appearing in a haze of memory beyond the subject are two little girls playing naked in the woods, clearly meant to represent Mortimer-Lamb's Pictorialist photos of Molly and her friend Barbara Biart in their childhood. Surmounting all is a long view of the Second Narrows Bridge, visible from the window.

As the years passed, one of the warmest notes of appreciation came from Bess Harris, wife of Lawren Harris and herself an artist. Mortimer-Lamb had given her a painting that she, as an invalid, had hanging across from her bed where she saw it from morning till night. "Your painting delights me," she wrote. "I find that lying on one's back with responsibilities and everyday concerns nonexistent for the time the most enjoyable and rewarding way to look at paintings—one responds more freely. Your painting responds too. It becomes more and more intriguing and subtle. It is at once a positive statement and elusive. That in itself is an enchantment. I do thank you from my heart for providing me with a fresh experience of beauty. There is no greater gift."[36] This seems to be extraordinary praise from a woman living in a house otherwise hung with many of the acknowledged treasures of Canadian art.

At this stage in his life, Mortimer-Lamb lived to paint, though he was never content with his productions. He covered his panels over and over again, slowly bringing to life the "familiars" of his intimate world—the cat, flowers from his garden, and, as always, the serene presence of Vera. Shadbolt expressed it succinctly: "He was inside what he did. It was his act of love. The light does not fall on the objects in his work, it emanates from within in clear radiance."[37]

By 1967, the tenor of life had changed in the domestic world of Mortimer-Lamb and Vera. Vera began to show signs of dementia, and

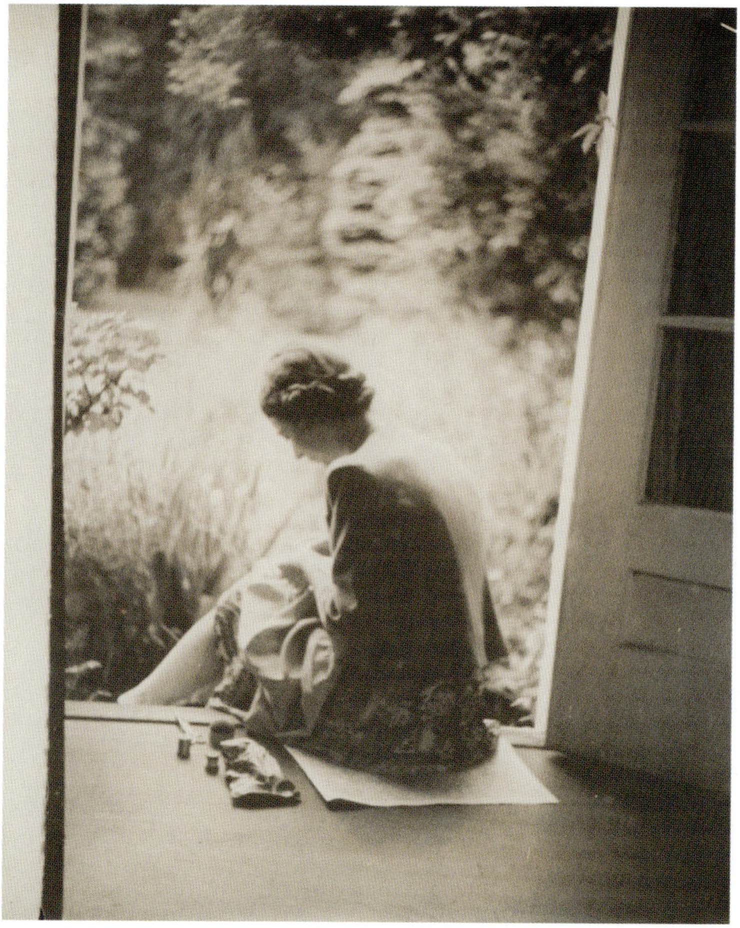

85 Mortimer-Lamb, *Vera mending.*

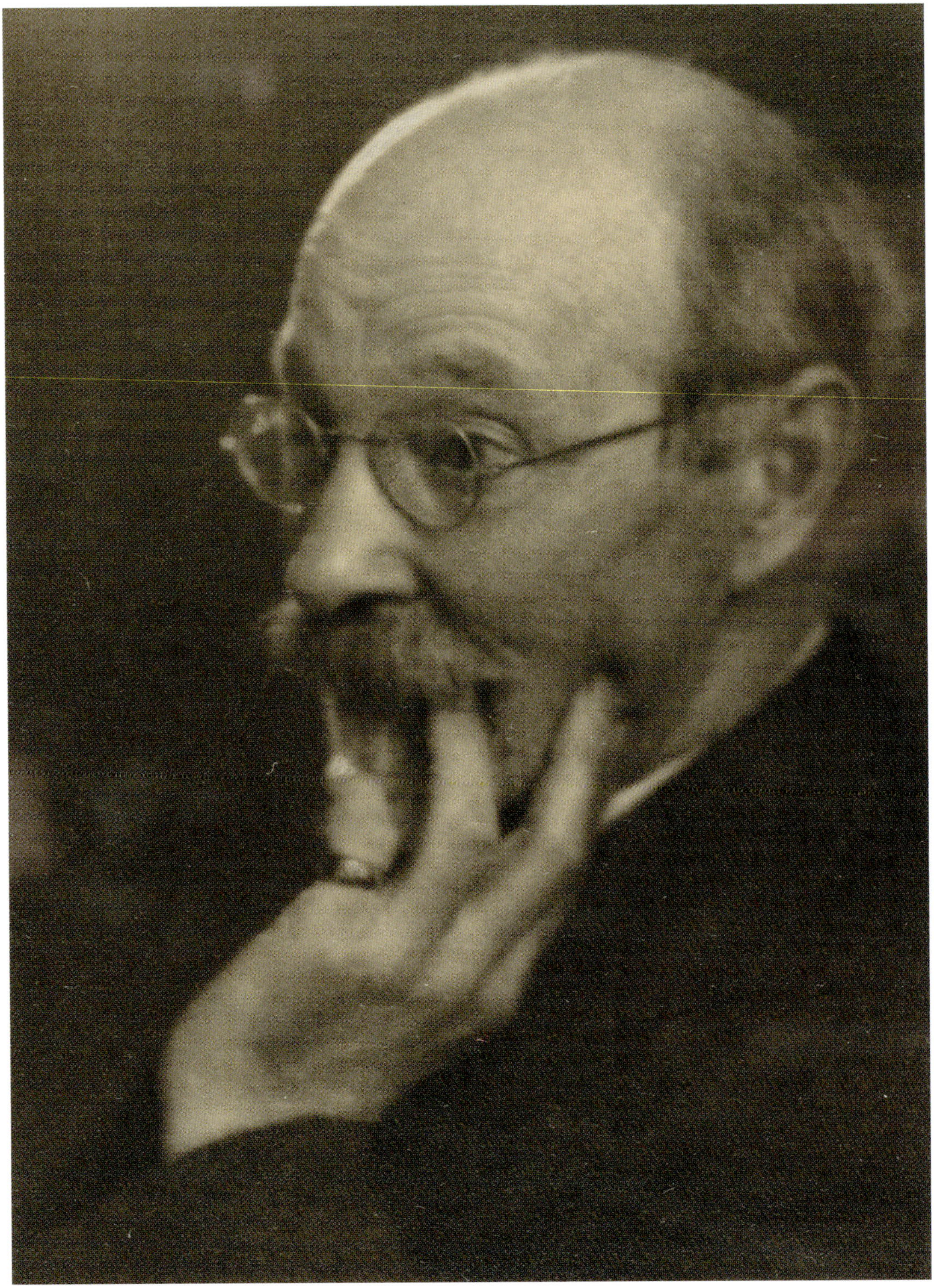

86 Harry Upperton Knight, *Harold Mortimer-Lamb.*

Molly and Bruno Bobak reported that she believed Tommy Douglas, a contemporary political figure, was hiding in the refrigerator. She showed many signs of paranoia and this degeneration frightened Mortimer-Lamb. Vera was greatly helped by the attentions of his third son, Lawrence, but late in 1967 she was committed to Essondale, a psychiatric hospital (later known as Riverview) on the north bank of the Fraser River. "It's sad to say," said Molly, "but she had a frontal lobotomy—nobody would ever do that nowadays . . . After the lobotomy she seemed perfectly well, but she was never really the same."[38]

And for the art lover, time finally ran out. Harold Mortimer-Lamb died on October 25, 1970, at the age of ninety-nine. He was survived by four sons, a daughter, seven grandchildren, and six great-grandchildren. By way of a memorial, an exhibition of his paintings and photographs was held at the Burnaby Art Gallery in May 1971. At the opening, most of his children were present, as was almost the entire first graduating class of the Vancouver School of Art, a tribute to the "Varley Era." Mortimer-Lamb's life was over, but his legacy lived on.

Jack Shadbolt wrote a touching eulogy in the Vancouver *Province* about this friend and neighbour whose paintings he so admired: "What had produced in this perceptive yet conservative, this kindly yet petulant, this shrewdly practical yet artistically sensitive man of the later years those qualities that inspired such consecration? Could it be that somehow he had never lost his romantic vision?"[39] Truly, in ninety-nine years of engaged and broad experience with the world, Harold Mortimer-Lamb never lost his romantic vision. He was, in every way, an art lover.

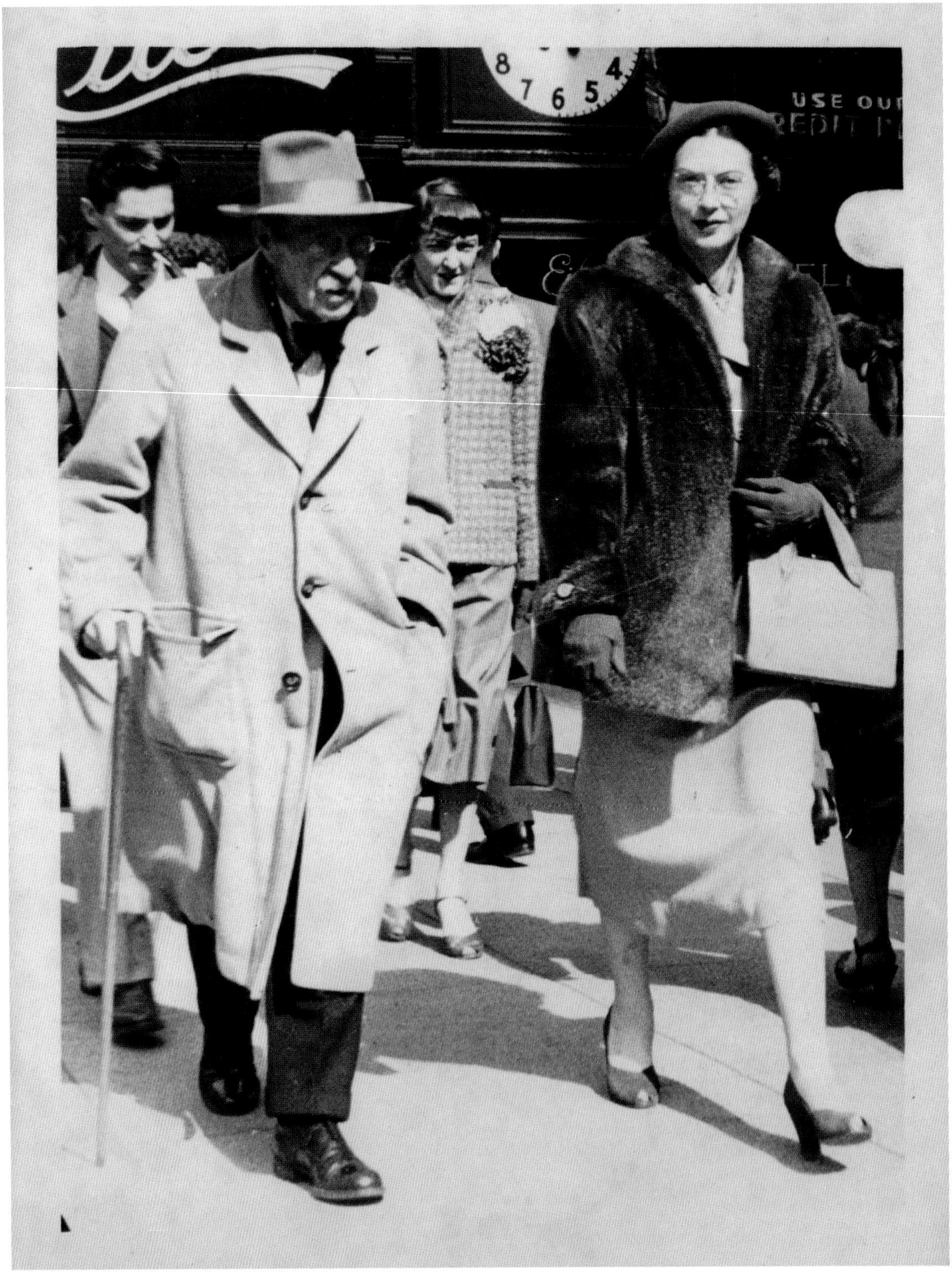


87 Unnamed street photographer, *Harold Mortimer-Lamb and Vera in Vancouver.*

# Epilogue

Vera lived on alone in the big house on Burnaby Mountain, and a neighbour kept an eye on her in her final years. It was said that she slept on the floor by her husband's four-poster bed, so devoted was she to him even after his death. One day in 1977 her brother came to visit from Seattle. Molly wrote that "she served him a steak dinner on an English round table with a folding leaf—it was early eighteenth-century English, I believe. He got up to go to the bathroom, and when he came back he found she had choked on a piece of steak and died. It was a spring day in February and the little daisies were out in the lawn. I will always remember that when I think of Vera's death."[1]

Mortimer-Lamb had left his possessions to Vera with the understanding that after her death they would be given to the Art Gallery of Greater Victoria as the Harold and Vera Mortimer-Lamb Bequest. This bequest included their household art, books, and papers and a substantial sum of money. After Vera's death, Colin Graham drove over from Victoria and, with a small moving van, brought back their lifetime collection of treasures. Eventually, 192 works of art were added to the collection in Victoria, not to mention the many that have been purchased since with money from the estate. Graham brought back Mortimer-Lamb's letters and clipping files and more than 260 of his photographs. The Harold and Vera Mortimer-Lamb Bequest included a donation of $110,000 as an art-purchase fund, the only restriction being that it could not be used to buy sculpture or abstract art. Beyond what is housed in Victoria, the Vancouver Art Gallery has over the years catalogued 30 items as gifts from Mortimer-Lamb and Vera, while the Vancouver Museum lists 35 pieces from a single donation in 1957.

# ENDNOTES

Unless otherwise noted, all letters cited here can be found in the Harold Mortimer-Lamb Papers held in the British Columbia Archives in Victoria.

### CHAPTER ONE: THE EARLY YEARS IN BRITISH COLUMBIA

1 Molly Lamb Bobak, personal interview, December 5, 2000.

2 Ibid.

3 Harold Mortimer-Lamb, "Reminiscences," p. 6.

4 Ibid., p. 17.

5 Ibid., p. 5.

6 Sophie Pemberton (Deane-Drummond) to Harold Mortimer-Lamb, December 1954.

7 Vancouver *News-Advertiser*, February 19, 1905.

### CHAPTER TWO: MONTREAL

1 Harold Mortimer-Lamb, "Reminiscences," p. 8.

2 C.D. Graham, *Arts Victoria* (Victoria: Art Gallery of Greater Victoria, May 1978), p. 13.

3 Harold Mortimer-Lamb, "Reminiscences," p. 9.

4 Harold Mortimer-Lamb, *Photograms of the Year* (London: Royal Photographic Society, 1905), p. 81.

5 F.J. Mortimer, *The Amateur Photographer and Photographic News* (London, July 6, 1909), p. 36.

6 Harold Mortimer-Lamb, *Photograms of the Year* (London: Royal Photographic Society, 1913), p. 34.

7 *The Amateur Photographer and Photographic News* (London, August 11, 1904), p. 12.

8 Harold Mortimer-Lamb, "Photography by Night," *American Annual of Photography* (New York, 1908), pp. 285–6.

9 Ariane Isler-de Jongh, "The Night Photography of Harold Mortimer-Lamb," pp. 157–9.

10 *The Amateur Photographer and Photographic News* (London, July 12, 1910), p. 41.

11 Anthony Guest, *The Amateur Photographer and Photographic News* (London, July 19, 1910), p. 71.

12 Anthony Guest, *The Amateur Photographer and Photographic News* (London, July 24, 1911), p. 96.

13 *The Sketch* (London, November 11, 1911), not paginated.

14 Laura Muntz to Harold Mortimer-Lamb, June 3, 1926.

15 Molly Lamb Bobak, personal interview, December 5, 2000.

16 Sidney Carter to Alfred Stieglitz, January 8, 1907, Sidney Carter Papers, The Alfred Stieglitz Archive.

17 Laura Muntz to Harold Mortimer-Lamb, June 3, 1926.

18 Montreal *Star*, undated clipping, March 1912.

19 Homer Watson to Harold Mortimer-Lamb, not dated.

20 Harold Mortimer-Lamb, "Reminiscences," p. 1.

21 Alfred Stieglitz to Harold Mortimer-Lamb, December 11, 1913.

22 Harold Mortimer-Lamb in *Camera Work* 47 (New York, July 1914), not paginated.

23 S. Morgan-Powell, Montreal *Star*, March 29, 1913.

24 Harold Mortimer-Lamb to the editor, Montreal *Star*, April 7, 1913.

25 A.Y. Jackson to Harold Mortimer-Lamb, April 15, 1913.

26 Harold Mortimer-Lamb to the editor, Montreal *Star*, April 24, 1913.

27 Harold Mortimer-Lamb in *The Studio* 52 (London, September 1914), p. 313.

28 Harold Mortimer-Lamb in *The Studio* 64 (London, August 1915), p. 212.

29 Harold Mortimer-Lamb to Eric Brown, December 9, 1913.

30 Harold Mortimer-Lamb to H.E. Young, September 30, 1913.

31 H.E. Young to Harold Mortimer-Lamb, December 11, 1913.

32 Harold Mortimer-Lamb in *The Studio* 77 (London, August 1919), p. 119.

33 Molly Lamb Bobak, personal interview, December 5, 2000.

34 Ibid.

35 The Canadian Mining Institute, report for 1920.

### CHAPTER THREE: VANCOUVER

1 *Farm and Home*, Vancouver, undated, 1925.

2 Harold Mortimer-Lamb, "Reminiscences," p. 19.

3 Molly Lamb Bobak, personal interview, December 5, 2000.

4 Ibid.

5 Molly Lamb Bobak, *Wildflowers of Canada*, p. 16.

6 Cindy Richmond, quoting Jack Shadbolt in *Molly Lamb Bobak: A Retrospective*, p. 28.

7 Molly Lamb Bobak, *Wildflowers of Canada*, p. 11.

8 Harold Mortimer-Lamb, "Reminiscences," p. 24.

9 A.Y. Jackson, *A Painter's Country*, p. 113.

10 Maria Tippett, "Who 'Discovered' Emily Carr?" *Journal of Canadian Art History* 1, no. 2 (Montreal, Fall 1974).

11 Harold Mortimer-Lamb to Eric Brown, October 24, 1921.

12 Harold Mortimer-Lamb in the Vancouver *Province*, February 8, 1925.

13 Eric Brown, letter published in the Ottawa *Journal*, February 25, 1925.

14 Harold Mortimer-Lamb in the Vancouver *Province*, October 23, 1923.

15 Charles H. Scott, Vancouver *Sun*, May 24, 1931.

16 Molly Lamb Bobak, *Wildflowers of Canada*, p. 20.

17 Molly Lamb Bobak, personal interview, December 12, 2000.

18 Letter from the Committee for Pictorial Photography and Fine Art, New Westminster, to Harold Mortimer-Lamb, January 6, 1925.

19 Sheryl Salloum, *Underlying Vibrations: The Photography and Life of John Vanderpant*, p. 23.

20 Harold Mortimer-Lamb to Arthur Lismer, January 28, 1926.

21 Sheryl Salloum, *Underlying Vibrations: The Photography and Life of John Vanderpant*, p. 23.

22 Harold Mortimer-Lamb to Arthur Lismer, March 8, 1926.

23 Harold Mortimer-Lamb to Arthur Lismer, National Archives of Canada, quoted in Salloum, p. 24.

24 Sheryl Salloum, *Underlying Vibrations: The Photography and Life of John Vanderpant*, p. 24.

25 Arthur Lismer to Harold Mortimer-Lamb, August 10, 1925.

### CHAPTER FOUR: FRED VARLEY IN VANCOUVER

1 Peter Varley, *Frederick H. Varley*, p. 61.

[2] Molly Lamb Bobak, personal interview, December 12, 2000.

[3] Molly Lamb Bobak, *Wildflowers of Canada*, p. 24.

[4] Ibid.

[5] F.H. Varley to Vera Weatherbie, October 9, 1931, Varley Papers, Art Gallery of Alberta, Edmonton, Alberta.

[6] F.H. Varley to Vera Weatherbie, November 8, 1939, Varley Papers, Art Gallery of Alberta, Edmonton, Alberta.

[7] McKenzie Porter, "Varley," *Maclean's* (*Toronto*, November 7, 1959), p. 66.

[8] Quoted in *Varley*, a film in the series *Passionate Canadians*, directed by Allan Wargon for the National Film Board of Canada, 1953.

[9] F.H. Varley to Harold Mortimer-Lamb, June 6, 1936, Varley Papers, Art Gallery of Alberta.

[10] F.H. Varley to Maud Varley, October 19, 1936, Varley Papers, Art Gallery of Alberta.

### CHAPTER FIVE: HAROLD AND VERA

[1] Molly Lamb Bobak, personal interview, December 12, 2000.

[2] Harold Mortimer-Lamb in the Vancouver *Province*, November 7, 1931.

[3] A.Y. Jackson, *A Painter's Country*, p. 138.

[4] Harold Mortimer-Lamb in the Vancouver *Province*, November 7, 1931.

[5] Frank Kermode to Harold Mortimer-Lamb, September 26, 1937.

[6] Molly Lamb Bobak, *Wildflowers of Canada*, p. 24.

[7] Ibid., p. 24.

[8] Ibid., p. 25.

[9] Jack Shadbolt, Vancouver *Province*, May 8, 1971.

[10] Molly Lamb Bobak, *Wildflowers of Canada*, p. 25.

[11] Molly Lamb Bobak, *Wildflowers of Canada*, p. 17.

[12] Molly Lamb Bobak, *Wildflowers of Canada*, p. 29.

[13] Harold Mortimer-Lamb, "Reminiscences," p. 66.

[14] Molly Lamb Bobak, *Wildflowers of Canada*, p. 32.

[15] Harold Mortimer-Lamb, "Reminiscences," p. 47.

[16] Jim Varley, quoted in Maria Tippett, *Stormy Weather: F.H. Varley, a Biography*, p. 247.

[17] F.H. Varley to Vera Weatherbie and Harold Mortimer-Lamb, undated letters, *circa* 1939, 1941, 1943.

[18] Ibid.

[19] R.C. Rowe, *Canadian Mining Journal* (Toronto, March 1946), p. 194.

[20] B.C. Binning to Harold Mortimer-Lamb, January 22, 1946.

[21] Molly Lamb Bobak, personal interview, December 12, 2000.

[22] Ibid.

[23] Doris Shadbolt, "Painter of an Intimate World," *Canadian Art* magazine, vol. 5, no. 1 (Toronto, 1947), p. 19.

[24] Harold Mortimer-Lamb, "Reminiscences," p. 57.

[25] Ibid.

[26] Molly Lamb Bobak, personal interview, December 12, 2000.

[27] Harold Mortimer-Lamb, "Reminiscences," p. 66–70.

[28] Jack Shadbolt, exhibition press materials for *Harold Mortimer-Lamb*, Vancouver Art Gallery, June 1952.

[29] Colin Graham, exhibition catalogue of *Harold Mortimer-Lamb: Paintings* (Victoria: Art Gallery of Greater Victoria, 1978), p. 5.

30 Doris Shadbolt, CBC Radio interview transcription, October 2, 1958.

31 Colin Graham, unpublished memoir, 1974.

32 Molly Lamb Bobak, personal interview, December 12, 2000.

33 Colin Graham to Harold Mortimer-Lamb, January 19, 1957.

34 Jack Shadbolt to Harold Mortimer-Lamb, March 9, 1957.

35 A.Y. Jackson to Harold Mortimer-Lamb, Christmas card, 1962.

36 Bess Harris to Harold Mortimer-Lamb, not dated.

37 Jack Shadbolt, Vancouver *Province*, May 8, 1971.

38 Molly Lamb Bobak, personal interview, December 12, 2000.

39 Jack Shadbolt, Vancouver *Province*, May 8, 1971.

### EPILOGUE

1 Molly Lamb Bobak, personal interview, December 12, 2000.

# BIBLIOGRAPHY


Atanassova, Katerina. *F.H. Varley: Portraits into Light*. Toronto: Dundurn Press, 2007.

Blanchard, Paula. *Emily Carr*. Vancouver: Douglas & McIntyre, 1987.

Bobak, Molly Lamb. *Wildflowers of Canada*. Toronto: Pagurian Press, 1978.

Brooke, Janet M. *Discerning Tastes: Montreal Collectors 1880–1920*. Montreal: Montreal Museum of Fine Arts, 1989.

Carr, Emily. *Growing Pains*. Toronto: Clarke Irwin, 1946.

Clark, Michael. *Vancouver Artists—Vision in the Making*. Vancouver: Emily Carr Institute of Art and Design, September 1995.

Graham, Colin. *Harold Mortimer-Lamb: Paintings* (exhibition catalogue). Victoria: Art Gallery of Greater Victoria, 1978.

Hill, Charles. *The Group of Seven: Art for a Nation*. Toronto: McClelland & Stewart, 1995.

Hill, Charles. *John Vanderpant Photographs*. Ottawa: The National Gallery of Canada, 1976.

Housser, Frederick. *A Canadian Art Movement: The Story of the Group of Seven*. Toronto: The Macmillan Company of Canada, 1926.

Isler-de Jongh, Ariane. "The Night Photography of Harold Mortimer-Lamb." *The History of Photography*, Volume 20, Number 2 (Summer 1996).

Jackson, A.Y. *A Painter's Country*. Toronto: Clarke Irwin, 1964.

Mortimer-Lamb, Harold. "Reminiscences." Harold Mortimer-Lamb Papers. Victoria: British Columbia Archives.

Mastin, Catherine (general editor). *The Group of Seven in Western Canada*. Toronto: Key Porter Books, 2002.

McLeish, A.B. *September Gale: A Study of Arthur Lismer and the Group of Seven*. Toronto: Dent, 1955.

Reid, Dennis. *A Concise History of Painting in Canada*. Toronto: Oxford University Press, 1973.

Richardson, Letia. *First Class: Four Graduates from the Vancouver School of Decorative and Applied Arts, 1929*. Vancouver: Women in Focus, 1987.

Richmond, Cindy. *Molly Lamb Bobak: A Retrospective*. Regina: MacKenzie Art Gallery, 1993.

Rombout, Luke, et.al. *Vancouver: Art and Artists 1931–1983*. Vancouver: Vancouver Art Gallery, 1983.

Salloum, Sheryl. *Underlying Vibrations: The Photography and Life of John Vanderpant*. Victoria: Horsdal & Schubart, 1995.

Shadbolt, Jack. *Correspondences* (exhibition catalogue). Calgary: Glenbow-Alberta Institute, 1991.

Stieglitz, Alfred. The Alfred Stieglitz Archive. New Haven, Connecticut: Collection of American Literature, The Beinecke Rare Book and Manuscript Library, Yale University.

Tippett, Maria. *Stormy Weather: F.H. Varley, a Biography*. Toronto: McClelland & Stewart, 1998.

Tuele, Nicholas. *Sophie Pemberton* (exhibition catalogue). Victoria: Art Gallery of Greater Victoria, 1980.

Watson, Scott. *Jack Shadbolt*. Vancouver: Douglas & McIntyre, 1990.

Watson, Scott. *Jack Shadbolt Drawings*. Vancouver: Douglas & McIntyre, 1994.

Varley, Christopher. *Frederick H. Varley*. Ottawa: National Gallery of Canada, 1979.

Varley, Peter. *Frederick H. Varley*. Toronto: Key Porter Books, 1983.

# LIST OF ILLUSTRATIONS

# INDEX

# ACKNOWLEDGMENTS

This book is based on the Harold Mortimer-Lamb Papers, which were donated with his estate to the Art Gallery of Greater Victoria. The collection contains materials of many sorts, saved by Mortimer-Lamb for the use of whoever might write his biography. Where not otherwise noted, the facts that make up this story are to be found among these papers. While the papers and photographs were stored at the gallery, they were the subject of extensive research by Ariane Isler-de Jongh, a historian of photography, who worked for years to prepare an exhibition of Mortimer-Lamb's photography. Though she was unable to arrange this, she generously shared with me the fruits of her research in 1996 and, in 2011, she gave me her papers relating to the project.

Not being constituted as an archive, the gallery passed on the letters, published notices, and photographs to the British Columbia Archives, located in Victoria, in 1992. The photographs, numbering over 260, include both family photos and exhibition prints by Mortimer-Lamb and others. It is to these papers that anyone looking further into this story must turn.

The most important informant for this book has been Molly Lamb Bobak, daughter of Mortimer-Lamb and Mary Williams. Molly wrote a memoir of her early life in her book, *Wildflowers of Canada*, and in a number of interviews told me everything she could remember about her "Dadda." She also made available his photographs, which had hung in her home, and his earliest photo albums. Molly gave me encouragement at every stage to tell this story and generously permitted me to quote from her writing and interviews as well as use material for which she holds the copyright. Throughout the writing of this book, Molly's daughter, Anny Scoones, also helped me in every way, finding photos and carrying messages across Canada on my behalf.

The purpose of this book is to shine a light on the remarkable and tightly integrated art collection donated by Harold and Vera Mortimer-Lamb to the Art Gallery of Greater Victoria in 1977. Almost every major event in Mortimer-Lamb's life is illustrated by significant works of art created by the participants, often presenting multiple views of the same situation. For example, the Savary Island trip in 1935 is represented by a painting of the scene by Fred Amess, an etching of the setting by E.J. Hughes, portraits in pencil of Mortimer-Lamb by three of the participating artists, and photographs of the day by Mortimer-Lamb. All of these were donated to Victoria.

My work with the Art Gallery of Greater Victoria was made possible by the deeply committed stewardship of Jon Tupper, the director. With aplomb he secured key loans from the National Gallery of Canada, the University of British Columbia, and the Vancouver Art Gallery. Crucially, he was willing to become involved in a project that included essential participation by the British Columbia Archives and the independent publisher of this book, TouchWood Editions. My staff liaison at the gallery began with Chief Curator Mary Jo Hughes and has continued with her successor, Michelle Jaques, and my every wish has been granted. Collections Manager Stephen Topfer prepared photographs of material from the gallery's collection, and Registrar Lori Graves navigated the vaults for me. At the BC Archives, my work has been facilitated by Provincial Archivist Gary Mitchell and Kathryn Bridge, Director of Visitor Services, as well as the CEO of the archives and museum, Jack Lohman.

Sheryl Salloum, the biographer of John Vanderpant, provided me with useful information and permission to quote from her book. Scott Watson helped identify the hand of Jack Shadbolt in Mortimer-Lamb's sketch-book. I am also grateful to Charles Hill of the National Gallery of Canada, who encouraged, advised, and inspired me as this project unfolded.

Since 1978, the research and preparation of this book has been my own labour of love. No grants have been applied for or received.

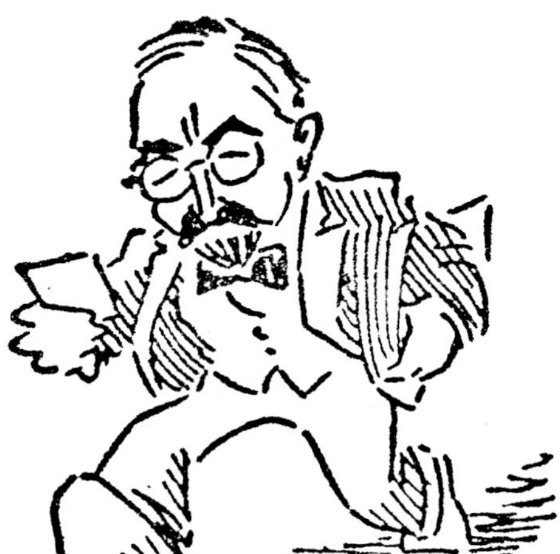